Growing Great Employees

Growing Great Employees

Turning Ordinary People into Extraordinary Performers

Erika Andersen

Portfolio

PORTFOLIO

Published by the Penguin Group

Penguin Group (USA) Inc., 375 Hudson Street, New York, New York 10014, U.S.A. • Penguin Group (Canada), 90 Eglinton Avenue East, Suite 700, Toronto, Ontario, Canada M4P 2Y3 (a division of Pearson Penguin Canada Inc.) • Penguin Books Ltd, 80 Strand, London WC2R 0RL, England • Penguin Ireland, 25 St. Stephen's Green, Dublin 2, Ireland (a division of Penguin Books Ltd) • Penguin Books Australia Ltd, 250 Camberwell Road, Camberwell, Victoria 3124, Australia (a division of Pearson Australia Group Pty Ltd) • Penguin Books India Pvt Ltd, 11 Community Centre, Panchsheel Park, New Delhi–110 017, India • Penguin Group (NZ), Cnr Airborne and Rosedale Roads, Albany, Auckland 1310, New Zealand (a division of Pearson New Zealand Ltd) • Penguin Books (South Africa) (Pty) Ltd, 24 Sturdee Avenue, Rosebank, Johannesberg 2196, South Africa

Penguin Books Ltd, Registered Offices:
80 Strand, London WC2R 0RL, England

First published in 2006 by Portfolio,
a member of Penguin Group (USA) Inc.

10 9 8 7 6 5 4 3 2 1

LIBRARY OF CONGRESS CATALOGING IN PUBLICATION DATA
Andersen, Erika.
  Growing great employees : turning ordinary people into extraordinary
  performers/ Erika Andersen.
    p. cm.
  Includes index.
  ISBN 1-59184-151-8
  1. Supervision of employees. 2. Employees. I. Title.
  HF5549.12.A525 2006
  658.3'124—dc22   2006046788

Printed in the United States of America
Set in ITC Galliard
Designed by Amy Hill

To Dad, for believing in me

To Mom, for the love of language

To M, for your kind gift

To Scott, Rachel, and Ian, for being my home

Contents

Acknowledgments

I'm indebted to many, many people in a variety of ways:

Jim Levine, agent extraordinaire—your personal passion for the topic warms my soul. Thank you for every conversation and every effort. And the sox.

Adrienne Schultz, my editor, for being a delight and telling me about *occhi di lupo*.

Adrian Zackheim, my publisher—glad you liked the book, even though it's not about options trading. And it *is* a great cover.

My pre-Proteus bosses, for lessons learned: Prentiss, Tim, Peter, Dot, and Bob.

All my smart, honest, cool clients, for letting me help and helping me grow.

My wonderful Proteus colleagues, past, present, and yet to be—for every step we take together toward our hoped-for future.

Jeff: your good brain and good heart sustain me daily.

My dear siblings—and that includes you, Anne.

And always, every day, to Scott, Rachel, and Ian.

Introduction

Here's a little experiment. Find any ten people who have some responsibility for others' work success—managers, HR staff, team leaders. One at a time, ask them what the hardest and most challenging part of their job is. Tell them they can say whatever they want, they don't have to be politically correct, and no one is writing down their answers. I'll bet you anything that nine out of the ten will say something about "dealing with the people stuff." And the tenth will say something else, simply because he or she has only been in the job two weeks and hasn't gotten to the people-stuff part yet!

If life were fair, employees would be perfect. They would do exactly what we asked them to do, exactly when we asked them to do it—except, of course, for the fantastic ideas they would cook up on their own, the ones that would knock everybody's socks off, rejuvenate our tired products and services, and increase the bottom line by double digits. They would be cheerful-kind-brave-reverent-thrifty; they would evolve smoothly from entry-level to VP with no bumps along the way, handing us completed performance reviews once a year that perfectly reflect their efforts and results, and include their own entirely appropriate developmental plans. . . .

.   .   .

Back to reality. Your employees are, like you and I, flawed and hopeful human beings whose success is at least partly dependent on your skill as a manager; human beings who will thrive with skillful and consistent attention and wither without it. Kind of like plants. (Thus the gardening metaphor you'll notice throughout the book, from which I intend to wring every last drop by the end of the final chapter.)

So, in that spirit, I've written this book for everyone who is responsible for helping another person succeed at work: managers, team leaders, human resource professionals, coaches, mentors, even managers-to-be. I want to share with you the best of what I've learned as a coach and consultant, a business owner, a manager of people from entry-level to highly skilled professionals—and as an employee.

Why Now?

Part of what I've learned over the past thirty years is that the covenant between employees and companies has changed dramatically. When I was first starting out in the American work world, managers and the companies they represented expected that employees would simply show up and do what they were told—even if that meant moving every couple of years, families in tow, or working for a truly awful boss, or standing by while white males got plum jobs and plum salaries and everybody else didn't. Companies expected that people would do practically anything for their paycheck . . . and leave their dreams and feelings in a box by the door, thank you very much. Now—poor economies and other uncertainties notwithstanding—employees expect much more. They expect to be treated fairly, to be given both a clear sense of what their job is and the resources to do it well, and to be helped to grow and develop as professionals. And if they don't get these basic work-related needs met at one job, they are likely to look elsewhere.

In other words, employees (especially the more skilled and talented ones, the ones you want to keep) now tend to see themselves as having more leverage in the job equation. They bring something the company wants (themselves, with all their skills, experience, and talents), and the company brings some things they want (a place to have influence and make money, but also opportunities to learn and advance, professional connections, and mentoring). Most of the things that make employees want to work for a particular company can be provided by a skillful manager. I can help you be that kind of manager.

How We'll Approach This

When I began to mention to people that I was thinking of writing this book, the response was fascinating. Almost without exception, friends and colleagues in the business world would say something along the order of, "Oh, wow. When you finish it, I want a copy. I want ten copies." And when I asked why they were so interested? Well, that takes us back to the beginning of this introduction: if you ask any ten people who have some responsibility for managing people what the hardest part of their job is . . .

So then, this book is a distillation of the teaching and coaching I've done with individuals and groups throughout my career. And it's a mix of the same elements I use in that corporate work: conversation, ideas, experiments, calls for self-reflection, and—perhaps most important—skill development. Managing well requires skills—just like cooking, or playing the piano, or, yes, gardening—and I hope to teach you some of those skills. Since you and I aren't sitting in a room together, we'll have to be a bit creative about how we work together to develop your people management skills. I've put the skills in an order that seems best to me, and in a number of cases the later chapters build on skills and understanding that will have been addressed in earlier chapters. But for those of you who don't like to read in a straight line, and who would prefer to dip in and out . . . please be my guest. Here's a quick summary of what's in each chapter:

Chapter 1. Preparing the Soil: This chapter focuses on listening, which I see as the foundation of managerial success. I'll use the gardening analogy of preparing the soil before planting a garden; no matter how good the seeds or how well you care for them, if the soil has not been loosened and enriched, in order to create the best possible environment, not much will grow. Listening well (and sincerely) is the key to creating an environment that supports employee growth. I'll start by helping you become aware of how listening (or not listening) affects relationships and results. Then I'll show you how listening is a skill that can be learned and used by anyone who sees the benefit in doing so. You'll work through a skill-based model for listening, and I'll share a case study that helps show the different paths a conversation can take, depending on whether a manager listens or doesn't. This first chapter also contains a "bonus skill"; a skill of internal preparation called managing your self-talk—a way of making sure that what you say to yourself is supportive of the results you're trying to achieve.

Chapter 2. Plan Before You Plant: This chapter explores the importance of clarifying your needs and expectations—both organizationally and for a given job—before recruiting. I'll draw the analogy to the need for planning a garden in order to make it yield what you want. I'll first explain the idea of establishing core competencies, the key capabilities needed for anyone to succeed in your organization. Then I'll share an approach for identifying these core competencies in your organization, and I'll show how doing so can help ensure that you create the kind of workplace you want to have. I'll walk you through the process of creating your own core competencies. Then you'll learn the importance of describing a job clearly in order to find the right person for that job, and I'll offer a template and an approach for creating simple, practical job descriptions. I'll talk through a case study of how one client, faced with the need to hire someone for a complicated new job, used the job description tool to clarify his needs so he could find the right person.

Chapter 3. Picking Your Plants: How does a gardener know which plants will take root and flourish and which ones won't? That's the focus of this chapter—using the interview process to make sure that you're hiring the people most likely to succeed in the job, in your department, and in the company. You and I will focus on the skill of behavior-based interviewing, the basic principles of which most managers can learn and apply for themselves. I'll help you use your core competencies and job descriptions to decide which questions you want to ask, and how to ask them. Most important, you'll learn how to make use of your listening skills so as to ensure the effectiveness of this approach. Finally, I'll explain and demonstrate (through examples) how to "rate" each interviewee in a way that's aligned with your core competencies and job description. This chapter will include actual case studies of ineffective and effective interviews—and their outcomes.

Chapter 4. Not Too Deep and Not Too Shallow: When a gardener has chosen his or her plants, the next step is to make sure they're planted well—not too deep and not too shallow. This chapter focuses on how to start new employees off on the right foot by making sure they're "planted" at the right depth. An employee who's not given key information about systems, relationships, and expectations is "planted too shallow," and will have a hard time getting what he or she needs from the organization in order to grow. An employee who's overloaded with information and unrealistic expectations is "planted too deep," and is likely to suffocate—paralyzed by too much, too soon. You'll learn an approach to orienting new employees that gives them key information and experience, and sets clear and reasonable expectations. I'll also show you how to use listening to tell whether or not the employee is getting what's necessary. The chapter closes with a step-by-step guide for implementing this approach with your next new employee.

Chapter 5. The Gardener's Mind: Successful gardeners have a certain mind-set: they trust in their own skills and they trust in the power of nature; they know that rain falls, the sun shines, and seeds grow. They know that nature and their plants will do a lot of the work, and that they'll need to help nature along and take best advantage of what nature offers. This chapter explains the mind-set of a successful coach, which is very similar to that of a successful gardener—believing in people's potential and wanting to help them grow. I'll use the gardening metaphor to show why this mind-set is critical to growing great employees, and what can happen if the coach doesn't have that mind-set. You'll learn a way to investigate your own mind-set, and to shift it, if necessary, by managing your self-talk about your employees. Finally, I'll provide a suggestion about how to sustain the "coach" mind-set.

Chapter 6. A Mixed Bouquet: High-yield gardening requires attending to the individual needs of each kind of plant, and growing great employees requires the same thing. All too often, leaders use a "one size fits all" approach to managing and developing their employees—which may work well for some, but won't work at all for others. This chapter offers a listening- and observation-based approach to discovering how to best manage each of your employees. You'll learn to use this approach to determine an employee's strengths and passions, as well as his or her Achilles' heels. You'll also be able to find out what motivates each employee, and what each employee finds demotivating. At the end of the chapter, you'll find a suggestion for remembering your most important discoveries.

Chapter 7. Staking and Weeding: This chapter focuses on key "maintenance" skills for growing employees. These are the managerial equivalents of the things a gardener does to keep a garden thriving—staking, weeding, spraying, deadheading, etc. They may not be the most fun or creative aspects of management (or gardening) but these preventative measures nip problems in the bud and give employees a chance to bloom. You and I will explore the skills of making agreements with your employees and giving them feedback, first explaining why each skill is helpful and how they work together to keep your employees moving in the right direction. Then we'll teach an approach to making agreements that yield realistic expectations to which the employee is committed and that he or she feels capable of fulfilling. I'll build on this to teach you how to give feedback (both positive and corrective) about whether an employee is fulfilling his or her agreements, in a way that your employee will find "hearable" and actionable. You'll get real-life examples of both skills in use, and you'll have a chance to prepare to have a real-life feedback conversation with one of your employees.

Chapter 8. Letting It Spread: The most lush and exuberant gardens are those allowed to spread—to indulge in their natural tendency to expand into new seedlings and new shoots. One of the most powerful ways to grow great employees is to delegate authority and responsibility to them—to "let them spread." This chapter will show how delegation, when done well, increases employee capability, creates commitment and pride, and frees the leader for higher-leverage, more strategic work. I'll offer a model for delegation that builds on skills learned in previous chapters (especially listening, agreements, feedback, and determining the best management approach for a given employee). I'll then walk you through how to apply the model, and share a case study of a leader who used it to unleash the growth potential in a key employee.

Chapter 9. Plants into Gardeners: In being a leader, there's a possibility that doesn't exist in gardening; some of your plants have the potential to become gardeners! This chapter focuses on how to help your employees focus on developing new skills and abilities, including management and leadership. I'll share a model for coaching that builds on the delegation discussion of the previous chapter, as well as the "coach mind-set" ideas of chapter 5. You and I also will talk about situations where you, the manager, are the best resource for an employee to acquire new skills or knowledge; I'll offer an approach to teaching, based on concepts we've discussed earlier, and give you a chance to think through how you could teach something important to one of your employees.

Chapter 10. How Does Your Garden Grow? Making a wonderful garden requires balancing the gardener's effort with the power of nature. As applied to developing employees, this means finding the appropriate balance between your responsibility and the employee's responsibility for his or her growth. This chapter offers a summary of the core responsibilities you can expect any employee to fulfill. I'll also discuss a "management decision tree" based on the skills in this book, an approach to making sure you've taken every reasonable step to balance your efforts as a manager with an employee's efforts to support his or her own growth. This chapter is less skill-based and more conceptual than most of the previous ones, exploring the issue of personal responsibility, and helping you think more clearly about how your actions and assumptions can support or hinder an employee's taking charge of his or her professional development.

Chapter 11. Some Plants Don't Make It: Even skilled gardeners have some plants that don't thrive, despite their best efforts. It's true of leaders, too; sometimes even excellent managers and leaders have employees who don't succeed. This chapter reviews the "management decision tree" introduced in chapter 10 and discusses how to proceed when you've determined that you've done what you can, and a particular employee is not going to thrive in a given job. This chapter focuses on giving you a process and tools for taking the difficult step of termination in a way that's fair and respectful and that minimizes damage to the rest of the organization.

Chapter 12. The Master Gardener: Reading this book is a start. Now it's time to try these ideas and approaches in your real world. Some readers—you, perhaps?—might want to take it even further; growing great employees might be, or might become, something of a passion for you. I'll talk about the idea of mastery—of personally gaining mastery in those areas that are important to you, and how you can continue to use this book as a resource. I'll also help you make a plan for continuing to develop toward mastery as a manager of people. Finally, you'll create a key phrase or phrases you can use to remind yourself why and how you want to grow great employees.

I hope you'll find this book useful, enjoyable, and thought-provoking in equal measure. And if you'd like to tell me how it strikes you, or find out more about my company and what we do, I'd love to hear from you: Feel free to e-mail me at connect@proteus-international.com.

Bon voyage!

Erika Andersen
Kingston, NY
June 2006

Growing Great Employees

CHAPTER 1

Preparing the Soil

(Or, There's No Such Thing as a One-Minute Gardener)

This is where the gardening metaphor kicks in. You may also have noticed that the chapter title combines the gardening metaphor with a good-natured swipe at a popular management book. And, it's true: growing a garden and growing employees both require time, thought, skill, and knowledge. However, both yield benefits that make the effort entirely worthwhile. In the garden, the right effort yields plants that thrive and are productive. In managing people, the right effort yields employees who thrive and are productive. Thriving and productive, in the world of work, means motivated, self-sufficient, capable, and good with others. When you think about the alternative, which most managers have experienced—that is, employees who are unmotivated, overly dependent, not capable and/or difficult to work with—taking the time and energy needed to become a good manager starts to seem like a very smart investment.

So, why can't you be a one-minute manager/gardener? Well, what if a gardener, looking out at his weed-filled, gasping-for-moisture flowerbed, shook his head in disgust and said, "What is up with those flowers? They're so needy! Why can't they just get it together?" We would think that person was being just a tad unrealistic. And yet, with our employees, we're often irritated that they can't just "do it on their own." Now, don't get me wrong. If you put the right plant/employee in the right spot, it will be relatively easy to grow. (And, conversely, no amount of gardening skill or effort will make a cactus thrive in a swamp!) But even when employees are a good fit for the company, for the job, and for your management style—they're still going to need some support from you to do their best.

Which brings us to the foundation of your success as a manager (drum roll). Any good gardener knows that the secret of good gardening, the inescapable foundation for excellent results, lies in soil preparation—unglamorous as that may be. No matter how good the plants are, no matter how much you water or fertilize later on—unless you start by creating a rich, open environment for your plants to grow in, you are likely doomed to failure. Therefore, the wise gardener, before ever making that first, exciting trip to the garden center to pick the plants of his or her dreams, spends time creating great soil. You do this by digging it up to loosen it and to see what it's like, and then digging things into it. Great soil is loose and open, so the plants can burrow their roots into it easily, and it has natural nutrients incorporated into it as needed—compost, rich topsoil, etc.—so that the plants get the nourishment they need.

For a manager, *listening* is preparing the soil. It's your key to creating a working environment that supports optimal growth. Listening to your employees first allows you to "dig it up and see what's there." That is, it gives you a chance to find out what people actually know and don't know, what has and hasn't been done, where the concerns and misunderstandings are—as well as the enthusiasm and clarity. Listening gives you the best sense of who your employees are and what they're capable of doing. In the process, it creates an atmosphere of mutual respect—one where people feel valued and encouraged to express their ideas, opinions, and concerns. When they are genuinely listened to, employees tend to put down roots and to thrive—to be loyal and committed, and to be more enthusiastic about achieving great results.

.   .   .

Over the years, when I've talked about listening as the foundation of managerial success, I often get puzzled or disbelieving looks, initially. This idea seems to fly in the face of much that people hear or assume about managing. Many of us have grown up with the idea (and seen it demonstrated way too many times) that managers are the people who talk, and employees are the people who listen. It's that whole fearless leader thing: too often, when people get to be managers, they think they're suddenly supposed to have all the answers—and be continually giving them! In my experience, that's not what works best. The best leaders I've worked with do a lot of listening—to their customers, to colleagues in their industry, and to their employees. Just recently, I watched a client of mine, someone for whom I have a lot of respect as a person and as a results-oriented businessman, sit in a meeting with a group he had just been brought in to manage. He only talked about 10 percent of the time. He started out by letting people know that he wanted to get their understanding of the current state of the business, and hear about what they thought were the key issues. He then focused on people as they spoke, and he took notes. When he did speak, he asked insightful questions or made statements that built on what people had said. At the end, he thanked everyone, and clarified a few next steps. As people left the room, I could tell they felt more relaxed and hopeful. He had communicated very clearly and powerfully to them what kind of a manager he was going to be. Much more powerfully than if he had told them, "I value you, and I'm interested in your point of view." He showed them, by listening.

From here on, we're going to be strengthening your listening skills, teaching you how to be the kind of manager I've just described. There will be times when I encourage you to put the book down and do something or think about something. If that's not your style (to read in fits and starts), don't worry about it. Just keep on reading. At the same time, I do hope that you'll try out the activities I suggest at some point, because understanding something intellectually is very different from being able to put it into practice . . . and I want you to be able to do this!

Learning to Listen: A Model

In any conversation that includes an "issue"—even if it's only a few minutes long—two things usually happen: you gather information and you try to deal with the issue that's been raised. Let's build a model based on these two things people generally do when engaging in conversation:

INFORMATION GATHERING	ADDRESSING ISSUES
paying attention	brainstorming
inviting	making agreements
questioning	giving feedback
restating	coaching
	problem-solving

Simple model. Unfortunately, because most of us have been taught to believe that "manager" means "person with all the answers," it's often difficult for us not to jump into addressing the issues too early, before we've gotten the information we need. And whether or not you do this out loud is largely irrelevant in this context: once you've formed a strong opinion and are thinking about what should happen next, it's hard to take in fully what the other person is saying (especially if it doesn't line up with your point of view).

Listening gives you a clear alternative to addressing the issues too soon, and a way to stay neutral while you're gathering the necessary information.

No Voodoo—Actual Skills

The very good news is that listening in this way is learnable. It's not a "you have it or you don't" kind of thing . . . and I speak from my own hard-won personal experience, and my experience in teaching and coaching hundreds of managers. Just as a gardener can learn to put the right nutrients in the soil, or a tennis player to hit a stronger backhand, you can learn to listen more consistently and more effectively—and reap the benefits of doing so. The skills of good listening aren't difficult or complicated—but they do require, for most people, new ways of behaving. These new ways of behaving, in a few words:

LISTENING IS:
Paying Attention
Inviting
Questioning
Restating

I'll spend the rest of this chapter offering you ways to learn to do, or to get better at doing, these four things. I'll offer a reasonable explanation for everything I recommend, and then I'll encourage you to try it out in real life, as I said earlier. And as you try it out, see how it works—notice whether it helps you to be a better manager and developer of people.

Before we dig into these four skills, here are a few red flags—things *not* to do when practicing listening:

Interrupt—even if you're excited by what the other person is saying, or you disagree strongly . . . keep listening. Interrupting will make it hard for the other person to complete his or her thoughts. It's distracting and, if done enough, annoying.

Divert—offering advice, asking questions about another topic, throwing in your own war stories, etc., is likely to pull the speaker off of his or her own train of thought and onto yours.

Monologue—remember, listening is focusing on the other person's thoughts, ideas, and feelings. Hard to do if you're always the one talking!

Listening Skill 1: Paying Attention
The first skill of listening is so simple and obvious that it may seem unimportant. However, paying attention to someone when he or she is

speaking is the first effort you can make to keep the focus on that person.

Paying attention is an uncomplicated thing, and most of us do it naturally when we're curious and involved. By knowing what it entails, understanding how important it is, and doing it consciously and consistently, we can use it to help us get curious and involved in what the other person is saying.

Some of the key elements of paying attention are:

physical focus: making eye contact, turning toward the other person, not doing other tasks.

verbal focus: not carrying on other conversations (even via e-mail . . .).

mental focus: making effort to follow the other person's thinking and understand their feelings (versus daydreaming or thinking about what you're going to say when they take a breath).

TRY IT OUT

At this point, I want you to put the book down and do an experiment. Find a friend, family member, or colleague, and ask for a few minutes of their time. Tell them you're going to talk to them about something you're interested in, and you want them to do everything they can (without interrupting, and short of leaving the room) to *not* pay attention to you, while you try to keep talking.

OK? Go do it.

So, how did that feel? How easy or hard was it to keep talking? I suspect it was somewhat difficult to keep talking, and that you felt unheard or unappreciated . . . even though you were the one who set the conversation up that way!

Now, the embarrassing part. Think about all the times an employee, teammate, spouse, or child has come to you wanting your attention, and you've done to them (in some version) what you just had done to you. Ouch.

Paying attention is simple and relatively easy to do. In fact, we all know how to do it—and we do it sometimes. All this makes it easy to underestimate its importance in building strong, open, respectful communication with employees. I'm hoping you're thinking about it differently now than you were a few minutes ago.

Listening Skill 2: Inviting
Paying attention is like being home when someone comes to visit. The next skill, "inviting," is like opening the door and asking them to come in. Paying attention lets people know you're present; "inviting" encourages them to speak.

As with paying attention, inviting is something most people do automatically when they're relaxed and interested, and when they have a good relationship with the person who's speaking. Making this a conscious skill gives you the option to use it whenever you want, in order to create more positive, productive interactions.

Some key elements of the skill of inviting are:

physical "gestures": nodding, matching body language and expressions.

verbal "gestures": nonword sounds, encouraging phrases; brief questions that specifically encourage the speaker to begin or continue speaking.

Here's how this looks and sounds. Let's say you're standing at the company Christmas party, talking to your boss's boss, who's new to the company and to you. As you speak, she stands facing you, drink in hand (like you), and nods in agreement. When you mention something you think is a problem (probably with a concerned look on your face), she frowns in sympathy and says, "Mm-hmm." When you pause, wondering if she's getting bored, she asks, "So, what else bothers you about that?" And when you say that you find it challenging to deal with the folks in

Memphis, she raises her eyebrows and nodding, says emphatically, "Oh, OK!"

I suspect you would feel invited to keep talking.

Let's try the same scenario, without the inviting. You're standing at the company Christmas party, talking to your boss's boss. As you speak, she stands turned slightly away from you, arms folded, and looks a little preoccupied. When you mention something you think is a problem (probably with a concerned look on your face), there's no change in her expression. When you pause, wondering if she's getting bored, she doesn't say anything. Losing steam and getting a little uncomfortable, you note that you find it challenging to deal with the folks in Memphis. She stares at you blankly.

She's paying attention, but I don't imagine you feel invited to continue.

Like paying attention, inviting is a simple, almost invisible skill. And, as in our scenario, it can make the difference between creating an environment where employees feel encouraged to express their thoughts and ideas, and one where they don't.

TRY IT OUT

Sometime today, spend five minutes—with your spouse, a friend, a colleague, an employee—simply paying attention and inviting while they talk about something that's important to them. Note the effect it has on them, and on you. Note whether you hear more of what they say and whether they say things you haven't heard before.

Listening Skill 3: Questioning

In listening, questions are like atomic power: a great force for good or evil. Depending on how and why a question is asked, it can greatly hinder or greatly help the listening process.

Questions that hinder listening are those that aim to support your existing point of view (e.g., "Isn't it true that distribution is the main problem?" or, "Don't you think you could have addressed that sooner?"). They are simply statements of what you already think, followed by a question mark. These kinds of questions put the speaker in the position of responding to your point of view, rather than sharing his or her own.

Listening questions arise out of curiosity. They are an expression of your intention to hear the speaker's point of view (e.g., "Do you see distribution as part of the problem?" or, "What are some ways you might have addressed that sooner?").

Here's a way to think about the differences between questions that hinder and those that foster listening:

LISTENING QUESTIONS	NON-LISTENING QUESTIONS
information-gathering	information-sharing
curiosity-based	giving directives
asking for speaker's P.O.V.	asserting a P.O.V.

One of the best ways to tell what kind of question you're about to ask is to listen to your own self-talk. A curiosity-based question that focuses on finding out your employee's point of view will tend to come from self-talk like, "Hmm, I wonder what she meant by that?" or, "Now, that's interesting—I'd like to know more." In contrast, non-listening questions tend to be preceded by self-talk like, "I don't agree. I think . . ." or, "I need to set him/her straight."

Are you actively interested in hearing more about what your employee has to say? Do you want to hear it even if it contradicts your own opinions and ideas? Then your questions will probably be listening questions: information-gathering, curiosity-based, and asking for the speaker's point of view.

Now, don't get me wrong. I'm not saying you shouldn't express a point of view. I'm just saying don't mangle the two things together. When you're listening, listen! And when you want to express your point of view, just do it . . . don't add a question mark at the end in order to pretend to be open-minded.

Think of two people with whom you talk fairly regularly. The first person should be someone who puts you on the defensive; with whom you often feel as though you're being asked to justify your point of view. The second person should be someone with whom you feel really comfortable; someone you feel accepts you as you are and is interested in hearing your point of view.

Next time you talk with each of these people, notice what kinds of questions they ask you—listening, or non-listening. I suspect you'll find that the person with whom you feel more comfortable tends to ask more listening questions.

Listening Skill 4: Restating

The final skill of listening is the only one that generally requires a conscious effort to learn. Unlike the first three—paying attention, inviting, or asking curiosity-based questions—restating isn't something most of us already do. It is, however, an extremely useful skill, particularly when you're trying to understand complex or new ideas, or demonstrate your understanding. Restating is simply summarizing, in your own words, the essence of what the speaker has just said.

RESTATING IS:
In your own words
The essence
Only when needed

Restating completes a feedback loop between speaker and listener. Without it, you tend to simply assume that you understand what the speaker is saying. That assumption, as you can imagine, isn't always true. How many times have you left a meeting or a conversation thinking that you and another person had the same understanding only to find out later (after the packaging was orange and fuchsia, or the money was spent without checking with finance) just how wrong you were!

When you briefly restate the essence of the speaker's message in your own words, you are far more likely to avoid such frustrating (and often expensive) misunderstandings. Interestingly, when your restatement is accurate, the speaker's reaction will often be "Yes, exactly!" It's very gratifying, as the speaker, to know that the person listening really has understood your point of view. This is yet another way to create that great "soil"—an environment of mutual respect and understanding—where excellent work can get done and people can enjoy working together.

So, how does restating sound? You might be thinking to yourself, "Won't I seem goofy if I just repeat what the other person has said?" Remember, it's not just parroting back—it's the core of what's been said, in your own words, and only when needed. (If someone says, "It's a nice day," you wouldn't say, "So, you think the weather is nice today.") Restating doesn't have to be "techniquey" or stiff.

For example, an employee of yours might come into your office one day and say, "I don't want you to think I'm just dragging my heels on this or anything, but I'm just not sure this new direct mail reward campaign is the right way to go. I know that it's important to sales to have this done and get it out quickly, before the new line comes out, but I don't think the customers will respond to it like the VP of sales is hoping they will. I wish we could either talk it through a little more with sales, or test it out with some actual customers . . . or, I don't know, it just seems too rushed. You know, it's a lot of time and money to put into something and have it tank. What do you think we should do?"

Now instead of just leaping into fearless-leader-problem-solving mode, you restate. You take a deep breath and say, "You're feeling conflicted about this. You know the sales folks are eager to move, but you're worried it could turn out badly without more thought or research." I suspect your employee would say something like "Yes!" or "Exactly!" And as a result you'd be sure that you understand their point of view before responding, and they'd know you understand, as well. Ah, clarity! A great starting point.

But what if your restatement doesn't capture the essence of what the other person has said? Does that mean you've failed? Not at all. Maybe after your succinct restatement, above, your employee says, "Well . . . kind of. I guess the thing I'm most worried about is that they'll blame us if it turns out badly, rather than taking responsibility for their own decision." Very interesting. That's a whole new level of information that you probably wouldn't have gotten to without restating.

So, the good news is: restating is extremely valuable, even when your restatement is "wrong," because it tends to keep moving the conversation toward greater and greater clarity.

Yet another benefit: your restatement invisibly requires your employee to reflect on his or her own words and to take responsibility for what he or she is saying. After the conversation above, it would be easy for you, as the manager, to say, "So, how do you think you should handle this?" or, "Where do you think we should go next?" (Curiosity-based questions!) Restating helps set up your employees to learn to solve their own problems, instead of simply coming to you as the solver-of-problems. As the old adage goes, it helps you "teach to fish" versus just "giving fish." (We'll talk more about this in chapter 9.)

TRY IT OUT

Sometime over the next twenty-four hours, someone will most likely start a conversation with you about something that they're very interested in. (Note: this will be an even more useful practice if it's something you're NOT particularly interested in.) As they begin to talk, try out all four listening skills—paying attention, inviting, curiosity-based questioning, and restating. (If you're feeling really curious and motivated, you can put the book down and go find somebody to do this with right now!)

After the conversation is over think about the following:

How did your use of the listening skills change the speaker's behavior?

What did you notice about the speaker or the topic that was new for you?

Which of the skills felt most awkward?

Which felt most useful?

Now that you've got the basic skills under your belt, I encourage you to try them out in a variety of situations: at work, at home, with friends.

What's Self-Talk?

I mentioned self-talk earlier in this chapter, when we were talking about the skill of questioning, so now let me take a moment to tell you what it is and why it's important to you as a manager.

OK. First of all, I assume you're aware you talk to yourself? Don't feel bad. Everyone talks to themselves. There's a running commentary in our heads: sometimes we're aware of it, more often we're not. The unfortunate thing about this internal voice is that it often says things that are unsupportive or unhelpful; messages that make it more difficult for us to behave in productive ways. Here's an example. Let's sa9y an employee comes into your office. And let's say further that this employee has a tendency to focus on problems he is having with other employees and that he tends to talk to you about it rather than to them. As you look up and see this person standing in your doorway, what are you likely to say to yourself?

A number of possibilities may have just run through your head; at least one of them was probably something along the lines of, "Oh, no, here he is again. Always complaining." So, if you said that to yourself as this employee came into the office, how would you be likely to feel? I suspect it would be negative: probably irritated or impatient, maybe resentful. And, feeling like that, how might you greet your employee? Pursed lips, a sigh, perhaps a brusque, "What's up, John?" or even, "John, this isn't a good time." In any case, you'd be unlikely to be very open to anything he has to say—whatever it might be. And what impact might that have on him and on your relationship? Not so positive, I would think.

Now, wind the tape back, and imagine that, when you look up and see John, you very consciously say to yourself, "You know, I want John to learn how to resolve issues he has with his colleagues, rather than complaining to me about them. And, to be fair, it could be that he's not here to complain." How might you feel after saying this to yourself? Perhaps: resolved, clear, firm. Maybe even open. And how might you then approach him? By gesturing him into the office, asking him to have a seat. Perhaps saying, "What's on your mind, John?" Much more paying attention and inviting, I would imagine. In this scenario, there's a far higher likelihood that you would have a positive conversation, that John would feel heard, and that he'd walk away having learned something, or being a little clearer about the need to behave differently. When you change your self-talk, you can have a really significant impact on how you feel and then on how you behave. Being able to manage your self-talk is key to being an effective people manager: like listening, it underpins everything we'll be talking about throughout the book. Here's what I mean: if you try to use the skills and approaches we'll cover in this book, but all the while you're saying things to yourself like, "This will never work," or "I'm no good at this," or even, "My employees don't deserve this much thought and energy on my part," it's unlikely that you'll be successful in your efforts.

Now, the most effective way to change your self-talk is to get underneath it and question the negative assumptions and beliefs that cause it. For instance, in the example we explored above, the initial self-talk most likely arose from two beliefs: that John was going to complain and there was nothing you could do about it. The revised self-talk arose from two different beliefs: that John might or might not be coming to complain, and that you could provide John with a viable alternative to complaining.

In chapter 5, "The Gardener's Mind," we'll go into depth about how to change negative or counterproductive beliefs, and you'll see how self-talk changes almost automatically as a result. For now, I'd like to suggest that you make an effort to become more aware of your self-talk—negative or positive—as you read these next few chapters.

That way, when we get to chapter 5, you'll have some really great, visceral personal examples to work with as you learn the skills of "changing your mind."

OK, Back to Listening

As a parting image for this portion of our journey together, I'd like to share with you a scenario that demonstrates the power of listening (or not listening). This first interaction is, sadly, representative of many conversations I've seen and heard over the years. Imagine the following:

> Allen sticks his head into his boss's office. "Is this a good time?" he asks. "There's something I'd like to talk to you about."
>
> "Sure," Jessica says, looking up from her computer, then back down. "Come on in." He comes in and sits down in the chair facing her desk. She continues to work, and he waits, not knowing whether to begin. "It's OK," she says. "I'm just finishing this e-mail. What's on your mind?"
>
> "Well," Allen starts off, "it's Natalie. I'm a little concerned about how she's doing with this new vendor. She's . . ."
>
> Jessica interrupts, still looking at her computer. "Yeah, I don't know about Natalie. I didn't want to say anything, but she seems a little in over her head . . ."
>
> Allen jumps in, alarmed. "No, no, she's great, I mean, I think she's doing great overall—it's just that this new vendor is very tough . . ."
>
> "Yeah, well, that's what her job is all about, isn't it?" Jessica seems to have finished the e-mail—she's no longer typing—but she's still looking at the computer, moving her mouse. "I mean, we hired her to make sure the vendors don't take unfair advantage of us, right?"

"Of course, of course," Allen responds, "and she's doing a really good job on that. In fact, she just renewed the ACME deal last week and was able to negotiate a lower rate than we had last year—and I wasn't even sure we could hold it at the same level."

Jessica finally looks at him, frowning a little. "Now, Allen, I really need you to lead the charge on cost control. You know that. And if you don't express confidence to your folks that we can negotiate better deals . . . well that's not good."

"Jessica, come on. I'm the one who encouraged her to go for a lower rate." Allen sounds a bit defensive and just a tad irritated.

"Well, good. I'm glad she did OK on that ACME deal, because the jury's still out on her, as far as I'm concerned." She looks at her watch. "Oh, wow—I've got a meeting with Jeff in a couple of minutes. Listen, let's catch up some other time, OK? I've got to get ready for this."

Allen gets up and walks to the doorway. He turns to say good-bye, and perhaps ask when they can finish the conversation, but Jessica has picked up the phone and is punching in numbers. She waves distractedly in his direction. "See you tomorrow."

Allen tries not to sigh as he walks out.

Unfortunately, that scene is being repeated, with variations, in offices all over the world at this very moment. Now, imagine instead that Jessica is the kind of manager who knows that growing great employees is critical to her success, their success, and the business's success, and she knows both how to listen and how important it is. Let's run the tape again:

Allen sticks his head into his boss's office. "Is this a good time?" he asks. "There's something I'd like to talk to you about."

"Well," Jessica says, looking up from her computer, "it's not a great time; I've only got about ten minutes. Will ten minutes be useful, or can it wait?"

He smiles and comes in. "I'll take ten minutes. I just want to get your thoughts about something." He sits down in the chair facing her desk.

"OK, shoot," she says, leaning forward and folding her arms on the desk.

"Well," Allen starts off, "it's Natalie. I'm a little concerned about how she's doing with this new vendor. She's great with people who are civil, but this guy is so tough."

Jessica encourages him. "Tough as in . . . ?"

Allen shakes his head. "Oh, you know, just a bulldog. Keeps selling, selling, selling. Doesn't really answer her questions. She's great at communicating to vendors what we need, and negotiating terms, ordinarily, but this guy just . . . you know, Natalie's young, and she's petite, and I think this guy is seeing her as a kid he can steamroll."

"OK," Jessica says, "she just can't get through to him."

"Right," Allen continues. "And it's just this one guy. Otherwise, I'm so impressed—she negotiated a lower rate with ACME than we had last year."

Jessica nods. "Wow, that's great! OK, so from your point of view she's doing really well, except that she's run into this one tough vendor and can't get him to listen to her."

"Exactly."

"So, where do we go from here?" Jessica is looking directly at him, waiting for his response.

"Well, that's what I was wondering. Can I give her the authority to say she'll take the business away from him if he won't change his approach?"

"What do you think?" Jessica asks. "Do we have a good alternate vendor?"

"We do, actually. I just wanted to make sure I wasn't missing something."

"Nope, sounds to me like you've thought it through. If that's what you guys need to do—go for it." She looks at her watch. "Oh, wow—I've got a meeting with Jeff in a couple of minutes." She looks back at Allen. "Did you get what you needed?"

"Yeah, thanks. This was very helpful." Allen gets up and walks to the doorway. He turns to say good-bye, but Jessica has picked up the phone and is punching in numbers. She stops, looks up, and smiles. "See you tomorrow."

Allen waves, turns, and heads for Natalie's office.

The power of listening. Jessica fully understands the situation, Allen has solved his own problem and has the clarity to help Natalie solve hers. And, for those of you who are still thinking quietly to yourselves, "Yeah, but I don't have time to listen" . . . please note: the two Jessica-and-Allen conversations above are, word for word, exactly the same length.

BIG IDEAS

Listening is the foundation of success in managing people. As a gardener prepares the soil in order to allow the plants an ideal growing environment, listening well creates the ideal human growth environment, one where people feel capable, valued, and respected.

Listening well requires a set of learnable skills, like playing tennis or cooking, or—you guessed it—gardening. The skills of listening are:

Paying Attention: giving the person who is speaking your physical and mental focus.

Inviting: using verbal and nonverbal signals that encourage the speaker to keep talking or go deeper.

Questioning: asking genuine, curiosity-based questions to discover the speaker's thoughts and feelings about the topic he or she is discussing.

Restating: summarizing the essence of the speaker's message, in your own words, to make sure you've understood, and to let him or her know that you've understood.

Listening to your employees may take more time initially than *not* listening to them—but it will certainly save time in the long run; time that would otherwise be spent clarifying misunderstandings, overcoming resistance, or correcting mistakes.

Self-talk: how you talk to yourself about situations can have a dramatic impact on how you feel and how you act—and you can manage that internal dialogue by addressing your underlying assumptions and beliefs about the situation. We'll explore this idea in much greater depth in chapter 5.

CHAPTER 2

Plan Before You Plant

I have a friend who can't seem to grow a good garden. She's smart, she has good taste, she wants a nice garden . . . but it just doesn't happen. Her garden always ends up looking a bit thrown together—a collection of random plants; some struggling to survive, some shouldering out their neighbors. The problem is, she's a "winging it" kind of gardener. She sees a plant she likes, buys it, and plops it in, hoping it will look like the beautiful picture on the sign at the garden center. A little planning would make a huge difference for my friend's garden. If she thought about just two things before buying a plant, she could make a really nice garden. First, what kind of a garden does she want to create? What does she want it to do—to produce flowers for cutting, perhaps, or simply to provide beauty and fragrance? And second, how does she want it to look and feel—informal and loose, formal and structured, lots of bright flowers, or mysterious and cool? Let's say she decides that she wants a garden that is beautiful to look at and quite easy to maintain. She wants lush foliage and soft-colored flowers. This gives her a great place to start making important choices. Already, she knows that she's not going to go for plants that are difficult to grow, or those that have stiff or sparse leaves, or ones with bright-colored flowers. And all of them will have to be sun-lovers, because her garden doesn't get a lot of shade.

Now she just has to think a bit more about some specific "jobs" or roles different plants will play in her garden. For instance, she'll need some big, loose-growing plants for the back of the garden, to provide the core of the soft, lush look she wants. Then, she'll need some mid-sized pastel-flowering plants for the middle of the garden, and some low-growing, spreading plants to continue the cozy look and easy maintenance at the front of the garden.

Having decided these things she'll have the basic understanding she needs to make a lovely garden. She can go to the garden center and look at plants and their information tags, and decide whether a particular plant would help to create the kind of garden she wants. She could decide first whether it suits the overall look and feel of the garden she's trying to create, and then whether it will fill any of the more specific "jobs" she's outlined for different parts of the garden. Of course, gardening is a subtle art, and there are lots of other details she could learn and think about, but just those two things would guide her in a very useful way.

Too often, new employees get "plopped in" to a department or company based on a similar lack of planning, and too often, these perfectly good people fail to thrive because of it. You can end up with a department (or even a whole company) of people who seem like a hodgepodge of random employees—some struggling to survive, some shouldering out their neighbors. Fortunately, the same two relatively straightforward planning steps I've noted above are as helpful for groups of employees as they are for groups of plants. For a manager, these planning steps translate into (1) deciding what kind of a workplace you're trying to create, and then (2) clarifying the specific jobs your successful workplace requires.

What Kind of a Garden Would You Like?

My friend with the less-than-successful garden hasn't answered the important question, "What kind of a garden do you want to create?" As a manager (of one person, a hundred, or a thousand) the question to ask yourself is, "What kind of a workplace do you want to create?" This question actually has two related parts, which we talked about above in the garden example. The first is, "What do you want your garden to do?" which translates, for the manager, into: "What do you need to achieve in your workplace?" The second is, "What do you want your garden to look and feel like?" The analogous question for a manager is, "How do you want people to work together in order to get there?"

I assume you're already reasonably clear about the first question. Most managers are pretty clear about what they need to achieve—the results they're being held accountable for—for example, some measure of profitability, growth, productivity, sales, or customer satisfaction. How to get there is generally less clear to people, but equally critical to success. For instance, perhaps it's important to you—given the work you're doing and the kind of manager you are—that everyone work very well as a team, and that they continually look for innovative solutions to challenges that arise. You want employees who can demonstrate "teamwork" and "creativity" or "innovation." Perhaps, for another manager, one with different goals and a different style, it's more important that everyone work independently to achieve their results, and that they stay very rigorous about following existing procedures. This manager would need employees whose core competencies include "independence" and "precision" or "rigor."

Imagine what happens when managers don't think through these preferences, or don't make them explicit in the hiring process. You might hire someone who has all the technical qualifications you need, who is an honest, smart person with the right experience, but who relies on "independence" and "rigor" to do her job, when what you're looking for is "teamwork" and "innovation." That plant would almost certainly fail to thrive in your garden and in a few months, everyone would be shaking his or her head and saying—"You know, it's so sad. She's a great person, but she's just not a fit for the culture." "Not a fit for the culture" is business-speak for the problem we're describing; where the person's core competencies, the "how" that he or she uses to get work done, don't match up to the invisible, unexpressed "how" of the company or department.

You can save yourself and others enormous amounts of time, money, and emotional trauma (just think how much it costs, on a whole variety of levels, to hire someone and then let them go six months later) by thinking through your preferences about how the work gets done—and then making them explicit. Even though the example above is very simple, and focuses on only a few elements, you can see that making clear decisions about what kind of workplace you're trying to create would help you choose who to hire, and make it more likely that those you hire would be best-suited to helping you create the kind of workplace you need. I'll devote the next part of this chapter to teaching you an approach for deciding how to determine those core competencies that define the kind of workplace you want to create.

Selecting Core Competencies

*A **core competency** is a capability that someone needs in order to succeed in a given organization or department.*

I think you've probably understood that already, but I thought it might be helpful to put it into a single sentence. First, let me offer you a simple approach to defining the core competencies that are most important in the people you manage:

SELECTING THE
CORE COMPETENCIES FOR YOUR TEAM
Find Exemplars
Look for Clues
Work from a List

Finding exemplars simply means looking for people already in the environment who demonstrate the characteristics you want. These people can then become your mental model of the kind of people you're looking for, and you can spend time getting very clear on what it is about how they work that fits so well for you and your department. It's great if you can find more than one person, and even better if they're in quite different jobs. That way, the capabilities they share are less likely to be a function of their particular jobs, and more likely to be an indicator of what you like about how they do work, period.

In addition to having exemplars to think about, it's also useful to **look for "clues"** in the environment. The implicit preferences about how work gets done in a particular place often show themselves in the form of common phrases, slogans, positive jokes, or even values statements. For example, you and others in your department or company might pride yourselves on never letting anything fall through the cracks; or there might be a running joke about how everyone else wants to work in your department because you all have fun, even when things get rough.

Finally, it's helpful to **have a list** of possible core competencies to work from as you're thinking about your exemplars and clues—something to spark your memory and focus your thinking.

TRY IT OUT

Let's experiment with this. In the space below (or on a separate piece of paper, if you're one of those people—like me—who don't feel comfortable writing in books!), note a couple of people now in your department or business who approach their work in a way that appeals to you; that exemplifies the kind of workplace you'd like to create:

Person #1
Person #2
Person #3

Now, think about clues in the environment that help define the core competencies that are important to your team. What are some phrases, jokes, slogans, or comments that are used to talk about the positive aspects of how work gets done in your company or department?

———————————————————————————
———————————————————————————
———————————————————————————

Below, you'll find a list of possible core competencies. Using your exemplars and your clues, above, as reference points, pick the four to six you think best capture the essence of how you want work to get done in your department or company.

Teamwork	Customer Focus	Respect
Judgment	Leadership	Honesty
Creativity	Initiative	Flexibility
Precision	Independence	Clarity
Focus	Results-orientation	Toughness
Accountability	Analytical Thinking	Humor
Realism	Passion	Optimism
Resilience	Vision	Ingenuity
Open-mindedness	Intuition	Drive
Sensitivity	Self-sufficiency	Diplomacy

Please understand that the list above is provided as a starting point for your thinking. You may find competencies on this list that perfectly capture the qualities you're looking for or, on the other hand, looking at this list may help you think of other competencies that are even more accurate in describing the workplace you want to create.

Defining Your Competencies

Once you've selected your four to six core competencies, it's important to define them in behavioral terms. That way, you and everyone else—the people who work for you now, your future employees, the people who will help you hire those people (HR, outside recruiters, etc.)—will have the same expectations. You'll all have a common language about what success means in each of these core competencies.

Defining your core competencies in behavioral terms means thinking about how that core competency would look and sound in the real world and then, creating three to five brief descriptive statements to summarize that look and sound. You can use your exemplars to help you do this.

Here's how this works. Let's say one of the core competencies you've chosen is teamwork. You think about or observe one of your exemplars—someone you think is particularly skillful in this area—demonstrating teamwork, and you realize he does the following things:

- achieves results through working with others,
- engages in consistent, two-way communication with team members,
- successfully handles conflicts with others.

All three of these statements are behavioral; that is, you could say with reasonable accuracy whether and to what extent someone was doing these things, simply by observing her behaviors. The art here is really to make these statements as clear, simple, and behavior-based as possible. For more help on how to do this, look in chapter 7, "Staking and Weeding," under the section called "Camera Check."

TRY IT OUT

On a piece of paper, write the first core competency you've selected. Imagine one of your exemplars demonstrating this competency and that you are videotaping him or her doing it. Now, "watch the tape" mentally and make notes to yourself about the key words or actions you "see" on the tape. Use these notes to write three to five descriptors—brief behavior-based statements that define the essence of this competency.

Repeat this process for each of your four to six selected competencies.

Finally, when you're finished, I suggest you share your competency/descriptor list with a few people whose judgment (and discretion) you trust. Ask them to read it with a particular person in mind, someone with whom they work closely. Have them think about whether this person demonstrates the competencies as you've described them. Then have them give you feedback about ways in which your document was helpful or easy to use; anything they found confusing or unclear in trying to use it; and any suggestions they have for making those things clearer and less confusing.

Now, What About the Plants?

As a gardener, having clarified what kind of garden you want to create—what you want it to "do" and the look and feel you want—you're ready to go out and buy some plants. Right? Well, not quite. Before you hit the garden center, it's important to think more specifically about the roles you need various plants to play. For instance, in the example at the beginning of the chapter, I noted that my gardening friend would need certain kinds of plants at the front, middle, and back of her garden. These plants, in addition to demonstrating her core competencies—soft flower colors, sun-loving, easy maintenance, lush growth—would need the characteristics that would allow them to do their unique "jobs" in the garden. For instance, the plants at the back of the garden would need to be taller and looser-growing, to provide a lush background. On the other hand, the plants in the front would need to be much shorter, and spreading rather than staying the same size, to support the lush look and provide ease of maintenance.

That same kind of clarity is needed when hiring people to work in your department or company. Once you're clear on your core competencies, the next step is to define what each person will do—the role he or she will play in the workplace. Without this, you're still going to have a confused workplace. Maybe everyone will have the capacity to work in a team, or think outside the box, or get results. But without a fairly straightforward definition of roles and responsibility, those core competencies aren't going to be best utilized.

I'm suggesting that you create job descriptions. Now I know that in most organizations, job descriptions have a bad reputation, so you may be rolling your eyes and sighing right now.

Job descriptions are thought of as useless at best and actively counterproductive at worst. Even in organizations where job descriptions exist, they tend to languish at the back of a drawer, unused, until they're so out-of-date that people couldn't use them if they wanted to!

I think that most people think job descriptions are stupid because: (1) most job descriptions *are* stupid—they're way too complicated and either too theoretical or too task-level specific; and (2) job descriptions generally don't tell you what you need to know in order to figure out whether a specific candidate will be right for the job they describe.

I'm going to teach you an approach for writing job descriptions that are realistically simple and practical, and that serve as a screen for interviewing, hiring, and (after you've found the right candidate) establishing clear performance agreements. Having clear core competencies and good, usable job descriptions will allow you to hire people who will be most likely to succeed in your workplace—giving you the optimal place to begin growing great employees.

Key Responsibilities

In my experience, most jobs contain a handful of what I call key responsibilities. These are the *results the person in that job is responsible for accomplishing*. I want to make a distinction here between tasks or efforts and responsibilities. Let's listen in on two different executive assistants talking about their jobs; the first person is describing his job in terms of the tasks he performs, while the other is focusing on the overall responsibilities her tasks help to fulfill:

Anthony Assistant: task-focused
"I'm very busy. I answer all the incoming calls for the department, and route them either to my boss or her two direct reports. If the call is for my boss I find out what the person wants, and then either deal with it myself, or pass it on to her, as appropriate.

I also do a lot of filing, both electronically and on paper. I file everything having to do with the ongoing projects my boss and her two direct reports are working on; all the proposals, invoices, correspondence, statements of work, etc. Oh, and then whenever there's a report due, like the monthly financials for the department, or if my boss is preparing a presentation for the board, or anything like that, I create it for her on the computer—on Power-Point, or Excel, or whatever's most appropriate, and then make sure it's printed out and that there are copies for everybody. And the meetings where they go over the presentations, that's part of what I do, too—set those up and make sure the room has everything that's needed. Oh, and not just meetings to make presentations, but any meetings or parties we have. And then just miscellaneous stuff—things they want me to find out, or look up; you know, get them information about new products or approaches. And fairly often there are follow-up activities to do as a result of the things they've had me research . . ."

Alice Assistant: responsibility-focused
"Well, one of my main responsibilities is communication between our department and the rest of the organization. Whether it's by phone, e-mail, or in the form of presentations or reports, I work with my boss to make sure that needed communication goes in all directions in a timely and accurate way. Then I'm also the department archivist: I'm responsible for maintaining a complete and up-to-date filing system for information relating to all the projects our department is working on. My boss has also made me responsible for organizing any events or meetings the department holds. Finally, I complete a variety of projects as assigned by my boss or her direct reports."

Take a minute to think about the differences you notice between the first paragraph and the second. What assumptions do you find yourself making about the first person, as opposed to the second? Often, people who read these paragraphs have some of the following reactions:

Anthony:

· seems disorganized.
· would need more direction and structure to do his work.
· seems less capable and productive.

Alice:

· seems more professional and responsible.
· seems clearer about the big picture.
· would be able to work more independently to complete her job, requiring less direction.

Using responsibilities (vs. tasks) as the basis for a job description yields all the benefits of the second paragraph, above; not only does it provide a clearer, more organized overview, it also clarifies the scope of the job and the skills and characteristics needed to do it well. That's helpful in recruiting and hiring; in actually doing the job (as above); and in managing the person doing it.

Finally, it's results-based versus effort-based. Here's what I mean. Anthony believes part of his job is to answer the phone (an effort). Alice believes part of her job is to assure clear and timely communication with the rest of the organization (a result). Anthony could certainly answer the phone every time it rings, without assuring clear and timely communication. For instance, he could provide insufficient information, or take a number down wrong, or leave someone on hold for a long time. He could be unclear, or come across as distracted. If his boss gave him feedback about these things, Anthony might be genuinely puzzled. "But, I'm answering the phone," he might say. "That's my job."

Alice would understand that all the elements above—providing sufficient information, taking down numbers correctly, getting people off hold quickly, being clear and focused—are within her responsibility, because they go toward creating the result she's accountable for: assuring clear and timely communication.

So, I'm sure you've figured out by now that I advocate creating job descriptions that focus primarily on responsibilities/results! As you'll see, the job description template on the following pages will allow you to create a simple map that summarizes the most important elements of a job: the information most needed for hiring, for doing the job, and for managing the person in the job.

KEY JOB DESCRIPTION ELEMENTS
Relationships
Responsibilities
Abilities

The first element, **relationships,** outlines the key ongoing interactions this person will have within the organization. The second element, **responsibilities,** we've discussed at length. You'll also describe the core tasks within each of the key responsibilities, and about how much time the person will be devoting to fulfilling each responsibility. (It's useful for someone to know the specifics of the job—as long as those tasks are organized within the responsibilities they help to fulfill, and aren't simply a random list of efforts.) Finally, a good job description will contain a list of the **abilities** needed to do the job well, including practical skills and knowledge, as well as the core competencies you've outlined for your department or company.

TRY IT OUT

Below, you'll find the job description template we've been discussing, along with brief definitions for each element. Read through it, if you would, then I'll ask you to try using it.

JOB DESCRIPTION TEMPLATE

Job Title (*what this position is called*):

_____

Manager (*who manages this person's performance*):

_____

Direct reports (*what position[s] report directly to this position, if any*):

_____

_____

_____

Other key teams/positions (*other teams or individuals with whom this person will need to work closely in order to be successful in this position*):

_____

_____

_____

Key responsibilities (*the four to six major results this person must produce or accomplish*):

_____

_____

_____

_____

_____

[Note: On another page, you can list "Time and tasks," the specific efforts required to complete the responsibilities, and the time required to make these efforts.]

Abilities (*the skills, knowledge, and capabilities needed by someone in this position in order to fulfill his or her responsibilities*):

Skills and knowledge (*practical abilities or information required*):

_____

_____

_____

_____

Competencies (personal capabilities required):

_____

_____

_____

_____

First, use the template above to describe your own job. That's the easiest way to get familiar with the tool, since you know more about your job than anyone else's. Start at the beginning, with your title, your manager, and so on.

You may find the key responsibilities area challenging—it's new territory for most people to describe the results they're supposed to accomplish versus the tasks they do. Here's a way to make sure you're focusing on results. Write down something you think is a responsibility, then ask yourself: "Why do I do this?" Then write that answer down, and ask again: "Why do I do this?" Keep asking "why" until your answer is some version of, "to make the company successful." Then go back one answer, and that's most likely your responsibility in this area. (For example, a salesperson might write down "to make twenty cold calls a week." If he then asks, "Why do I do this?" the answer might be, "to find new sales opportunities." If he then asks again, "Why do I do this?" the answer might be, "To generate sales revenue." And if he asks again, "Why?"—well, it's, "To make the company successful." Go back one, and—voilà—the key responsibility is "to generate sales revenue.")

Once you've used the template to describe your own job, and you're reasonably satisfied with the outcome, notice any positive impact it has on your understanding or your actions. You might want to share your job description with your boss, assuming you have a reasonably good and mutually supportive relationship with him or her, and ask how it lines up with the way he or she sees your job.

At this point, you'll probably feel fairly comfortable with the template, and you can begin to use it to more clearly define the jobs of those who work for you now, or new jobs for people you are planning on hiring.

Bringing It Together: An Example

To further encourage you to make use of this approach, I'd like to share an example of how a manager might use the core competencies and job description tools to fill a new and critical job.

Jorge Lopez has just been made GM of the Central Region for a young company called SENSIA that makes portable DVD players. The company has grown so quickly that the main office in San Francisco isn't capable of meeting demand, and the senior team has decided to open offices in Chicago and New York as headquarters for the new Central and Eastern regions. Jorge, in Chicago, has most of his senior team in place—the heads of sales, finance, and production—but he needs to hire a head of HR, and he wants to make sure that he gets it right. He has a skeleton crew of about twelve people right now, just getting the office and the production facilities set up, and he's been tasked with hiring about eighty more people over the next four to six months. If the company keeps growing as it has been, they'll be hiring even more people over the next year or two. Jorge knows that the success of the regional office depends on finding and keeping the right employees. He sees the HR director as key to that.

He's reading a new book called *Growing Great Employees,* and he decides to start by working with his team to create core competencies for their region. Jorge figures this will be useful not only for finding the right HR director, but will help them to hire the right people for every open position. (They're hoping when the SENSIA CEO hears about their work . . . but that's another story.)

Anyway, after some discussion, the Central Region team comes up with their five core competencies: teamwork, flexibility, innovation, decisiveness, and honesty. They feel these competencies are represented in the company's best employees, and that these qualities will create the kind of workplace they want and need in order to meet their goals.

The Corporate VP of HR has already suggested a structure for their HR function: a director, a training specialist, a compensation and benefits administrator, and an HR coordinator. They like this structure and decide to go with it. Now, Jorge asks his team to help him create the job description for the regional director of HR. They talk about the best HR people they've known in the course of their own careers, and the results those people were able to achieve. Then they talk about some of the specific things this person is going to need to accomplish in order to help them build a strong regional office. They question themselves to make sure they're focusing on results (versus tasks) in the key responsibilities area, and then think through the key tasks under each responsibility. They decide to propose an allocation of time for the next six months only—during the time when the office is being staffed and all the systems are being set up. They agree they'll have to reassess the time needs with the HR director after the first six months.

Finally, they look at abilities. They think about and agree on the skills and knowledge needed to fulfill these responsibilities. Agreeing on the competencies is easy; they just use their new core competencies, and then add "discretion," which they feel is critical for the head of HR.

Once they've drafted the job description, they send it to the VP of corporate HR for her input. She's surprised and pleased at what they've come up with: she suggests some revisions based on her more in-depth knowledge, and lets them know they've created a very clear roadmap. She and they feel confident they'll be able to use the job description to find the kind of person they want and need in this critical job.

I don't want to leave you hanging—so, here's the job description they created:

Job Title: Director of Human Resources, Central Region

Manager: Jorge Lopez, GM Central Region

Direct reports: Central Region HR staff, including HR Coordinator, Training Specialist, Compensation and Benefits Administrator

Other key teams/people: Central Region Senior Team; Corporate VP of HR

Key responsibilities

- Create and maintain an effective approach to *recruiting and selection* throughout the region.
- Support Central Region managers in proper *hiring and orientation* of new employees.
- Work with managers to *retain and develop* employees through effective performance planning and review, supported by appropriate training and development and appropriate Employee Relations (ER) support.
- Support managers in making appropriate *promotion and transition* decisions, in order to help assure the right person is in the right job.
- *Manage regional HR staff* to fulfill their responsibilities and develop professionally.
- Work as a full member of the regional senior team to fulfill the business goals.

Time and tasks

Recruiting and Selection—35 percent over the next six months
- Help managers to identify personnel needs and create job descriptions for those needs.
- Develop approaches for sourcing new candidates (working with Corporate HR team to avoid duplication of effort).
- Help managers to develop interview questions and coach them in interviewing skills.
- Interview candidates with managers as feasible, and for all managerial positions.

- Help managers select most appropriate candidates, based on interviews and experience.

Hiring and Orientation—20 percent over the next six months
- Support managers in creating clear performance agreements with new employees.
- Work with managers and comp and benefits administrator to create clear, legal, and equitable employment agreements.
- Work with managers and facilities to assure that new employees have all essential tools and resources when they begin work.
- Support new employee success by providing orientation, in collaboration with managers and HR training specialist, that offers necessary information and understanding.

Retain and Develop—15 percent over the next six months
- Support managers to make effective use of the performance review process.
- Create a system, in collaboration with Corporate HR, for handling ER issues appropriately and quickly.
- Establish a system for employees to get needed training and/or coaching.
- Work with senior team to continue improving Central Region approaches to all human resources issues, especially succession planning.

Promotion and Transition—10 percent over the next six months
- Support managers in identifying need for change in employee status (promotion, firing, part-time to full-time, etc.)
- Work with comp and benefits administrator to build equitable and consistent promotion and transition guidelines.
- Coach and/or help managers to conduct promotion and transition discussions.
- Provide outplacement services for any released employees at director-level and above.

Manage Regional HR Staff—10 percent over the next six months
- Provide ongoing feedback and coaching for each HR employee, including timely performance reviews and bonus discussions.

- Support employee development plans as agreed.
- Assure that all HR Central Region staff function as an effective team to support the work of the region.
- Create and maintain an environment of collaboration and mutual respect within the HR department.

Work as a Member of the Regional Senior Team—

10 percent over the next six months

- Offer the team information and perspective on HR issues as appropriate.
- Support all decisions made by the team by fulfilling agreed-upon commitments.
- Work with team members to create organizational and reporting structures.
- Work with team to create appropriate, simple, legal HR policies and procedures.
- Act as "team coach," helping to resolve conflicts or difficulties in collaboration.

Abilities

Skills and/or Knowledge:

- management and coaching skills
- communication skills (listening, feedback, presentation)
- interviewing skills
- collaboration/teambuilding skills
- writing skills
- strategic thinking
- ability to create and maintain HR systems and procedures
- current management and team theory and practice
- basic human psychology

Competencies

- teamwork
- flexibility
- innovation
- decisiveness

· honesty
· discretion

Good Garden, Good Workplace

I'm sitting in my friend's car, and we're on our way to the garden center. She now knows what kind of garden she wants to create: her garden's "core competencies" are lush, low-maintenance, sun-loving, softly colored, and fragrant. She knows the "job descriptions" for the plants at the back, middle, and front of her garden. She's focused, confident, and excited, and feels as though she can select from what's available to make the garden of her dreams.

Well, at the moment, this is just my dream (to tell the truth, my friend has yet to admit to herself that her garden isn't so great). However, like you (having read this chapter), Jorge is now ready to go out and find the employee of his dreams, in order to create the workplace of his dreams. Let's follow Jorge and our metaphor . . .

BIG IDEAS

For a gardener, creating a dream garden requires knowing what kind of a garden you want to create, and then what kinds of plants will help you to create it. For a manager, creating a great workplace requires getting clear about the workplace you're trying to create and what kinds of jobs and people will help you to create it.

Selecting core competencies—capabilities required of every employee—allows you to create the kind of workplace you envision. They will define "how work gets done" in your workplace, and serve as a screen for recruiting, hiring, development, and promotion. You select core competencies by:

Finding exemplars: looking at the people now in the organization who most embody the workplace you want to create, and noting their key capabilities.

Looking for clues: noting verbal indicators—in-jokes, key phrases, or comments—of the positive aspects of "how work gets done" in your organization.

Working from a list: like the list of possible core competencies provided in this chapter.

Creating and using clear and simple **job descriptions**—based on responsibilities versus tasks, specifying the most-needed skills and knowledge, and including the core competencies—will help assure that you hire the people who are most capable of helping you create the workplace you envision.

CHAPTER 3

Picking Your Plants

S o, let's pretend that my friend has taken all my wise gardening advice, and now we're at the garden center; she's looking at plants. She sees one that she likes the look of—it's small, with glossy green leaves and tiny blue flowers. She picks it up and looks at the tag. "It says this plant stays fairly small and has a spreading habit. That's good for the front of my garden, right? Oh, wait—it needs a lot of shade. Too bad." She sets it back down. We walk a few more feet and she sees something else she likes. It's a tidy plant with fuzzy green leaves and lots of little daisylike white flowers. Again, she looks at the tag. "This one is for full sun; that's good. It stays low—about six inches—and doesn't spread, but forms good-sized clumps. It says it's very hardy and doesn't need much water. That sounds perfect for the front of the garden, doesn't it? I like it—it's very soft and casual-looking." Smiling, she puts it in her cart.

Unfortunately for us, prospective employees don't come with tags. Well, I guess a résumé is sort of a tag, but not a very helpful one. A résumé is kind of like a plant having a tag that says "I grew really successfully in some other people's gardens." How, then, do you find out whether an employee will take root and flourish in the workplace that you're creating?

Since people don't have accurate information tags, at some point in the distant past we humans invented interviewing. We figured we could ask people questions and they'd tell us the truth, and then we'd know whether they'd do well in the job and in our workplace. The problem with this is that people quite often say things about themselves that aren't true. Sometimes it's because they don't see themselves very clearly (they may believe they are great managers, for example, when in fact they aren't) and sometimes it's because they so much want the job that they say what they think you want to hear rather than what's precisely accurate. And sometimes, sadly, people just lie.

In any case, the result is that regular interviewing—that is, I ask you some questions about whether you'd be good at this job and whether you'd like it, and you say yes—doesn't work very well.

Fortunately for us, an approach called scenario-based interviewing has developed over the past ten or fifteen years. It's based on the premise that the best way to find out whether someone is a good fit for a job and a workplace is to put the person in a situation where he or she has to demonstrate the needed skills, knowledge, or characteristics rather than simply saying that he or she has them. Though this approach is often explained in a rather complicated way, the essential principles are straightforward, and using them can dramatically increase your chances of finding the right person for the job.

Even if your company uses an outside recruiting firm or has internal recruiters as part of your HR staff, you'll still have to interview the candidates they find for you. And knowing how to apply the principles of scenario-based interviewing will help you select the best-suited of the candidates (or, perhaps, help you decide that you need to see some other candidates).

How Does This Work?

By now, you know how fond I am of examples. And examples are the quickest way to understand the differences between scenario-based interviewing and "regular" interview questions. So let's go back to Jorge, our GM who's looking for an HR director. He's found three candidates, and he's interviewing them. Let's imagine first that he uses "normal" interviewing techniques, and asks each of the three this same question in his or her interview:

> *Jorge:* This is going to be a very demanding job. We're going to need a lot from you, especially at the beginning. Would you feel OK about doing a lot of the hands-on stuff yourself while you're hiring your own staff? Understanding, of course, that you'd get support from me and the rest of the senior team. And we already have some great people on board.
>
> *Candidate 1:* Oh, sure. That's not a problem.
>
> *Candidate 2:* Well, yes, of course.
>
> *Candidate 3:* Yes, if that's what it takes.

Hmm. Not a lot of difference there. It's hard to tell much about the candidates from these responses. Now let's look at an alternative.

> *Jorge, using scenario-based interviewing:* We're really at the beginning stages of setting up this regional office. You're the first person we're hiring in the HR department, although we have corporate's OK to hire three more HR people. Over the first few months especially, there would be a lot of hiring and setting up of systems . . . including hiring your own group, all while undertaking all the regular day-to-day HR responsibilities. How would you approach that?

Candidate 1: Well, I don't think it would be a problem—I've worked in much bigger organizations, where the HR job is very, very complex. I would use what I've learned in my career to date, focusing first on hiring my own group, then on working with them to set up necessary systems and procedures. Then, when those things were up and running well, we could turn our attention to staffing the rest of the group.

Candidate 2: I would lean heavily on corporate HR. I'm sure they have many of the systems in place already that we would use, and it would be silly to reinvent the wheel. If not, I have lots of other resources—including people at my old job—so that we could build the systems you need. And the day-to-day responsibilities wouldn't be difficult, I don't think; that's what I'm used to.

Candidate 3: I like to work collaboratively. I'd want to start by sitting down with you and the other members of the senior team to get a good sense of your priorities—what's most critical, what's important, what can wait a while. Then I'd draft a top-level six-month HR plan, based on the priorities, and get all of your input and agreement. Then I'd work the plan. And hopefully, hiring at least one other person in HR to help me would figure pretty early on in the plan!

Like magic, three different people emerge. You begin to get a real sense of their individual strengths and weaknesses in this area and of how their approach would (or wouldn't) suit you and the workplace you're trying to create. The magic is actually quite simple:

SENARIO-BASED INTERVIEWING STEPS
Establish the scenario
Ask a "what if" question
Stop and listen

If you look at the first example, you'll notice that Jorge's normal interview didn't really do any of these things. First, he threw out a couple of quick and generic sentences: "This is going to be a very demanding job," and, "We're going to need a lot from you, especially at the beginning"—not enough to establish the scenario in any meaningful way. Then he asked a question with both a clear "right" answer and a proposed course of action: "Would you feel OK about doing a lot of the hands-on stuff while you're hiring your own staff?" Really, that question is a statement (remember about "non-listening" questions in chapter 1? If you haven't yet read the first chapter, you might want to go back and do that at this point); what he's really saying is, "I assume you're going to need to do lots of the hands-on stuff at first, and I want you to be OK with that." Very few people in a job interview are going to say "no" when asked directly if something is OK with them! Finally, instead of simply stopping and listening to the answers, he kept on talking, giving reassurances and information that established even more strongly what the "right" answer was. No wonder they all said basically the same thing in response. He might as well have held up cue cards.

Now look back at Jorge using the scenario-based approach. He started by establishing the scenario; giving the candidates a good overall sense of the environment and the challenge. He said, "We're really at the beginning stages of setting up this regional office. You're the first person we're hiring in the HR department, although we have corporate's OK to hire three more HR people. Over the first few months especially, there would be a lot of hiring and setting up of systems . . . including hiring your own group, all while undertaking all the regular day-to-day HR responsibilities." He's given the candidates a context within which to answer his question.

Then, he asked the all-important "what-if" question. We call it a "what-if" because the essence of this kind of question is, "What would you do if you were in this situation?" In this example, the actual question was, "How would you approach that?" but that's just another way of asking the candidates what they would do in the situation. The beauty of the what-if question is that there's no right answer. It's a true curiosity-based question, which the person being interviewed has no choice but to answer from his or her own experience and understanding.

Now, Jorge could still have blown it by continuing to talk, telegraphing the "right" answer and therefore making it easy for the candidates to take the easy route—the route of giving him the answer he was looking for. He didn't do that, though. He asked the question, then stopped, looking at each candidate with respect and curiosity, silently inviting them to answer the question in their own way. And look what happened.

TRY IT OUT

This approach works in lots of arenas—not just hiring employees. For instance, you can use it to find out how your kids might handle a particular situation, or how a prospective service provider (a lawyer, housecleaner, carpenter, banker) would deal with you, or even how a colleague might approach a challenge you're working on together. Below, you'll find a way to use scenario-based interviewing in your daily life, as well as with prospective employees.

Think of a situation, challenge, or project with someone in your life (child, spouse, colleague, service provider), where you want to find out more about his/her understanding or approach.

Write below the name of the person and the challenge or project.

Person:

_____

Challenge/project:

_____

_____

Now think about how you might offer context to this person for the what-if question you'll ask about this challenge or project. What do they need to know in order to answer the question from their own understanding? Make notes to yourself below about how you'd like to verbally set up this scenario for the person:

Scenario:

_____

_____

_____

Finally, think about and write down your what-if question. Remember to make it a real curiosity-based question, rather than one with an implied or obvious "right" answer.

What-if question:

_____

_____

Just to help you in doing this, here's an example:

Person: my son, Ian, 18

Challenge/project: getting a job to help pay his expenses at college

Scenario: (1) We've talked about you getting a part-time job during the school year. (2) It's important to me that you help pay for some of your expenses, since we're paying for everything else. (3) Of course, it needs to be something that won't interfere with your schoolwork.

What-if question: What's your plan for finding that kind of a job?

Once you've completed the exercise above, I encourage you to go try it out. And one last thing—after you've asked your what-if question, _stop talking_. No matter how good your scenario-setting and what-if questions are, if you keep talking you'll most likely give the person what you think is the right answer, and then you won't find out what they think or know.

Go Back to the Job Description

In the activity above, I encouraged you to choose a situation, challenge, or project with someone in your life (child, spouse, colleague, service provider), where you want to find out more about his/her understanding or approach. When you use this approach for interviewing job candidates, the overall situation, challenge, or project is ready-made: you want to know how they'll approach this job and your workplace. That's a lot broader, though, than me wondering how my eighteen-year-old is going to find a part-time job at college. How can you break it down to make sure you ask questions that will allow you to discover how a candidate will approach the most important aspects of his or her job?

The job description you've created is the perfect resource for your what-if questions. Remember, it includes the key responsibilities, important skills, and your core competencies—the most important places for you to focus your questioning. Again, let's go back to Jorge, our HR-hunting GM. The first key responsibility on the HR director's job description is "recruitment and selection." Jorge rereads that key responsibility and the tasks under it to remind himself of what he needs to know about the person's approach and skills in this area:

Create and maintain an effective approach to recruiting and selection throughout the region—35 percent over the next six months
  · Help managers to identify personnel needs and create job descriptions for those needs.
  · Develop approaches for sourcing new candidates (working with Corporate HR team to avoid duplication of effort).
  · Help managers to develop interview questions and coach them in interviewing skills.
  · Interview candidates with managers as feasible, and for all managerial positions.
  · Help managers select most appropriate candidates, based on interviews and experience.

Working from the information above, Jorge uses our model to create a scenario-based interview question:

Person: HR director job candidates

Challenge/project: addressing our near-term staffing challenges in a way that will also work long-term

Scenario: (1) We need to hire eighty-plus people in the next four to six months. (2) We'll be looking to you for an approach that makes sure we get the *right* people, now and in the future. (3) We want managers to be able to participate as fully as possible in this process.

What-if question: How would you approach this challenge?

In the same way, Jorge could use the model, and the job description, to create a good scenario-based question for each key responsibility. Finally, he could create a few more questions, if he needs to, that focus on important cultural issues, or specific demands of the job at this point in time. In fact, the scenario-based question Jorge asked earlier in the chapter—about how the person would handle the overload of having to staff and set up systems while fulfilling all the day-to-day HR responsibilities—is a good example of that kind of additional question.

Creating the "Plant Tag"

Now you're ready to create an interview sheet that will become, in effect, your plant tag—you'll use it as a place to gather and record the critical information from each interview, and it will serve as your record of how you feel each candidate will approach the key responsibilities of the job, and whether he or she has the necessary skills, knowledge, and competencies. The interview sheet consists of the following:
· The person's name, your name, and the date.
· Each of your scenario-based questions, with space after each to take notes, while the person is speaking, about what you're learning from his or her answers.

· A space for recording your immediate post-interview impressions about whether and to what extent this person demonstrated the skills, knowledge, and competencies you need in the job.
· A space for giving the person an overall rating, based on the interview.

Here's a sample; this is what the interview sheet would look like for the HR position that Jorge is working to staff. (Please note, I've included only the questions we've discussed here. Of course, the actual interview sheet would have seven to eight questions in all.)

Interview Sheet: Director of HR, SENSIA Central Region

Candidate:_____
Interviewer:_____
Date:_____

Questions:
1. We're really at the beginning stages of setting up this regional office. You're the first person we're hiring in the HR department, although we have corporate's OK to hire three more HR people. Over the first few months especially, there would be a lot of hiring and setting up of systems . . . including hiring your own group, all while undertaking all the regular day-to-day HR responsibilities. How would you approach that?

_____
_____
_____
_____

2. We need to hire eighty-plus people in the next four to six months. We'll be looking to you for an approach that makes sure we get the *right* people, now and in the future. We want managers to be able to participate as fully as possible in this process. How would you approach this challenge?

_____

_____

_____

_____

3.–?) Etc. . . .

Post-interview Impressions:
Based on the candidate's answers, and any other impressions you received during the interview, rate this person 0–3 in each of the skills and competencies necessary to this job, listed below. (0 = unacceptable, 1 = growth area, 2 = strength, 3 = key strength.) Leave blank any skills or competencies you weren't able to observe.

Skills and/or Knowledge:

_____ management and coaching skills

_____ communication skills

_____ interviewing skills

_____ collaboration/teambuilding skills

_____ writing skills

_____ strategic thinking

_____ HR systems and procedures

_____ management/team theory and practice

_____ basic human psychology

Competencies:

_____ teamwork

_____ flexibility

_____ innovation

_____ decisiveness

_____ honesty

_____ discretion

Now, based on all you've seen and heard, give this candidate an overall rating:_____

Up a Notch: Scenario-Based Simulations

Wouldn't it be great if you could try a plant out in your garden? Take it home, plant it, see whether it grows well and how it looks with your other plants . . . and then, if it doesn't work, you just dig it up, take it back, and get another one to try.

I haven't been able to convince my local nurseries that this is a good idea, but you can do a version of it when you're in the hiring process: you can use a variation on scenario-based interviewing to "try out" prospective employees.

Remember that the point of scenario-based interviewing is to create verbal scenarios where candidates have to *speak* from their own experience and understanding, rather than just giving "right answers." You can use the same approach to create actual situations where the candidates have to *act* from their own experience—and this kind of scenario-based simulation is even more effective than a scenario-based interview.

Think about it. Most often, we know whether or not an employee is a good hire within the first few weeks after they start work. We see how they interact with others, how they respond to challenges that arise, how they prioritize, what their work ethic is. The problem is, if they're not right for the position or the organization, this is a bad time to find out—it's expensive both emotionally and financially for them, for you, and for the organization.

Using a scenario-based simulation approach, you can create a reasonably good replica of some key elements of those first few weeks—before you make the decision to hire the person. You can actually have them "do the job"—or at least a few important aspects of it—for a few hours, and see how it goes. It's like taking someone out in a flight simulator before having her pilot a real plane. Or, to continue our gardening metaphor, using a computer modeling program that will tell you how a particular plant is likely to fare in your garden's conditions (light, temperature, moisture, soil) before planting it.

Now I have to say, before we get into this, that if you only use what we've talked about so far—if you work from the job description to create scenario-based interview questions, make an interview sheet, stop talking after you ask your questions, and record your post-interview ratings—your success in hiring the right people will probably increase significantly. However, if you want to make it even more likely that the people you hire will be a great fit for their jobs and the company, you might consider creating a scenario-based "job model," which I'll explain below.

This is more complicated than the interviewing approach, though, and does require more inventiveness, time, others' involvement, and preparation. Take a look and see if it's right for you. If not, skip to the next chapter—I won't be offended.

The Job Model

The most important variables in creating a job model or simulation are the elements you've defined in the job description—the key responsibilities, skills/knowledge, and competencies for this job. Let's refer once again to our friend Jorge. He may decide that the two most important key responsibilities for him to find out about during the hiring process are (1) how the candidate would interact with the rest of the senior team, and (2) how the candidate would respond to the staffing challenges facing the HR function. He might feel these two key responsibilities are the most critical right now, and that in simulating these, he will also be able to observe whether and to what extent each candidate demonstrates the core competencies of teamwork, flexibility, innovation, decisiveness, and honesty. He'll also be able to observe each person's use of three of the skill/knowledge areas in the job description: communication skills, strategic thinking, and knowledge of HR systems and procedures.

In order to set up the job model, you use an approach quite a bit like the one for the scenario-based interviewing process.

CREATING A SCENARIO-BASED JOB MODEL
Establish the scenario
Build the model
Run the model and observe

If you recall, in scenario-based interviewing you establish the scenario by thinking through the verbal context you'll share that will allow candidates to answer your what-if questions. In scenario-based modeling, **establish the scenario** means deciding the key job situations that will allow candidates to demonstrate (or not demonstrate) the abilities and characteristics you're targeting.

Building the model, the next step in this process, means creating an actual situation that provides a simulation of the key job situations you've determined above.

Run the model and observe is like "stop and listen" in the interviewing approach—it simply means inviting the candidate into the model and watching what happens. You will also need something like the interview sheet—a place to note what you saw and felt, and rate the candidates on their demonstration of key skills, knowledge, and competencies.

Let's look at an example. For that, we'll rely again on Jorge. Here's how he might use the approach outlined above to create a simulation that would model the critical parts of the HR job that he's focusing on.

Establishing the scenario

Jorge decides on the three key job situations he wants to simulate in the scenario—those things he most wants to be able to observe the candidates doing:
- working with the senior team
- responding to staffing requests
- creating a staffing plan

Building the model

Based on the above, Jorge decides to create the following model, which includes all three of the situations he selected above. "We could have the candidates meet with a few key people in the organization to listen to their current *staffing requests,* then come to a *senior staff meeting* to tell us what they've learned and ask any questions they have. At the end we could have them tell us what their next steps toward creating the *staffing plan* would be. We could also have them participate in a *senior staff discussion* about some other issue, as well, just to see how they'd interact with the group."

Then he decides what it will take to actually create the model above. "So, to build this model we need to get a few people to agree to participate—that is, to meet with each of the two or three final candidates and discuss their staffing requests and then meet with me to debrief.

Then we need to create instructions for the candidates—probably written instructions—so they'll all be operating with the same information. We need to decide as a senior team what other issue we want to discuss with the candidates (in addition to staffing) and how we want to discuss it. Finally, we need to decide how we're going to debrief and rate the candidates after the simulation."

Run the model and observe

Having set up the model in the way he outlined above, Jorge invites his three final candidates, one at a time, to participate in the simulation. When he debriefs afterward, both with the people who had shared their staffing requests, and with the other members of the senior team, he finds there is almost complete consensus in favor of the third candidate. Everyone felt very comfortable dealing with her. They rate her very highly on the five core competencies, especially teamwork, and each person feels she is both knowledgeable about HR processes and procedures and very open and responsive to their needs. While all three candidates were strong, the third one really shone in the job model exercise, and Jorge feels confident about making her an offer.

TRY IT OUT

I suggest that you start experimenting with this approach using a lower-level job. The tasks and responsibilities of the job will be smaller in scope and more easily designed into a model. Once you get the hang of it, you can use this approach for any job.

I'll walk you through using the job modeling approach with an entry-level administrative person; next time you have occasion to be involved in hiring a person like this, you can see how it works:

Establish the scenario: Select a few situations that are a part of this job, ones that you feel will best allow the candidates to demonstrate their capability in the key responsibilities, and write them below.

[For example, in an entry-level administrative job, some situations might be: dealing with a series of requests; meeting with the manager to get clarity about a project; or dealing with people over the phone.]

_____
_____
_____

Build the model: Design a simulation or simulations using the situations you've listed above. Decide who needs to be involved, what they need to do, how you will communicate the purpose and "rules" of the activity to the candidates, and any other elements necessary to making this a useful job model. Feel free to use the space below to make notes for yourself about how you intend to build the model.

[For instance, using the situation above, you might create an inbox for the candidates to work through, one that contains items or requests that require them to demonstrate the skills you're looking for—word processing or other computer skills, making travel arrangements, setting up meetings, making phone appointments, etc.]

Run the model and observe: Invite your final candidates for the job to complete the simulation; immediately after each one goes through the model, rate them according to how well they demonstrated the key responsibilities, the required skills/knowledge, and your core competencies.

Whether you share the candidates' results with them is up to you. In our company, we share successful candidates' results with them as part of their orientation process—using the feedback approach you'll read about in chapter 7.

At this point, I hope you feel reasonably confident that you have a way to create the hiring equivalent of the "plant tag": some solid tools and guidelines for helping you find out which of your candidates can best help you create the workplace you're envisioning.

Now let's make sure you know how to get them headed in the right direction, once you've hired them . . .

BIG IDEAS

Gardeners are lucky: plants come with tags that tell what they like and don't like, their strengths and weaknesses, and how they're likely to perform in a given circumstance. While job candidates don't come with tags, scenario-based interviewing can give you much of the information—about an employee's actual skills, knowledge, and core competencies—you need to make better, more informed hiring decisions.

You create scenario-based interviews by using the following steps:

Establish the Scenario: provide a verbal context that will allow the candidate to answer your "what-if" questions.

Ask a "What-if" Question: ask the candidate some version of, "What would you do in this situation?"

Stop and Listen: once you've asked the question, stop talking or you may send what you think is the "right" answer. Listen as the candidate answers the question from his or her own understanding and experience.

If you want to take this process a step further, you can use the scenario-based approach to create a job model simulation that will allow candidates to demonstrate their understanding and experience to you, rather than simply speaking about it.

CHAPTER 4

Not Too Deep
and Not Too Shallow

B ack at my friend's house we're at the exciting part—making the
garden. The soil is ready, and we have the plants that will create
the look and feel she wants. Of course, some of her existing
plants are a good fit for what she's trying to create, and so we're building around those, as well. She also ended up buying some seeds for annual flowers that will fill in the empty spaces this first year while her new
perennial plants are small. I glance over and notice that she's planting
the seeds way too deep, and I encourage her to plant them nearer the
surface. So then she just kind of sprinkles them on the ground. At this
point I realize there's an art to this, and I need to share it with her.

I point out to her the planting instructions on the seed packet; it says
these particular seeds need to be planted one to one and a half inches
deep. The soil's already prepared and loose, so she can just poke little
holes in the ground with a twig or pencil, drop the seeds in, and pat the
soil smooth over them.

Later, proudly surveying our handiwork over a cold glass of lemonade,
she asks me why planting depth is such a big deal. "Well," I respond, "if
you plant seeds too deep, they may not be able to grow all the way to the

light—they'll suffocate before they can break ground. If you just throw them on the surface, they might get blown away or eaten by birds—it's less likely they'll be able to survive long enough to put down roots."

Okay, I know you're sitting there tapping your foot, waiting for me to stop with the gardening stories already and make with the metaphor. Here it is: putting plants or seeds in the ground is like getting an employee started in the job and at the company.

If, at this critical point, you don't give the employee the information, guidance, or resources he or she needs to get started properly, that person may never get established in the environment. At best he or she will waste time, money, and emotional energy trying to figure out what's what, and at worst he or she will feel abandoned and unsupported enough to leave. That's "planting them too shallow."

If, on the other hand, you pile on huge quantities of information or advice ("Here's our fifteen-chapter policies and procedures manual: I'd like you to read it over the weekend . . ."), or set up unrealistic short-term expectations ("All our new employees need to be at full productivity within the first three days . . ."), they may feel so overwhelmed that they give up: becoming paralyzed with fear or literally quitting the job. That's "planting them too deep."

Planting Them Just Right

You've spent all this time, money, and energy to get clear about the kind of workplace you want to create, and to recruit and hire the best people to help you build it. It's in your best interests, and theirs, to give them what they need to get started well. Given that, what does "planting them right" look like?

Think about the last time you started a job in a new company. Or perhaps you've never had that experience—maybe you founded the company, or took it over from your parents. Or maybe you've been working for your current employer for so long, you don't remember what it was like to be a newbie. In that case, think of your college orientation, or your first meeting of a club or professional association.

What did you try to find out, in order to get comfortable and not feel like a dork? If you're like most people, there were three things on your mind:

Who do I need to know?
How do things happen around here?
What's expected of me?

Getting an employee started right basically means providing the answers to these "who, how, and what" questions. The only tricky part is knowing how much detail to provide at a given point; for instance, if you try to impart, on the first day, all the knowledge you've gained over the past ten years about "how things happen around here," the person's head will explode!

So, I'll spend the rest of this chapter offering you some understanding and guidelines for both the "what" (the content) and the "how" (the process) of orienting your new employees so that they're most likely to grow and flourish.

Answering the Critical Questions

A number of years ago, I agreed to teach my daughter how to drive a stick shift. It was the strangest experience. The first time we went out together, and I tried to tell her how to balance the clutch and the brake, I realized that driving a standard had become so ingrained in my body that I put no conscious thought into the mechanics of doing it. I just did it. I found myself saying to her, "Well, you just . . . hmm. I'm not sure—I think you . . . Here, trade places with me, so I can do it once." I had to observe myself driving and notice what I did, so that I could tell her.

In the same way, if you've been working in a company for a long time, you've very likely put a lot of knowledge "on automatic"—you just do things or know things and don't think about them. That's one reason it's often so frustrating starting a new job—your colleagues don't think to tell you the critical things, because they've forgotten that they know them!

An example: I was at a client company just a few weeks ago, and I overheard someone say to a new employee in her department, "Oh my gosh, don't send your expense reports in until you've gone over them with Alex. Didn't anybody tell you that?" And of course no one had told her that, because for everyone else it was as natural (and unconscious) as brushing their teeth or tying their shoes.

So, how can you become aware of the information and habits that are automatic for you—things that are critical to your new employee's success? Let's start with the three basic "who, how, and what" questions I gave you earlier, adding some thought-starters to help you dredge the important stuff up from your subconscious mind. Let's start with the "who":

Question 1: Who Do I Need to Know?

Thought-Starters:

> Who will this person be interacting with, and what will they be doing together?
> Who are the key people in the company, and what are their roles?
> Who else will be important to this person's success, and why?

Imagine how much time and stress it will save for this person to find these things out right away! Using these thought-starters also might lead you to think of other important "who" things—like who knows the most about a certain key process, or who used to have this new employee's job (and may therefore be a great source of specific information).

Next is the "how."

Question 2: How Do Things Get Done Around Here?

Thought-Starters:

> What systems or procedures does this person need to understand and use?

What cultural expectations exist in your company?
What is definitely not OK to do here?

The "how" area is a little more complex than the "who"; let's look at these thought-starters more closely. The first one, "What systems or procedures does this person need to understand and use?" focuses on the practical aspects of how work gets done. Here, you might want to think about routine processes this person will take part in—a weekly report, for instance, or a quarterly budget presentation. How do these work, and what will this person's role be in completing them? You'll also want to consider systems or processes this person will need to know how to use, all the way from reporting a sick day to surfing the company intranet.

For the next thought-starter, "What cultural expectations exist in your company?" it's very helpful to start by looking at your core competencies. Remember, these are all about the "how." For example, if one of your core competencies is teamwork, think of some practical examples, applicable to this person's job, of how teamwork happens in your workplace. For example, people filling in for someone who's out sick, or team members meeting regularly to share information about projects they're working on together. Under this thought-starter, you might also think about communication norms that are important for your new employee to know. For instance, if there's a conflict, do people confront each other directly, do they ask a third party to help them resolve it, or do they (not that this is a good thing) avoid talking about it altogether?

Then, "What is definitely not OK to do here?" These are the metaphorical landmines and danger zones—every company has them, and people know it. Don't worry about bumming out new employees by sharing some of the key no-nos; they'll thank you for it. For instance, if the finance guy is very moody, and sometimes flies off the handle if you ask him anything during the last week of the quarter . . . don't you think a new employee would rather be aware of that and be able to act accordingly? Or suppose people at your company get reprimanded for using a competitor's product? Knowing that is like having a map that reads "here be dragons"—you know not to go there. This question also covers any strong norms your company has about language, dress, etc. A colleague of mine once got a rather serious talking-to for using a fairly mild expletive in front of a client group . . . it "just wasn't done" at that company! On the other hand, we have some client companies where it's de rigueur for everybody to talk like a sailor.

A note about the "how" questions—in many organizations, HR does a good job of answering some of these questions, especially as they relate to employee policies and procedures, including benefits and compensation. I suggest you find out exactly what the HR orientation consists of in your company, so you'll know what else you may need to provide in this area.

Finally, the "what."

Question 3: What's Expected of Me?

Thought-Starters:

How does the job description translate into the day-to-day?
What short-term priorities are most critical?
How will you communicate with this person about expectations going forward?

Again, let's dig into these thought-starters a little bit. First, "How does the job description translate into the day-to-day?" I suggest, before the person starts work, that you go through the "tasks and time" part of the job description, and think about any tasks where you may have to clarify your expectations, so that the person really knows what successful completion would look like. Focus especially on tasks where the expectations may be higher than or different from what might be considered "normal" for a job like this. For example, let's say you're hiring a new assistant, and one of the tasks is "answering the department phones." Now, it may be that your department regularly gets calls from important clients, and it's really critical to you that they get put into voice mail as seldom as possible. It would be helpful if you make this clear to the new assistant, letting him know that phone coverage is a key expectation; maybe even to the extent that he needs to work out backup coverage when he's away from his desk.

Second, "What short-term priorities are most critical?" Even though the job description should do a good job of laying out the ongoing "shape" of the job, there may be parts of the job that are particularly important right now, or may be more time-consuming initially. For example, the HR director that our buddy Jorge is hiring will need to know that staffing is the key priority over the next few months, even though it's only one of six key responsibilities outlined on the job description. When you share these short-term expectations, it's useful to share "why" as well as "what." For instance, if a quality-control check isn't up to date because there hasn't been anybody in the position for the last few months and everybody else has been swamped, it's important to note that. Otherwise, the new employee might simply assume the company is generally disorganized, or that nobody cares about quality. Knowing why a priority is critical helps the employee give it the right level of attention, and make smarter decisions about how to complete it.

Answering the final question—"How will you communicate with this person about expectations going forward?"—is particularly helpful to new employees; it gives them a clear sense of how they'll know whether they're on track, especially during these first fairly nerve-wracking months. For example, will you have weekly one-on-one meetings to check in with the person, find out how their work is progressing, and provide feedback and support as needed? Or are you a more "ad hoc" kind of manager, where your employees need to catch you on the fly (your door is generally open), and you'll stop by their desks when you need to talk? In either case, will you have a more structured three- or six-month review meeting? And when should the person expect his or her first performance review (and what are performance reviews like at your company)?

The good news is, once you've thought these questions through in depth for one new employee, it's a lot easier for subsequent employees—partly because some answers will be the same for any new employee, and partly because just getting conscious about this kind of stuff makes it easier to do the next time. (I found it much easier to teach my son how to drive a stick shift, having already done it with my daughter!)

You may find it helpful to start a folder or binder that contains the key information you've thought through in these areas—then you'll have an easy reference to use the next time you're getting a new hire started. We'll talk more about this later in the chapter, as well.

TRY IT OUT

If you haven't used this approach to orientation in the past, you can practice it with employees who have been hired recently (within the past few months), as well as current or future hires.

Given that, pick someone you feel would benefit from having these "who, how, and what" questions answered:

Employee's name:

_____

Who do I need to know? Using the thought-starters explained in the text above, note below some of the key "who" information you want to offer this person:

_____

_____

_____

_____

How do things get done here? Beginning with the thought-starters and the explanatory paragraphs about this question, note below some of the key "how" information you want to offer this person:

_____

_____

_____

_____

_____

What's expected of me? Beginning with the thought-starters and the explanatory paragraphs about this final question, note below some of the key "what" information you want to offer this person:

_____

_____

_____

_____

_____

Now that you've surfaced some of the critical information to help get this person started (or to continue) as easily and smoothly as possible, I want to help you make sure you don't "plant them too deep" by trying to pile it all on at once. Let's look at how to share this critical information.

The Process: How People Learn

Most people have had great teachers, and OK teachers, and lousy teachers—and the difference is rarely about the subject matter. One year my son had a really bad math teacher. She shared the information without seeming to take any responsibility for whether the kids understood it. If they were lost it was their fault; if everyone failed the test—again, it was their fault. She was deadly boring (I heard her present at a parent-teacher night—yikes!) and offered the curriculum in huge chunks without much in the way of example or interaction. The next year, it was very different. His teacher seemed much better able to capture the kids' interest, and tried to make sure the kids were "getting" what he said. He was there to help after school, and if the material was complex, he would take it slower. My son was much happier, and he did much better.

I'm convinced that what we call "good teaching" is mostly about teaching in a way that aligns with the way people learn. My company has developed a simple model we feel captures the learning process; I want to share it with you, in order to help you be a good teacher for your employees, not only in their first few weeks and months, but throughout your time together.

The "LearningPath"

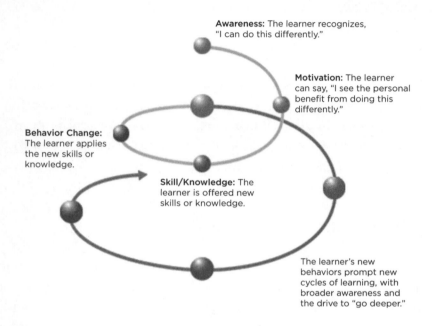

Awareness: The learner recognizes, "I can do this differently."

Motivation: The learner can say, "I see the personal benefit from doing this differently."

Behavior Change: The learner applies the new skills or knowledge.

Skill/Knowledge: The learner is offered new skills or knowledge.

The learner's new behaviors prompt new cycles of learning, with broader awareness and the drive to "go deeper."

We'll refer back to this model throughout the rest of the book, because so much of growing great employees depends on understanding how people actually acquire new skills and knowledge. You'll notice that we propose that learning begins with **awareness,** which we define as the person seeing, "I could do this differently." Then, the second step of learning is for the person to be **motivated** to say, "I see the benefit to me of doing this differently." When someone is a new employee, both awareness and motivation are generally already there—that's why new employees show up with those three initial questions. The person is ready and willing to get the information and skills he or she needs to succeed in this new job—to get the benefit of doing things differently.

So, then, with a new employee, you're generally ready for the third step; **providing new skills and knowledge.** That's the information we just talked about—the answers to the "who, how, and what" questions. Next comes the fourth step; the person's **behavior changes**—they start using the new skills or knowledge. (You might want to refer ahead to chapter 12 for a discussion of the various ways people like to take in the new skills or knowledge, under the section "Honor How You Learn.")

That's not all, though; notice what happens then. The process starts over again, on a deeper level: using the new knowledge and behavior, the person becomes even more aware of how much more there is to learn in this area, and more motivated to learn it. In the case of a new employee, this means he or she is now ready for the next level of specificity or complexity in his or her orientation to the new job and to your company. Then the process just keeps on repeating itself at deeper and deeper levels . . . if you're reasonably attentive to your new employees, you can meet their needs for deeper levels of skill and knowledge over the first few months of the job in such a way that their transition into "old hand" is almost seamless.

Understanding the cyclical nature of learning is especially important during these first few weeks and months on the job. It implies that the acquisition of new skills and knowledge is organic, like a tree growing ring by ring. Just as a tree can't go from sapling to spreading oak in one season, you can't just share your ten years of experience on the first day and expect the employee to be able to absorb it.

Here's an example. On an employee's first day, you might take him around to meet the key people he will be interacting with in his job. You introduce him by name and department, and provide a very brief summary of that interaction. For example: "Ed, this is Diane. She's the person we turn our expense reports in to every month, and she's our liaison to the finance department for any budgeting issues. Why don't you spend a little time just saying hello, and then we'll set up a more in-depth meeting for later in the week." Period. Enough info for now. You would consciously resist the temptation to add a couple of paragraphs about the budgeting process, or to whip out the end-of-month forecast-against-actual forms, etc.

During the first few days, you'd offer a similar top-level overview for each of Ed's initial "who, how, and what" questions. After that, you let him have a say in how and when to go deeper; he knows more, intuitively, about where he is in the LearningPath and how quickly he can move through it than you do.

For instance, toward the end of the first week, you might sit down with Ed and ask, "What more would you like to know at this point about how we interact with Diane and Joe in finance?" After you answer this next level of question, you might set up an appointment for Ed with Diane and Joe, letting them know that Ed would like to get to know them better and start to create a good working relationship.

The main principle here is to be attentive to a particular employee's capacity for absorbing new skills or information. You can do this in two ways: first, by noticing the signals they're sending you, and second, by using your listening skills to find out what they've understood.

Here's what I mean by being attentive to the signals the person is sending. When people are really focused on learning, they generally show it in their body language—and when they've had enough, and can't absorb anymore, they generally show that, too. Here are some clues to help you understand your employees' body language.

UNDERSTANDING "LEARNING" BODY LANGUAGE

Learning-focused	"Enough!"
Eyes focused	Eyes glazed/looking away
Body still	Body restless
Expression attentive	Expression blank

These signals are pretty easy to pick up on, if you're aware of them. Here's an example. Let's say you're talking to Ellen, your new salesperson, about the sales forecasting process. She's looking right at you, sitting forward in her chair, and glancing at the form when you refer to it. She looks puzzled for a moment, then asks you a question—and when you answer, she nods and her expression smooths out. She seems focused and attentive, both physically and mentally.

After about ten minutes, though, you notice she's starting to tap her fingers on the desk, or rub her face. She's looking less at you or the form, and her gaze is more unfocused, a bit glazed even. She looks down and away more often. She shifts in her chair and stifles a yawn. *Stop!* You can keep talking if you want to, but it'll be a waste of your time and hers, because she won't be taking it in.

When you lose someone's attention in this way, it's a good time to move on to something else. Have the person try something out, go back to their ordinary tasks, get up and stretch. If possible, continue the learning later.

This is also a good time to do the second thing I mentioned above—use your listening skills to find out what the employee has understood. (By the way, if you're reading this book out of order, at this point you might want to go back and read the first chapter, where we focus on listening skills.) One way to do this is by asking curiosity-based questions. For example, you could ask, "How do you see yourself making use of this form?" or, "What else do you need to know in order to feel confident about this?" One question not to ask is, "Do you have any questions?"—most people, if asked that question, will say, "No," partly because they don't want to look stupid and partly because that question is too generic to prompt their thinking.

Another way to use listening at this point, to discover what the employee has understood, is to ask him or her to restate. Remember, when we talked about the skill of restating in the first chapter, we noted that it's a great way to summarize and demonstrate your understanding. Well, asking others to restate is a great way to have them summarize and demonstrate their understanding. Some people worry that asking the other person to restate will seem like a quiz or an interrogation, but you can do it gracefully by providing a little honest context. For example you could say, "I want to make sure I'm being clear before I go on. Would you mind just summarizing, in your own words, the main ideas you've taken from what I've said?" or, "Just so I know what I may still need to clarify, what's your understanding of the sales forecasting process at this point?"

But let me go back a step—why bother finding out what the person has understood, anyway? If you look again at the LearningPath, you'll notice that it's all about what happens inside the person who's learning. One of the most important things I've learned during my years as a coach, consultant, and manager is that learning happens within the learner. I'll come back to this point again and again throughout the book. No matter how clear I am as a teacher, or how much I know, or how much I want to help—the only real measure of the effectiveness of my teaching is what happens in the mind of the person learning. So, if I actually want to make sure that learning is happening, I need to check in with that person at every step of the way: Is she aware of the possibility of new learning? Does he see the benefit of it for himself? Has she taken in the new skill or knowledge? Listening (paying attention, inviting, questioning, and restating) and requesting listening (asking the learner to restate what they've understood) are the easiest and most effective ways to find out whether and to what extent learning is happening.

TRY IT OUT

Below, I've reproduced a template that we use with clients (although we customize it for each client company's culture) as an orientation guideline for employees' first day on the job. It follows the principle of answering the "who, how, what" questions, and it prescribes an amount of information that seems appropriate for most employees on their first day. I suggest that you try using this with your next new employee, then adding or taking away elements as you see what works and doesn't work for you, your employees, and your culture.

Getting Your New Employees Started Right:
A Guide for Managers

What to do before the employee arrives:

☐ Make sure you have an accurate job description for the job; decide on the new employee's annual goals and any other necessary information about his/her role.

☐ Think about how you want to give the employee an initial sense of the company culture, building on whatever you shared during the interview process. (Remember to balance the great stuff with an accurate representation of the pitfalls and no-nos.)

☐ Arrange for the employee to attend any orientation offered by Human Resources.

☐ Make sure the employee will have the basic resources available from day one: e.g., desk, phone, computer, workspace, etc.

☐ Choose four to six people, inside and outside the department, with whom this employee will need to work closely and build strong relationships, and arrange for him/her to be introduced to each of them on the first day, and to spend thirty to forty-five minutes with them sometime during their first week.

☐ Select a "buddy" for your new employee—a peer to connect with and use as an initial resource for all the critical "how-to" questions; get the buddy's agreement to play that role.

☐ Make sure you have a welcome packet and a "goodie bag" of your company's products or products related to your industry to give your new employee.

☐ If you simply can't be there to spend the employee's first day with him/her, arrange a backup; ideally someone with whom the new person will be working closely (and meet with the employee yourself as soon as possible).

What to Do on the Employee's First Day:

☐ Clear your calendar, starting from the time the new employee will be finished with the HR orientation (if any).

☐ Be there to greet your new employee and show him/her to his/her workspace.

☐ Give a welcome packet to your employee and walk him/her through it. The welcome packet might contain:

· A welcome letter from the president or head of your department

  · The company mission and vision
  · The organizational chart and the office floor plan showing
    who is where
  · A list of relevant employee names, titles, and phone numbers
  · A press kit or annual report
  · The new employee's e-mail address, password, and work
    phone number

☐ Give the employee a quick tour of the office, pointing out
those elements that will be particularly useful or important for
him/her, and introducing him/her to people who you run
into along the way.

☐ Introduce your new employee to the senior support staff person in your area, and let him/her know that this person will
be able to answer "nuts and bolts" questions (making copies,
accessing the Internet, getting supplies, etc.).

☐ Give your employee a list of the four to six people with whom
you've set up initial meetings, and explain why you've chosen
them. Take your employee to the first meeting, introduce
him/her to the person, and ask the person to take or direct
the new employee to his/her next meeting when they're finished.

☐ Meet your employee at the office or cubicle of the last person
on the list, and introduce him/her to a "buddy," a peer who
can help with day-to-day concerns and questions about life at
your company.

☐ Allow an hour at the end of the day to meet with your new
employee to:
  · Answer any initial questions
  · Review the job description, then outline and agree on what you
    expect him/her to do or to accomplish in his/her first weeks
  · Share with him/her what you will do as a manager to support
    his/her success and what you expect from him/her as an
    employee

· Establish a time to sit down and debrief within the first two
  weeks
· Invite the new employee to his/her first team or staff meeting
☐ Wrap up the day by giving your new employee a "goodie bag"
  that might contain:
  · Samples of your company's products, or company premiums
  · Gift certificates to local stores, event tickets, etc.
  · Samples or gifts from your company's key partners or vendors
  · An invitation to any other new employee sessions your com-
    pany offers

Congratulations; your employee is now "planted at the right depth"
with the best chance of getting all that he or she needs to survive and
thrive in this new environment. Now the challenge is to keep this positive momentum going—and not just with this new employee, but with
every employee. In the next chapter we'll focus on what you can do to
be the kind of manager who keeps people growing.

BIG IDEAS

A gardener can dramatically help or hinder a plant's chances for survival, depending on whether he or she plants it too deep, too shallow, or just right. In the same way, how a manager gets an employee started can have a dramatic impact on his or her success. "Planting them too shallow" means not providing enough information, resources, or support. "Planting them too deep" means overwhelming employees with too much information or unrealistic initial expectations.

You can avoid "planting too shallow" by offering the answers to these critical questions:

Who do I need to know? The people and relationships that will be most important to this person's success.

How do things get done around here? The systems, procedures, and cultural "rules" this person will need to understand and use.

What's expected of me? The specifics about the performance for which this person will be held accountable, and how you'll stay in touch about those expectations.

You can avoid "planting too deep" by using the Learning-Path approach and your listening skills to provide new information and skills over time, in a way your employee can absorb and use.

CHAPTER 5

The Gardener's Mind

Some gardeners panic. They go out into the garden and see an expensive, newly planted bush languishing in the sun, and their stomach drops. They think, "Yikes! What do I do now?" Too often, they launch into a frenzy of "fixing"—adding fertilizer, digging up and replanting in a different place, drowning the bush with water. Or, shaking their heads and bemoaning their obvious "brown thumb," they watch hopelessly as the plant wilts and dies.

Successful gardeners generally have a different reaction. They know that transplanting is often tough on plants, especially in hot weather. They watch the bush carefully for a few days, making sure it has enough water—not overwhelming it, but enough—and if it still looks unhappy, they might create a bit of shade over it with a piece of cloth and a couple of sticks to give it a better chance.

In the same way, some managers panic when things don't go well with their employees. For example, let's say you've recently hired someone and you think they're doing fine. Then, you get some feedback from a colleague that this new person has made a pretty big mistake. You could do the manager version of leaping into fixing mode—which might take the form of staunchly defending your new employee and questioning your peer's perceptions or motives; or reading your new employee the riot act; or thinking about whether he ought to be moved into a different job; or . . . well, you get the drift.

A more confident manager might have a very different reaction. If you are such a manager, you might simply listen to the colleague's point of view, ask questions to make sure you're clear on the feedback, and then promise to address the problem. You might then think about whether this mistake is a result of something you've done (for instance, not explaining this part of the job clearly enough to your new employee). Finally, you'd sit down with the employee, share the feedback, and get his or her perspective on the situation. Then you'd work together to address the issue.

How you—as a gardener or a manager—respond to a less-than-optimal situation depends partly on your experience and your skill level. But it depends even more on your mind-set. I define mind-set as the beliefs you hold, consciously or unconsciously, about a situation or person, and therefore how you talk to yourself about it.

To explain this a little more clearly, let's go back to that panic-stricken gardener. What do you suppose some of his beliefs might be, regarding his unhappy-looking plant? Given his reaction, we could infer that he believes (and says to himself) some of the following: "I'm not very good at this," "Growing plants is really difficult," "Plants are delicate and prone to dying," "I have to fix this immediately." On the other hand, the more seasoned gardener might be believing and thinking to herself, "I'm pretty good at this," "Growing plants isn't hard," "Most plants will grow well if you give them a few essential things," and, "With a little help, nature will often solve the problem."

It's not that different for managers. When managers react to difficult employee situations with defensiveness, anger, micromanagement, or passivity—the odds are good that they have negative beliefs, either about the employee or about themselves, and that these beliefs are determining their internal monologue. These managers don't have faith in the employee's ability to improve, or they don't have faith in their ability to help, or they don't believe it should be their responsibility to help. These beliefs lead to self-talk like, "Well, Ed screwed up again. He's never going to get this," or, "Why on earth did they give me this department to manage—I should have stayed an engineer," or, "What's wrong with these people? Can't they do anything right?" (Note: you may remember that we talked about self-talk in chapter 1, and noted that changing your self-talk can dramatically change how you feel and behave in a situation. In that discussion, I noted that we'd go into self-talk more in chapter 5, and look at it as a function of your beliefs or assumptions. So: we're there now.)

On the other hand, when managers respond with clarity and calmness to a difficult employee situation, it's almost a given that—in addition to having some necessary people management skills—they hold positive beliefs about the employee, and about themselves and their role as manager. We summarize the essence of these positive beliefs as "the mind-set of a coach," which is:

Believing in your people's potential and wanting to help them succeed.

This mind-set results in self-talk like, "I really think Joe can do this, I just have to help him get clear on what it will take," or, "Hmm, I wonder how Sally is getting in her own way here? I know she really wants to succeed. We should sit down together and figure this out."

I would go so far as to say that if you don't have this mind-set about someone you manage, you won't be able to manage that person effectively. I know that's a pretty definitive statement, but think about it from the employee's point of view. As an employee, have you ever had a manager who didn't believe in you? Who you felt wasn't on your side—that is, who wasn't invested in helping you be successful? What impact did that have on you?

If you're like most people, it was very demoralizing. I've had the experience of working for someone who didn't support me, and it was like walking up a mountain with a heavy backpack. I was already doing something difficult—trying to grow and succeed in my career—and the added weight of my manager's lack of faith and support made it that much more daunting. It also felt like a continual wearing-away of my own positive beliefs about my potential: it's much harder to believe in yourself when the person who's responsible for managing your work day-to-day doesn't believe in you. In my case, I finally left that job—and though it was many years ago, I still remember clearly the surge of hopefulness, energy, and creativity I experienced almost immediately.

I've also experienced having a boss who did believe in me; who thought I was capable and talented and who made it very clear—through his words and actions—that he wanted to help me succeed. And even though that was *very* many years ago, my memory of working for him—of how incredibly helpful it was, and how quickly I developed in the warm sun of his regard and support—is an inspiration to me in dealing with the people I manage even today.

This is the core of why I'm taking a whole chapter to talk about this. I've found, through my own experience as an employee and through my experience as a manager, and through watching gifted and successful managers develop their people, that the coach's mind-set is an extraordinarily powerful thing. People whose managers believe in them and want to help them succeed are like plants given sun and water and then allowed to grow—they often exceed even the most positive expectations. By having and maintaining the coach mind-set relative to your employees, you can help ensure they have the best possible chance of success.

Changing Your Mind-set

If you accept that this "coach mind-set" is crucial to managing someone well, then how do you go about acquiring it? That is, how do you alter your beliefs? We often speak as though it's impossible to change our beliefs. We say, "I can't help what I believe; that's how I was raised," or, "That's just what I believe." And when someone does change a belief, we seem to think it's somehow suspect. "You didn't used to think that way," we accuse.

Really, though, we all change our beliefs all the time. When you were a little kid, you thought your parents were perfect. I bet you don't believe that now. The first time you tried to do something difficult—drive a stick shift or ski a black diamond or cook a soufflé—you may have believed that you'd never be able to do it well. Having learned to do any of those daunting things, you may now a hold a very different belief.

Let's deconstruct this process of changing a belief. First, you believe something. Let's say it's, "I will never be able to dance the tango." If you don't care about learning to dance the tango, that belief probably won't change. But let's say you do want to learn; that you begin to think that some important benefit will come to you from dancing the tango. Maybe you think you'll be sexier or more sophisticated, or that your significant other will think you're cool. (Remember the LearningPath in the last chapter? We're talking here about motivation.)

So now you've got a problem. There's a dissonance between your belief ("I will never . . .") and your hope ("I want to . . ."). In order to resolve that dissonance, you start talking to yourself, trying to convince yourself to change your belief. I know it sounds weird, but we all do it. In your head, you say something like, "I bet I could learn to tango. I have a pretty good sense of rhythm, and I love Latin music. And besides, how hard could it be? Lots of other people do it." And if your argument to yourself is good enough, you'll probably go out and find a tango teacher.

You take tango lessons, it's not as hard as you thought—you do have a good sense of rhythm, and your teacher is great—and in a few months, voilà. You're tangoing away like a pro. Now your belief is probably something like, "I'm pretty darn good at dancing the tango, amazingly enough." A significant shift!

Now, it may be, sadly, that you find your initial belief was accurate, and you aren't able to learn the tango (unlikely, but possible). Even in this case, though, some good will have come out of questioning your belief—you now know that your belief is accurate, rather than just an untested limiting assumption that may or may not be true. So, for instance, when your spouse says, "Let's take tango lessons—I bet that would be fun!" you can reply, sadly but with confidence, "Honey, let's not waste our time. I can't tango—I've tried. How about swing dancing?"

As I think you can see, we do this "belief shifting" unconsciously all the time. If you were to make this process of changing your beliefs or mind-set conscious, here are the steps you'd follow—the steps I've just described.

HOW TO CHANGE YOUR MIND-SET
Recognize your initial belief
Question it
Gather new data
Test the data
Revise (or recommit to) your initial belief

Let's look at this model relative to our tango situation. In order to even try to learn the tango, you had to **recognize your initial belief** (which was, "I'll never be able to dance the tango"), and then **question it.** We generally start to question our beliefs when we see it's possible to believe something different (awareness) and that there may be some benefit to us in believing something different (motivation). "I'll never be able to dance the tango" becomes "I wonder if I could learn to dance the tango?"

Then you **gather new data:** you look to see whether there are facts to support changing your belief. In our tango example, the data was already at hand: you were able to note that you have a good sense of rhythm and a love of Latin music, and you reminded yourself that thousands of other people have learned. Then you **tested the accuracy of your data** by actually trying to learn; you found a tango teacher.

The new data was accurate, your test was successful; you learned to tango! So, you **revised your belief.** (And if your test had proved your initial belief that you would never be able to tango, you would have **recommitted** to it.)

The Coach's Mind

Here's what happens when you use this model to investigate and—if possible—revise your mind-set about your employees. Let's say you've decided that one of your employees—let's call her Jane—simply isn't capable of doing her job. It would certainly be beneficial—to you, to Jane, to the organization—if that belief wasn't accurate. So, you start by questioning your belief: you turn "Jane can't succeed in this job" into "Can Jane succeed in this job?"

Then you look for new data. You may be basing your negative belief on some experience you've had with Jane, or on some critical feedback you've gotten about her. Who can you ask, or where can you look, to find other information? You might want to have confidential conversations with some of your peers who interact with her, or do a survey of her clients, or ask HR what their impression is. You could ask to look at some of Jane's work that you haven't seen—maybe you've only been exposed to the problems, but the bulk of her work is great. You might also want to talk to Jane about how she thinks she's doing; to see how self-aware she is, how honest she's willing to be with you, and how open she is to feedback and growth.

At this point, you may find that much of the information points to a new belief—for instance, that Jane is simply too new in her position to be up to speed, or that she just needs (and is open to) some development. On the other hand, all the data you've gathered may reinforce your initial belief—that Jane doesn't have the right skills or mind-set for the job, and isn't capable of changing. In either case, you can now test the data.

If the information you've gathered supports a new, more positive belief, you let Jane know where she needs to improve, offer your support, focus on providing her with the learning and growth opportunities she needs, and see what happens. If the information is more negative, you might do a final test by having a serious conversation with Jane, making it very clear what she needs to do differently, and setting a time frame for change (we'll talk more about how to do this in chapter 7, "Staking and Weeding").

One caveat: if the information you gather is really negative—if it supports your initial belief so thoroughly that you're now convinced Jane simply can't succeed in this job—you may need to go right past the testing step and act on your recommitted-to belief. That is, if your data-gathering convinces you that she has no chance of succeeding, it's cruel to make her try. You should either let her go, or help her find another job that would suit her better. (Of course, you need to talk with your HR folks to make sure you're doing this in a way that's legal and ethical.)

So, that covers the first half of the coach's mind-set: "believing in your people's potential." As you can see, we're not talking about blind faith, or being a Pollyannalike cheerleader, we're talking about finding out whether or not it's realistic to believe in someone's potential, and then acting appropriately, based on what you discover.

How about the second half of that mind-set, "wanting to help them succeed"? What if you find that you don't want to help your employees succeed? Or that there's a specific employee whose success you don't support? In this part of the "coach's mind," you have to do a bit of self-reflection to discover your underlying beliefs. Here are some possibilities; beliefs you may hold that make it difficult for you to support your employees.

I don't want to help my employees succeed because:

· They should be capable of succeeding on their own, without my help.
· I don't have time to help them; I've got a job to do, dammit!
· I don't like them very much.
· I did it on my own; they should, too.
· I don't want them to get better than me.
· I like being indispensable.
· I'm not sure I'm capable of helping them, and I don't want anybody to know that.

As you can see, investigating this part of your mind-set requires some brutal honesty and can be somewhat embarrassing. Most of us don't like to admit that we think in ways that are so selfish and self-serving. The good news is: if you're honest enough with yourself to acknowledge such underlying beliefs, you can use the model to shift them.

TRY IT OUT

Below, I'll walk you through the process of changing your negative mind-set about one of your employees (or finding out whether your negative beliefs are justified). I suggest you pick someone for whom, in your own head, the "jury is still out"—someone about whom your negative beliefs are not set in stone. That will make it easier, this first time out, to try this process of changing your beliefs.

Choose someone who works for you, about whom you cannot at this moment truthfully say, "I believe in this person's potential and want to help him/her succeed."

Employee's name:

_____

Part I: Being Open to the Possibilities:
Recognize, Question, Gather New Data

My current beliefs: Note below your negative beliefs, either about this person's capabilities or your role and ability in helping them succeed:

_____
_____
_____
_____

Question: Below, note how you could turn those negative beliefs into questions:

_____
_____
_____
_____
_____
_____

Gather new data: Note below any sources (people, situations, work product) that might yield new information to answer your questions:

_____

_____

_____

_____

Now you need to look and listen; actually gather the new data. If you're really excited, you can put the book down, right now—or you can commit to checking this out over the next few days. When you've had a chance to gather some new data, go on to the next part of the activity.

Part II: Testing the New Data

What the data shows: Summarize below the essence of what you discovered, and whether it leads you toward a new belief or reinforces your previous belief:

_____

_____

_____

_____

_____

Testing: Write below a simple plan for testing out the data above (i.e., if you now have information that supports the idea that this person is more capable, how will you find out whether it's accurate?):

_____

_____

_____

_____

_____

Again, at this point you have to actually go and do what you've written down above. This may take awhile. When you've had a chance to complete your "test" of the new data, go on to the last part of the activity.

Part III: Revise or Recommit

What I believe now: Note your belief about this person now, post-test:

_____

_____

If you now hold a coach mind-set about this person, congratulations! You and he or she will benefit tremendously, and the rest of this book will offer you lots of skills and guidelines you can use to act on your mind-set to help that person succeed.

If, on the other hand, this exercise has shown you that your initial negative beliefs are well-founded, and you can't realistically believe in this person's potential or want to help them succeed—then please act to change this employee's situation. Either let them go or support them in finding another job for which they'll be better suited. Trust me, it's as uncomfortable and frustrating for them to be managed by you as it is for you to be managing them!

As you've probably already figured out, this approach to shifting your beliefs is not only applicable to employees, but to nearly every aspect of your life. Any negative belief you hold—about your kids, your spouse, yourself, the future—can be questioned and possibly changed, using this model. I'll give you a great example. Recently, an executive I coach was in the uncomfortable position of being in limbo about who his boss would be. He'd been working for one person—the president of a division of their company—for a number of years, and he loved working for her. She was an excellent leader and a great person, and they had a trusting and open relationship (let's call her Diane). Structural changes were happening at the parent company, and it looked as though he was going to be reporting to someone else (let's imagine his name is Jeff). My client didn't really know Jeff, and he didn't know the people who had been reporting to him. During the few months when this change was still unclarified, he felt as though he was being cut adrift. He hadn't had much contact with Diane (her job had expanded, and she was very busy), and he hadn't had much contact with Jeff, his future (probable) boss. The situation was complicated by the fact that the new boss was probably going to be managing another group like his, headed by his peer (let's call her Janet)—and no one knew how their two groups would be merged.

He said he wanted to talk, so we set up a meeting. I had hardly sat down when he started talking at top speed:

"Well, I know how this is going to shake out. Jeff's spending lots of time with Janet, and he's not open to my suggestions at all, so I imagine he's going to fire me and have Janet head both our groups. Also, he's just not a good manager—he's not like Diane; she always kept me in the loop and Jeff has barely spoken to me. I've offered to help with the restructuring and he hasn't responded. He's a control freak. Diane has told me to be patient—but I can see the writing on the wall. It's so frustrating; all these years of great results, and it doesn't count for anything. I guess I should get my résumé together and call a headhunter, and then . . ."

"Whoa, slow down," I interrupted. (I've known this person for years, and our relationship is such that I can just cut to the chase.) "Sounds to me as though you've decided all this based on very little evidence. Are you willing to question your negative conclusions here, or are you absolutely convinced?"

He sighed. "Well, I'd love for it not to be true. But I'm pretty sure I'm right."

"Is there enough room for doubt that you're willing to change 'Jeff's a control freak who hates me and I'm toast' to 'Is Jeff a control freak? Does he hate me? Am I toast?'" I asked.

He laughed. "Well, OK, yes. I can do that."

"Great." I took out a piece of paper. "So, where can you look to find the answers to those questions?" Seeing his puzzled look, I added, "For instance, how can you find out if Jeff is really a control freak?"

"Oh, I see. Hmmm, I could ask people who work for him what he's like as a manager. And I could be more observant about how he interacts with people at meetings. I've been pretty focused on the fact that he's not talking to me much."

I nodded, writing. "Great ideas. And how could you find out whether he hates you?"

He shook his head. "Shoot, I don't know. What am I going to do, ask him? 'Jeff, I don't want to put you on the spot or anything, but—do you hate me? Am I toast?'"

It was my turn to laugh. "Right, I see your point. Well, how about rethinking the data you already have?" Seeing another puzzled look, I continued. "Here's what I mean: why do you think he hates you?"

"He barely speaks to me, and he's spending a lot of time with Janet. And when I offered to help with the restructuring, he just shook his head. He said, 'Thanks,' but he was just being polite."

"OK, what are some other reasons he might be doing these things—other than sheer hatred for you?" Seeing that he was about to defend his existing belief, I held up my hands. "Hold on, go with me here. I know you believe these things prove he hates you, but do your best to think of some other explanation."

"Well," he said reluctantly, "I suppose he could be avoiding me because he doesn't have anything useful he can say to me at this point—he may not even have the authority to start the restructuring yet. But then, why is he spending so much time with Janet?" He stopped and thought for a minute, "You know, I just realized that Janet has a deal in the works that has to get finalized, no mat-ter what else happens. That could be what they're working on. . . ." He stopped again and looked at me, surprised. "You know, this stuff might actually be true."

I laughed again. "Amazing, huh?"

That was the breakthrough moment for him; he saw that his deeply held negative beliefs *might* not be accurate. He gathered some more data, we figured out some ways to test his newly gathered data, and he was—happily—forced to revise his negative beliefs. As of this moment, his new, more accurate belief is, "Jeff thinks Janet and I are both tal-ented, and he's looking for ways to restructure that take advantage of both our strengths. People like working for him, and I believe that as soon as he's able to move forward with the restructuring, he will."

In other words, my friend is most definitely not toast. And I've no-ticed that, since he shifted his mind-set, he's behaving differently around Jeff—less defensive, more relaxed, more collaborative. I'm sure this is having a positive effect on Jeff's beliefs about my friend, and it reinforces *my* belief that mind-sets—negative or positive—tend to become self-fulfilling prophecies.

Sustaining the Coach's Mind-set

Now, once you've revised your mind-set, how do you maintain it? Most of us have a tendency to slip back into negative beliefs—about others, ourselves, our capabilities, or theirs. How do you sustain your new, more hopeful and productive—and more accurate—beliefs?

You can consciously remind yourself of the process you've gone through to get to a more positive, hopeful mind-set. My mom called this "good mental hygiene," and it involves talking to yourself in a sup-portive way, like a friend and coach. For example, if my friend and col-league, above, finds himself slipping back into his "he hates me and I'm toast" mind-set, based on one flimsy piece of evidence (an unanswered e-mail, say), he can say to himself something like, "Now, wait a minute.

Remember all the indicators I've seen that he doesn't hate me and I'm not toast? Let's not blow this out of proportion. There are all kinds of reasons he might not have had a chance to respond to that e-mail."

Like a good gardener, you now know how to trust in the ability of your plants—your employees—to grow and thrive, and you can trust in your own ability to support them. Now we'll get more specific; in the next chapter we'll focus on how to find out what each "plant" needs in order to achieve its full potential.

Big Ideas

For gardeners, having faith in the power of nature and feeling comfortable in supporting that power creates a solid foundation for their gardening skills. In the same way, managers who approach their employees with a "coach's mind-set" have the best foundation for using their management skills.

The coach's mind-set:
Believing in your people's potential
and wanting to help them succeed.

If, as a manager, you find that you don't have a coach's mind-set toward an employee, you can question your own mind-set—and revise or confirm it.

Recognize: accurately state your current beliefs about this person.

Question: ask yourself whether or not your current belief is actually true—turn your belief into a question.

Gather new data: look for new information that might support an alternative belief.

Test the data: find simple ways to test the new data you're considering.

Revise/recommit: based on the new information and the results of your "tests," revise your belief or recommit to your original belief.

If you find that you can't realistically adapt the coach mind-set toward a particular employee, it's kinder to all concerned to either let that person go, or find a job for which he or she is better suited.

You can maintain a positive mind-set by using "good mental hygiene"—reminding yourself of why you believe as you do, and how it will help you and your employees.

CHAPTER 6

A Mixed Bouquet

I t's a sunny June afternoon in my friend's garden. We're sitting with tall glasses of iced tea, listening to birdsong and watching butterflies swoop and hover, and she is both pleased and proud. This is the second season since we re-created her garden, and for the most part, it looks wonderful. The blank spaces are starting to fill in, and some of the plants have spread quite a bit since last year. "The only things I'm not happy about," she says, "are the roses. I expected them to be full of flowers by this time of year." She points to two shrub roses, a peachy-yellow one and a white one, at the back of the garden. They look all right, but they haven't grown as much as some of the other plants, and the blooms are a little sparse.

"Have you fed them?" I ask.

She looks anxious. "Fed them?"

"Oops! Did we not talk about this?" She shakes her head. "I'm sorry I didn't mention it," I apologize. "Roses need more nutrients than most of the other plants you've chosen. All you have to do is water in a little rose food—it's a kind of fertilizer—a couple of times a year. It's easy;

you can buy it at the nursery or most hardware stores, and the directions are right on the bag."

Relieved, she nods and takes a sip of her iced tea, looking over the garden. Then, frowning suspiciously, she looks at me again. "Is there anything else you haven't told me? I mean, do any of these other plants have individual needs you haven't mentioned?"

I smile. "Well, yes, there's lots I haven't told you. But I didn't want to overwhelm you with information. And except for a few specific things you can assume are true, like the rose food, your plants will tell you what they need much better than I could. You've chosen plants that like sun, are pretty hardy, and don't need huge quantities of water—remember, that was part of our master plan. Beyond that, if you just pay close attention, and get a good book about plant care—so that you know how to understand what you're seeing and how to respond, if there's a problem—you should be OK."

My friend has started to look a little disappointed. "What's up?" I ask.

She sighs. "Well, I guess I thought that once we did all that soil preparation and planning, and got plants that were right for the kind of garden I wanted and for the space I have, that would be it."

I nod, realizing I may have done a not very good job of managing her expectations. "Look at it this way—if you hadn't done all that, you wouldn't have gotten the beautiful garden you have today. And the rest of what you need to do is pretty straightforward. You've got a great beginning; from here on, it's just a matter of staying attentive to your garden to make sure that each plant is getting what it needs to continue to grow and thrive." Now she's looking worried. "We're talking about a few hours a week, max," I reassure her, and she relaxes—a little. "I'm with you every step of the way on this," I add. "I'll show you how to notice what's happening in your garden and I'll teach you some simple ways to respond to what you see."

Looking happier, my friend salutes me with her iced tea. "OK, you're on."

If a manager were to have followed the recommendations we've discussed in the last five chapters, he or she would be in pretty much the same situation as my friend. That manager—let's say it's you—would have worked to create the kind of environment where people feel supported and respected. You would have clarified the kind of workplace you want to create and the specific jobs that people would need to do to make it happen. You would have made sure that the people already in place were clear about their jobs and how those jobs support the overall goals. You would have instituted a hiring process that brought in new people to help create your envisioned workplace, and you would have gotten them off on the right foot. Finally, you would have investigated your own mind-set relative to all your employees, and shifted it (or them) as appropriate.

Now you would be at the point where you would need to stay attentive to your employees and discover how to best keep each one developing and moving in the right direction. And—voilà—that's what this chapter is about.

Staying Usefully Attentive

My friend can spend twenty-four hours a day gazing at her garden, but if she doesn't know what she's looking for—or what it means when she sees it—that attention isn't going to help her keep her garden thriving. In the same way, you can keep an eagle eye on your employees, but if you don't know what you're looking for, or how to understand what you see, your attention may be wasted. Staying usefully attentive means **directing your attention toward those things that will yield you the best information** about how to support your employees' growth.

Let's deconstruct the part of that last sentence I've put in boldface type. First, there's **"directing your attention."** You already know how to do that, courtesy of the first chapter—the one about listening. A quick review: paying attention consists of physical focus (not trying to do other things), verbal focus (not talking about other things), and mental focus (not thinking about other things). If, at a given moment, you're paying attention to an employee or a group of employees in this way, odds are you won't miss much.

The next part of that sentence we're deconstructing is **"toward those things that will yield you the best information."** This is where we'll spend the rest of this chapter. I'm going to offer you a behavioral model—one that we've used in my company for many years as a tool in coaching individuals and building teams—that provides some simple and very "high-yield" things to look for. The model, which was developed almost fifty years ago, is called the Social Style™ model.*

The Social Style™ Model

As anyone who's ever worked with others can tell you, people approach their jobs in a variety of ways. Some people complete tasks quickly, some more slowly. Some like to gather a lot of information before acting, and some like to decide and act quickly. Some are very friendly and personal with coworkers, while others are more reserved and formal. There are people who focus on managing risk and taking the "safe" course, and others for whom breaking new ground is essential. Sometimes these differences can create freshness, balance, interesting relationships, and innovative solutions. But all too often, the differences in approach and focus among members of a group—or between managers and those they manage—lead to misunderstanding, mistrust, and frustration . . . not to mention poor results.

The Social Style model is a simple, practical tool for understanding these differences and for working well with people who are very different from you, so that all your employees' strengths can be well used, and every person can be managed in a way that works best for them and brings out their highest potential.

Like many useful inventions, the Social Style model was discovered by accident. In the early 1960s, two industrial psychologists named Roger Reid and Dr. David W. Merrill were working with a large insurance company in the northeastern United States to find out whether there

---

*The Social Style concept and profile are used with the permission of the TRACOM Group. We are grateful for their help in making these materials reflect the intent of the creators of the Social Style model. Our special thanks to Roger Reid for his insights and support.

were simple behavioral markers that could predict leadership potential. They reasoned that if they could screen for these hypothetical behaviors when hiring new managers, they could create a culture of highly effective leaders.

Unfortunately, they were completely unsuccessful in predicting leadership potential through behavioral assessment. Fortunately, they discovered something else: Reid and Merrill found that when they assessed people relative to three behavioral dimensions—which they called assertiveness, responsiveness, and versatility—they could predict many other useful things. For example, they could tell how people would be likely to approach tasks and relationships with others; what parts of a project they would tend to focus on and which would be less compelling for them; what some of their key interpersonal strengths and weaknesses would be; how they would like and need to be managed; and how they would tend to team and to manage others.

Over a period of years, Reid and Merrill tested and validated their model with a wide variety of men and women in many different work situations. The model's predictive value held true, even—with slight modifications—for cultures outside the United States and for nonwork situations.

Today the model is used in a variety of ways. For example, it can be taught as a way to help salespeople sell appropriately to customers of various styles. Teams can use the model to make the best use of all team members' strengths. Managers can use the Social Style model to become more self-aware, to recognize and build on their style-based strengths and mitigate the impact of their style-based weaknesses, and—important for our purposes here—to better manage employees of any style. Anyone, in any situation, can use the Social Style concept to begin to see him- or herself as others see them (a very valuable insight) and to behave in ways that create productive, enjoyable relationships with people of every style.

I want to give you some simple ways to take advantage of Social Style concepts in being usefully attentive to your employees; in order to do that, I need to give you a basic foundation in what the model is and how it works. If you're already familiar with the Social Style model—as many people are—feel free to skip this next section, or to read it as review.

The Three Dimensions of the Social Style Model

As I mentioned earlier, three behavioral dimensions form the core of the Social Style model. A behavioral dimension is an area of behavior within which people make different choices and have different capabilities. For instance, think of musicality as a behavioral dimension. Some people like to sing, some don't; some have excellent rhythm while some have difficulty keeping time to a simple beat; some people can convey tremendous emotion through music and some focus only on technique. All these behaviors can be ranged along the dimension of "musicality" from more to less.

The three dimensions Merrill and Reid focused on in creating the Social Style model were—in their words—assertiveness, responsiveness, and versatility. Let's look at each one separately.

Assertiveness means something very specific in this model. Merrill and Reid defined it as "the extent to which other people perceive you as trying to persuade or convince them about your point of view." In this model, people who are highly assertive are those who try to accomplish what's important to them by directly influencing others. People who are less assertive, in this model, accomplish what's important to them through other means; for instance, through creating new systems or processes, through gathering supportive data, or through sounding out others on their ideas. Merrill and Reid created a horizontal line, divided into four quartiles, along which a person's behaviors on this dimension could be placed.

ASSERTIVENESS

It's important to recognize that this definition is somewhat different from the general definition of assertiveness that's evolved in the United States over the past few decades. We've come to think of assertiveness as a good thing; we connect it with high self-esteem and an appropriate level of self-confidence. It's important to understand that in this model, higher and lower levels of assertiveness as Merrill and Reid defined it can be equally effective (or ineffective).

There are specific behaviors that go along with these differing levels of assertiveness: people who are more assertive tend to speak, move, and respond more quickly; to tell others their thoughts and opinions; and to be forceful in their gestures and decisions. People who are less assertive tend to speak, move, and respond more slowly; to gather ideas and information from others before expressing their own opinions; and to be more reserved and moderate in their gestures and decisions.

Responsiveness, in this model, means "the level to which you are perceived as controlling or revealing your emotions." People who are highly responsive are very easy to "read"; their face, voice, body, and words convey how they feel about things. People who are low on the responsiveness scale are much harder to read; they give few vocal or facial clues, and they don't talk much about emotions, preferring to focus on facts. Merrill and Reid created a vertical line, again divided into four quartiles, along which they placed people's behaviors on this dimension:

RESPONSIVENESS

LOWER

1

2

3

4

HIGHER

As with assertiveness, there are clusters of predictable behaviors that tend to go along with high and low responsiveness. People who are highly responsive also tend to be relationship- and people-oriented, fun-loving, intuitive, and holistic in their thinking. People who are low on the responsiveness scale tend to be more task- and fact-focused, serious-minded, logical, and linear in their thinking.

Reid and Merrill then laid the two dimensions over each other, creating a grid:

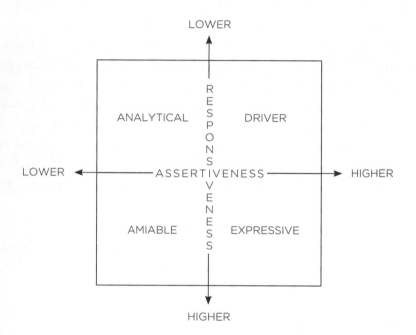

They discovered that each quadrant of the grid generally predicted a cluster of preferences, behaviors, and approaches that they termed a Social Style. The four styles defined by the grid are as follows:

Driver: Upper right quadrant: high assertive and low responsive. These people are fast-paced and decisive, and they can be impatient with those who don't keep up with them. Their favored approach is to act quickly, based on the information they consider relevant—and to make course corrections later if needed. They specialize in pragmatism, candidness, coolness under pressure, and completing tasks quickly. Others tend to perceive them as work-oriented, efficient, and demanding.

Expressive: Lower right quadrant: high assertive and high responsive. These people are fast-moving and adventuresome. They like to come up with new ideas. Their favored approach is to create a vision of the possibilities and then get others' support by selling the benefits of their vision. They specialize in energy, enthusiasm, humor, and risk-taking. Others tend to perceive them as persuasive, high-energy, creative, and impulsive.

Amiable: Lower left quadrant: low assertive and high responsive. These people are considerate and supportive. They like to take time to build rapport and to focus on team results. Their favored approach is to get consensus and to mediate—they believe that the best solution is one where everyone involved is "on board." They specialize in compassion, loyalty, mediation, and building trust. Others tend to perceive them as kind, skilled with people and teams, and somewhat self-effacing.

Analytical: Upper left quadrant: low assertive and low responsive. These people are cautious and thoughtful. They like to make sure that all the details are in place before moving ahead. Their favored approach is to minimize risk by looking at all the options before making a decision. They specialize in correctness, precision, prudence, and objectivity. Others tend to perceive them as cool, rational, and somewhat detached.

Many other behaviors and preferences can be predicted based on which of the four Social Styles is a person's "home base"; we'll talk about some of these in a few minutes when we focus on how to use the Social Style model to be usefully attentive.

Versatility, the third dimension, was defined by Merrill and Reid as the level to which you are perceived as being willing to change your preferred behaviors to make others more comfortable with you. This dimension is by far the most important in a developmental sense. While there is really no better or worse place to be on the dimensions of asser-tiveness and responsiveness—that is, no better or worse "style"—it is definitely better to have higher versatility.

For example, take a woman who is an Analytical—low responsive and low assertive. She is going to prefer a more deliberate pace; to plan and think carefully before making a decision; to look at all the facts. Let's say she's working on a project with a man who is an Expressive—high on both responsiveness and assertiveness. This colleague is likely to enjoy brainstorming new approaches, moving quickly, and being more infor-mal in his interactions.

If our Analytical is highly versatile, she is likely to speed up a bit in this interaction and be less formal, and to be more open to entertaining ideas that may not make logical sense to begin with, all in order to help her interaction with the Expressive go more smoothly and be more pro-ductive. If she is a low-versatile Analytical, on the other hand, she would keep her pace and decision-making approach the same as usual, focusing only on meeting her own style needs, rather than responding to the Ex-pressive's style preferences.

Merrill and Reid visualized versatility like this, again dividing the di-mension into four quartiles:

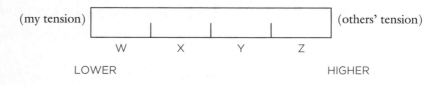

VERSATILITY

(my tension)   W   X   Y   Z   (others' tension)

LOWER   HIGHER

You'll notice that the low versatile end of this scale also says "my ten-sion." This means that others perceive low-versatile people as doing those things that reduce their own tension and make them feel more comfortable. Our low-versatile Analytical, above, is a good example of this. Facts, logic, and a deliberate pace make her feel most comfortable, and that's how she interacts with her Expressive colleague—even though it might be less comfortable for him. A high-versatile Analytical, on the other hand, would focus more on reducing the "other's tension," demonstrating the faster pace and less formal thinking that would probably feel comfortable to the Expressive. It's easy to see from the preceding example how a high-versatility person would be better able to build trust and rapport and to work more successfully with a wider variety of people.

When someone receives a Social Style profile as part of coaching or a workshop, they get an indication of how others rate their versatility. Without that profile, there's no sure way to measure your employees' versatility (or your own). So, for our purposes here, I'll share something I've learned over the years of using this model. One informal way to get a sense of someone's versatility is to notice how and to what extent they seem to modify their behaviors when dealing with others. If they seem good at "reading" people, and if they are able to speed up or slow down, and to be more informal or formal, as the situation demands, then they probably have fairly high versatility.

Why Is This Useful?

It's probably obvious to you this is just a thumbnail sketch of the model. However, let's apply the basic ideas we've covered in this overview to the subject of being usefully attentive to your employees. In the beginning of the chapter, I proposed the idea that being usefully attentive means **directing your attention toward those things that will yield you the best information** about how to support your employees' growth.

Now I'm going to give you a framework for directing your attention, based on the Social Style model. There are a few simple clues that provide a quick and fairly reliable fix on a person's Social Style, and knowing a person's style can give you lots of good information about what they need from you as a manager in order to succeed. Here are the clues, first for Assertiveness, then for Responsiveness. Since Social Style is a behavioral model, these clues are all fairly easy to observe in the course of interacting with a person.

ASSERTIVENESS CLUES

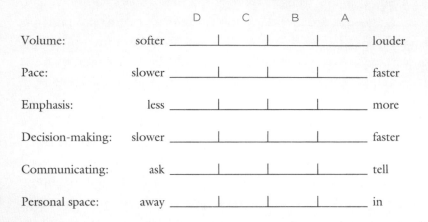

Volume: How loudly does the person speak? Also, how much "volume" do they have personally: do they slip quietly into a room, or do they have a "big" presence? People with less "volume" fall toward the left side of the assertiveness scale (soft would be "D," while moderately soft would be "C"). People with more volume fall toward the right (loud volume would be "A," moderately loud would be "B").

Pace: How quickly does the person speak, move, act, decide? For instance, if you ask some people a question, they'll start to answer even before you've finished speaking, while others will pause and reflect before they respond. People whose pace is slower fall toward the left side of the assertiveness scale (D or C); people whose pace is faster fall on the right (A or B).

Emphasis: With how much emphasis does this person express his or her point of view? For example, two people may feel equally strongly about a topic, but one will express her opinion by saying, "We have to . . ." or, "It's critical that we . . ." while the other person may say, "We might want to consider . . ." or, "It may be important to . . ." People who express themselves more moderately and less emphatically fall toward the left side of the assertiveness scale, while those who express themselves more strongly and definitively fall to the right.

Decision-making: How does this person make decisions? Some people feel most comfortable having the opportunity to gather information or opinions and think or talk through all the elements of a decision before coming to a final determination, while others feel comfortable assessing the situation and deciding more quickly. Those who prefer to take more time in decision-making fall onto the left side of the scale, while those who decide quickly fall on the right.

Communicating: In working with other people, how much does this person focus on telling others what he or she thinks or feels, and how much does he or she focus on finding out what others think or feel? For example, if you ask the person for his opinion about something, is he more likely to state it immediately or to ask some questions first? People who are more "ask"-oriented fall on the left side of the scale, while people who are more "tell"-oriented fall on the right.

Personal space: When you're interacting with this person, does he or she tend to "lean in" to the conversation physically, sitting forward or standing relatively close and gesturing toward you, or does he or she "lean away"—sitting or standing back and gesturing toward him- or herself? People who "lean away" fall on the left side of the scale, while people who "lean in" fall on the right.

RESPONSIVENESS CLUES

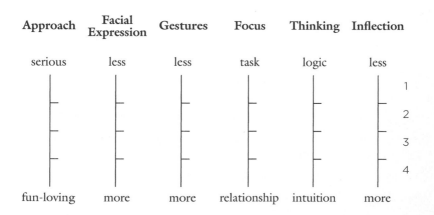

Approach: Generally, how does the person approach life? Do they seem more serious-minded (even if they have a good sense of humor), or do they seem more fun-loving (even when engaged in a serious pursuit)? People who are more serious-minded fall above the middle of the responsiveness scale (very serious-minded would be 1, while moderately so would be 2). People who are more fun-loving fall below the middle (very fun-loving would be 4, while moderately fun-loving would be 3).

Facial expression: How easy is it to tell what this person is feeling by looking at his or her face? For example, if you videotaped this person speaking on a topic about which they felt strongly, and then watched the tape without the sound, would you still be able to tell how they felt? People whose faces don't show much expression fall above the middle of the responsiveness scale (1 or 2); people whose faces show more of how they feel fall below the middle (3 or 4).

Gestures: How much gesturing or moving around does this person do when he or she is talking? Some people tend to be pretty "set," even when they're discussing something about which they feel strongly—they sit in one place and don't move their hands much. Other people use their hands freely to emphasize what they say, or stand up and move around to make a point. People who gesture less fall above the middle of this scale, while those who gesture more fall below the middle.

Focus: Where does this person put his or her primary focus when approaching work? Some people "lead" with task; in a new job, for instance, they'll start by making sure they're clear on the objectives and creating a plan of work. Other people "lead" with relationship; they'll begin a new job by making connections with others with whom they'll be working. Those who prefer to lead with task fall above the midpoint of the scale, while those who lead with relationship fall below the midpoint.

Thinking: In thinking through a project or problem, does this person rely more on intuition or logic? For example, if you ask someone how he

or she came to a decision, are they more likely to give you a rational explanation, or to tell you that it "felt right"? People who rely more on
logic fall above the midpoint of the scale; people who are more swayed
by intuition fall below the midpoint.

Vocal inflection: When this person is speaking, how much does his or
her voice vary—in pitch, speed, or volume? This is especially easy to notice on the phone; some people's voices stay within a fairly small range
of pitch, speed, and volume while others' voices vary a lot—you can tell
how they feel by listening to what's happening with their voices. People
whose voices have less inflection fall above the midpoint of the scale, while
people whose voices have more inflection fall below the midpoint.

TRY IT OUT

Below, I've described my interactions with two different people
(actual clients, who've been profiled in the Social Style model).
Using the clues I've just explained, assess each person's Social
Style. (At the end of the chapter, I've noted how these folks were
actually profiled, so you can see how your assessments of them
match up with their profiles.)

Ms. X

As I come into her office, Ms. X, a senior HR executive, looks up
and nods to me. "I'm sorry I'm a little late," she says gently, "it's
a bit crazy here today." She asks me to sit down while she finishes
writing an e-mail. She taps on her keyboard for a few minutes,
rereads what she's written, then pushes the send key. She gets up
from her desk and, bringing a couple of folders, walks over to her
conference table and sits down carefully across from me. She
smiles and says hello, then asks me for my understanding of why
we're meeting, to make sure we're on the same page. Her voice is
low-pitched and soft, and her expression, while pleasant and open,
is neutral.

The first item on our agenda is to discuss another senior executive at this company and how we might be able to help him build a more effective team. The person we're talking about really seems to be struggling—he's very bright and talented, but his people aren't happy—and they're increasingly less productive. Ms. X asks me my opinion, about both the executive and how he manages his team. As I speak, she listens attentively, making some notes on a piece of paper in one of her folders. After I've offered my point of view, I ask for her perspective. She nods thoughtfully, looks down at the page before her, and then responds. "What you've said makes a lot of sense," she says slowly. "I've thought about this a lot, and I agree that he needs to spend more time with his employees. He doesn't seem to recognize that they require more leadership and direction—that they're quite a bit more junior than he is." She stops and puts her pen down, sitting back and clasping her hands loosely in her lap. "Do you have a suggestion about how we might help him?" she asks.

I note that he would be an excellent candidate for executive coaching—he's open to feedback and has said to me on more than one occasion that he'd like to become a more effective manager and leader. Again, Ms. X nods thoughtfully. "Hmm, that might be a very good idea," she says, considering. "Let me think about how to present the possibility to him, and what would be the best way to bring the idea up to our president—his boss." She pauses again, thinking. "How about if I let you know whether we want to proceed on this next week?"

I reply that would be fine, and we move to our next topic . . .

Based on what I've written above, how might you assess Ms. X on each of the clues?

ASSERTIVENESS

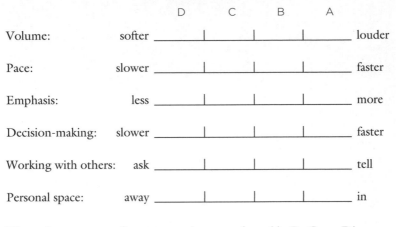

		D	C	B	A	
Volume:	softer					louder
Pace:	slower					faster
Emphasis:	less					more
Decision-making:	slower					faster
Working with others:	ask					tell
Personal space:	away					in

Note the average of your assertiveness clues (A, B, C, or D): ___

RESPONSIVENESS

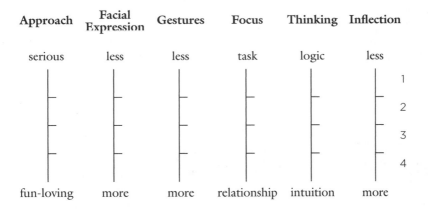

Approach	Facial Expression	Gestures	Focus	Thinking	Inflection	
serious	less	less	task	logic	less	1
						2
						3
						4
fun-loving	more	more	relationship	intuition	more	

Note the average of your responsiveness clues (1, 2, 3, or 4): ___

Now, on the "Social Style map" below, write "Ms. X" in the box where her assertiveness and responsiveness averages intersect. (For instance, "Joe," the made-up person noted on the map below, averaged "A," and "2.")

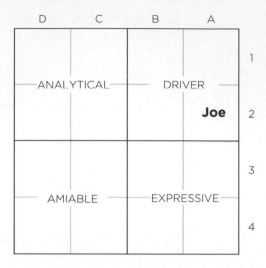

OK, let's try it again with a very different person:

Mr. Z

I meet Mr. Z in the hallway, walking toward his office. "Hey!" he calls. "I'm just coming from a meeting. How the heck are you?" He gives me a friendly pat on the shoulder. I tell him I'm having a great day, and we talk a little about our families as we arrive at his office. He motions me toward one of the comfortable chairs near his desk, as he settles into the sofa next to it. He sprawls comfortably, his long legs stretched in front of him. This is the first time I've been to see him since he took a new job running a start-up venture within a larger organization. Mr. Z gestures around the big office, a large window providing a great city view. "Nice digs, right?" He rolls his eyes, self-deprecating and half embarrassed. "You deserve it," I answer, smiling. He clasps his hands behind his head, sighing. "You bet. For all the hard work that I haven't done here yet." I laugh, and so does he.

"OK, down to business," he says, still smiling. He sits up and leans toward me, putting his elbows on his knees. "I want to do some kind of an offsite with all my folks. I need to spend some time with them, make sure we're all on the same page." He speaks quickly and enthusiastically. "We're going to be hiring a lot of new people over the next six months, and the people who are already here need to be the core. I want them to know who I am and feel comfortable with me and with each other. You got some ideas about how to do that?" He grins. "Wait, what am I saying—of course you have some ideas!" I smile back and note that I'd like to ask him a few questions first, so I understand more about what he wants to get out of the offsite. "Sure," he replies easily. "Oh, and while I'm thinking of it . . ." he gets up and goes over to his desk, sorts through papers for a minute, and picks out a sheet, which he hands me. "My current org chart," he notes, "including all the TBAs for the people we haven't hired yet."

"Do you want to do the offsite soon, or wait until you've got more of these positions filled?" I ask, looking at the org chart. He responds right away. "Well, I'm only missing one direct report—my finance person—and I've got two good candidates; I'm sure one of them will end up in the job. So let's do it as soon as that person's in place. I think if we scheduled it for early next month, it would be fine. Oh, wait." He smiles at me. "Do you have any time free early next month?" "I do," I respond. "How about if my assistant calls your office with my open dates?"

"Great!" he replies, nodding.

Based on this, how might you assess Mr. Z on each of the clues?

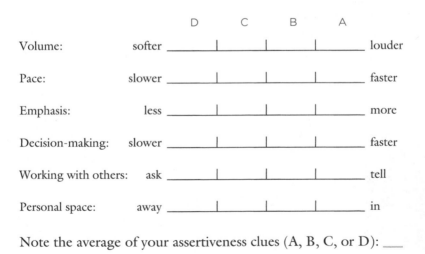

		D	C	B	A	
Volume:	softer					louder
Pace:	slower					faster
Emphasis:	less					more
Decision-making:	slower					faster
Working with others:	ask					tell
Personal space:	away					in

Note the average of your assertiveness clues (A, B, C, or D): ___

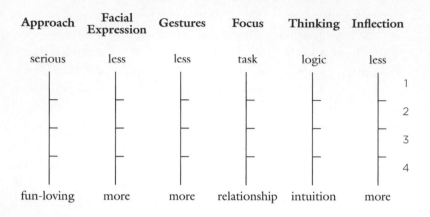

Approach	Facial Expression	Gestures	Focus	Thinking	Inflection	
serious	less	less	task	logic	less	1
						2
						3
						4
fun-loving	more	more	relationship	intuition	more	

Note the average of your responsiveness clues (1, 2, 3, or 4): _____

Now, on the Social Style map a few pages back (with Ms. X and the mythical Joe), write "Mr. Z" in the box where his assertiveness and responsiveness averages intersect. [Remember, the actual profiles for both Ms. X and Mr. Z are at the end of the chapter.]

TRY IT OUT (in real life, now)

OK, here's where the rubber meets the road. Using the clue sheets and style map on the following two pages, try profiling your employees, your boss, and yourself. One caveat: rather than trying to do it right now, I suggest you spend the next few days being "usefully attentive"; note how these people actually behave. Then, when you feel reasonably confident that you've observed enough to use the clue sheets, assess each person individually on the clues. When you're done, create the "map" of your work relationships on page 114.

Mapping My Team

Assertiveness

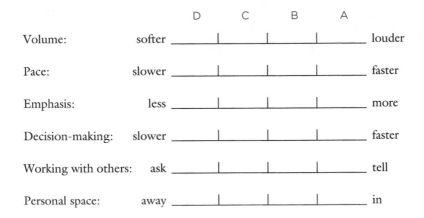

		D	C	B	A	
Volume:	softer					louder
Pace:	slower					faster
Emphasis:	less					more
Decision-making:	slower					faster
Working with others:	ask					tell
Personal space:	away					in

Responsiveness

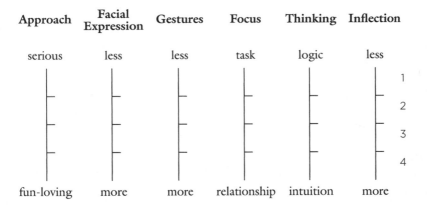

Approach	Facial Expression	Gestures	Focus	Thinking	Inflection	
serious	less	less	task	logic	less	1
						2
						3
						4
fun-loving	more	more	relationship	intuition	more	

Team Social Style Map

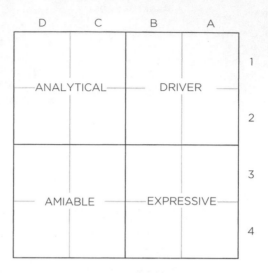

Tie-breakers

What if you're not quite sure of someone's style? For instance, what if you've clearly assessed someone as an "A," but they come out right in between a "2" and a "3" in responsiveness? How do you know whether this person is a Driver or an Expressive? Here's a useful tip I've developed over the years, based on an insight shared with me many years ago by a woman named Dot Bolton, my first teacher about Social Style. It's a kind of tie-breaker for those situations where you're not quite sure of someone's style.

People of each style seem to have a "bottom line" when working on a project: the thing that, if they have their choice, they're generally most concerned about achieving. If you're on the fence about someone's style based on the clues, ask yourself, based on your experience of them, which style's "bottom line" is more descriptive of that person. Here are the Social Style tie-breakers, the bottom line for each style:

Drivers want to **get it done.** They take deadlines seriously, plus they derive great satisfaction from completing tasks or projects and moving on to the next challenge.

Expressives want to **get it further.** They get excited about the idea of breaking new ground in their areas of interest, and rarely feel satisfied settling for the status quo.

Amiables want to **get to it together.** They really enjoy figuring out how to reach a goal without leaving people behind; they'd prefer to see everybody on board and committed to the result.

Analyticals want to **get it correct.** They see accuracy as being key to excellence, and generally don't feel comfortable with "close enough."

So in our example above, about the person you've assessed as either an A2 or an A3—Driver or Expressive—you'd ask yourself, "Is this person's bottom line *get it done* or *get it further*? And your answer would break the tie and let you know which style he or she is most likely to be.

So What? How to Respond

We've spent quite a bit of time and effort getting to this point in the chapter. Now you're probably able to figure out—with a fair degree of accuracy—someone's main Social Style. You may be asking, "So what? Is this more than just an interesting parlor game?"

Fortunately, yes—this is practical stuff. Once you have a fairly clear idea of someone's Social Style, you have lots of useful information about how they like and need to be managed, and about how to help them grow. If you recall, back at the beginning of the chapter when we were talking about my friend's garden, I suggested that if she got a good book about plant care, she'd know what to look for and how to respond to what she was seeing in her garden. So far in this chapter, we've focused on the "what to look for" part of being attentive to your employees. Now I want to give you some insight about how to respond to what you see.

The chart below offers a top-line approach to managing people of each of the four styles. On the pages that follow, I've expanded on these key ideas.

Style	How they like to be managed	What they need (but may not like)	Critical growth area
Driver	· Clear goals and time frames · Rewards for meeting goals and deadlines · Succinct meetings and direction · Autonomy	· To learn to dialogue · To be encouraged to gather more data · To be required to build consensus · To be held accountable for the "how" as well as the "what"	Look for others' perspective
Expressive	· Talking through decisions and plans · Being supported to innovate · Being acknowledged for contributions · Freedom to get results in their own way	· To learn to communicate the essence · To be encouraged to plan · To recognize the impact of their words and actions · To be held accountable for getting clear agreements	Do reality checks
Amiable	· Time to build teams and relationships · Knowing how decisions affect people · Well-defined structures and interactions · Support for their actions and decisions	· To learn to confront difficult issues · To be encouraged to say what they think · To recognize when a person or project can't be "saved" · To be held accountable for necessary decision-making	Take a stand
Analytical	· Sufficient information · Time to think through the implications · Lead time for making decisions · Calm and balanced feedback	· To learn to make quick decisions · To be encouraged to lead with the positives · To recognize when they need to "make a case" · To be held accountable for timely results	Share their thinking

Drivers

If any of your employees are Drivers, remember that they tend to focus on **getting it done.** They're likely to be the people you turn to when it's critical that something happen on time and on budget. If you give them clarity about what's expected and whether they've achieved it, provide as much autonomy as possible, and then reward them for reaching the finish line—they'll be quite satisfied and productive.

However, this important strength—this ability to move forward to accomplish goals quickly and efficiently regardless of obstacles—is also likely to be their Achilles' heel. The main reason Drivers can get complex stuff done quickly is that they tend to tune out distractions—and unfortunately, Drivers can often see other people and their ideas and concerns as a distraction! When they get too narrowly focused on moving things forward, they can be seen as autocratic, or as not taking time to consider alternatives, or as impatient or inconsiderate. So, you can support a Driver employee's growth by helping him or her learn to look for others' perspectives.

Learning to look for others' perspectives is the perfect antidote to the Drivers' tendency to put too much emphasis on forward momentum. Think of it this way: Drivers are compelled toward resolution. For most Drivers I've worked with and coached, it feels deeply and personally satisfying to complete things—projects, plans, buildings, agreements, meetings, etc. You need to help your Driver employee understand that actively seeking others' points of view will ultimately help him or her get things done; when people feel heard and included in planning and decisions, they're likely to be far more committed to the outcomes. Once a Driver sees this dynamic clearly, he or she will be motivated to do the things I'm about to encourage you to teach them. (Remember the LearningPath model I shared with you in chapter 4? We're talking here about helping your Drivers become aware they can approach work in alternative ways, and helping them become motivated to do so.)

First, teach your Driver employee the art of dialogue; you can do this by helping him or her learn how to listen (the sovereign skill for Drivers), and by making sure, at meetings you manage, that the Driver's peers get an equal chance to share their points of view and have those points of view considered and discussed. You can also encourage the Driver to gather more data than usual during problem-solving or planning, especially from those with other experiences or points of view. Gathering data is often easier than dialoguing for Drivers who are just learning to listen, because it's a more clear-cut task. They can make a goal out of understanding the other person's point of view and they're asking the questions, which will likely feel more directed and efficient to them. Just be careful to help them actively look for *new* points of view in this process, vs. simply reinforcing their existing conclusions. You may need to coach them to ask open-ended, nonleading, curiosity-based questions (as we discussed in the first chapter).

Another way to help your Driver employees look for others' perspectives is to require that they build consensus on important issues. This requires more skill than simply gathering data, and many Drivers can be helped to learn this skill by observing someone else who is good at building consensus and then debriefing what they observed afterward so that they can become aware of the key behaviors involved. The most important skill for building consensus is listening (which, they'll be pleased to realize, you've already started helping them to learn!)

Finally, in establishing performance goals for Drivers, be sure to hold them accountable for the "how" as well as the "what." In other words, if you give a Driver the goal of "increasing production by 20 percent over the coming year" (the what), be sure that you also include something about *how* you expect him or her to go about achieving that goal, like "without increasing employee turnover" or "by involving the employee base in deciding on and implementing productivity-increasing measures." Again, this provides a way to balance the Driver's task-focused, get-it-done approach with a focus on the role that others want and need to play in getting it done.

Expressives

Your Expressive employees, in general, will be most excited by the prospect of breaking new ground. Remember, their rallying cry is **getting it**

further. If you're looking for a fresh perspective, a sense of fun, an innovative way of approaching something—waking things up in general—you probably turn to your Expressive employees. They will enjoy being managed by you and do their best work if you give them as much freedom of movement as possible; let them think out loud, consider a variety of options, and accomplish the results in their own—sometimes quirky—way, rather than being constrained by unnecessary rules. Most Expressives also enjoy being regularly and sincerely acknowledged for their contributions—they want to know that someone "gets" them and the unique value they bring to the team.

As with the Drivers (and as you'll see, with the Amiables and Analyticals as well), their strengths, when overused or used to an extreme degree, can also be their greatest weaknesses. Their ability to think and act in innovative ways can slip into a stubborn unwillingness to look at the constraints, or follow even necessary rules, or take responsibility for the negative impact of their actions. You can help your Expressive employees to balance out these tendencies by teaching them to do reality checks.

By "doing reality checks," I mean looking at the downsides and implications of an exciting idea before recommending it or moving ahead with it. Because Expressives, as a group, are so focused on the possibilities inherent in a situation, they tend not to be looking at the pitfalls and consequences. You need to help your Expressive employees understand that thinking about what might get in the way of achieving the possibilities they can so clearly envision isn't just a buzz-kill—it will help them gain credibility, help them sell their ideas, and keep them from making embarrassing and costly mistakes. Again, following the LearningPath model, once your Expressives understand what's in it for them to do reality checks, they'll be much more open to your efforts to help them learn how.

A simple but powerful way to start getting your Expressive employees to "reality check" is to ask them to communicate the essence of their idea. Expressives often feel the potential power of an idea or approach, but have a hard time putting it into words. When they are requested to articulate it, they begin to see more clearly the strengths and weaknesses of the idea, and can begin to think about it more practically—while not losing their connection with the idea's inherent potential. I've found that asking them to summarize is more effective for this purpose than simply asking them questions ("Is it this?" "Is it that?"). Questioning an Expressive's not fully formed idea often results in frustration and defensiveness, while asking for a summary can help them clarify their own thinking. For instance, if your Expressive employee comes bursting into your office with a way to cut overhead by 50 percent, you can help them reality check (without destroying their enthusiasm) by saying something like, "Wow, that could be great. Can you talk me through the main points of how that would work?" With more senior employees, you could ask for a written plan (though they would still want to talk you through it!).

You can use the same approach to help them think through the impact of a proposed course of action on the people around them, which is another important kind of reality check for most Expressives. This can be as simple as asking, "How do you think the salespeople would respond to that?" or more pointedly, "Who might be unhappy or dissatisfied with that approach?" followed by, "How can we address their concerns?"

Finally, in establishing performance goals for Expressives, make it very clear that you are holding them responsible not just for innovative, ground-breaking accomplishments, but for achieving them in a way that doesn't create problems for others. For example, it's not OK to get new clients by promising things that manufacturing hasn't said they can deliver. It's not OK for the Expressive to offer all his or her employees a big bonus for meeting a deadline without first finding out whether the money is in the budget. In other words, hold your Expressive employees accountable not just for results, but for making the agreements with others that are necessary for achieving those results.

One thing to remember overall in managing your Expressive employees—especially when you're doing the things they need but may not like—is to lead with the positive. In using any of the approaches I've explained above, I almost guarantee you'll get the best results if you start by acknowledging something you genuinely like about what they've said (as in, "I love that you've put so much energy into this," or, "Wow, if that works, it would be great."). Then express your main concerns ("I'm worried about the financial implications of your idea") and then offer suggestions for resolving the concerns ("Could we do it on a smaller scale?") or ask them for suggestions ("How could we get some of the same benefits, with less investment upfront?"). Though this approach—Likes, Concerns, and Suggestions—is useful in a wide variety of situations, it's perhaps most useful in helping Expressives to do reality checks without demoralizing or derailing them. (I'm indebted to my dear friend and colleague Mitch Ditkoff for this model.)

Amiables

Amiables are, of all the styles, the people to whom teaming seems to come most naturally. Remember, their bottom line is **getting to it together.** Amiables tend to understand the power of getting people fully engaged in and committed to creating results. Most Amiables are good at seeing both sides of a debate, and at encouraging different types of people to work together. Give them the opportunity to build teams and relationships within a reasonably well-defined structure; provide the context they need to understand how the decisions they make will affect others; and be consistent in supporting their actions and decisions—and you will be rewarded with an extremely loyal and productive employee.

As with the other styles, these Amiable strengths have a dark side. When over-relied-upon, the Amiable's focus on mediation and consensus can turn into an unwillingness to confront difficult issues, and a perception by others that the Amiable can be taken advantage of, can't take decisive action, or doesn't have a strong point of view. The key way to strengthen and grow your Amiable employees is to help them learn to take a stand.

Taking a stand involves communicating and acting on a definitive position on issues about which you feel strongly, even when others may disagree, or when your position may put a strain on relationships. For example, most Amiables have a hard time firing someone, even when it's clear the person genuinely needs to be fired. For some of the Amiable executives I've worked with, this is their primary Achilles' heel; they let people stay in the organization long after it's clear to everyone around them that the person should be let go—sometimes long after that person's behavior has begun to have a negative impact on the business. In my experience, when Amiables have a hard time taking a strong stand on difficult issues, it's because they tend to focus on all the negative consequences of taking that stand. For example, in a situation where they can't bring themselves to fire someone, they might say something like, "Well, that person's been here a long time, and it would really devastate him. Also, it would create a lot of disruption in the team, and I think it might be difficult to find anyone better. And—even though he hasn't been performing up to par for a long time—he does have great relationships with two important clients, and I wouldn't want to damage those." When the problems that could result are all the Amiable is focusing on, of course it's unlikely he or she will fire the person.

So, a simple way to help your Amiable employees to take a stand is to help them look at the situation in a new way; to consider the negative consequences of not taking a stand and the positive consequences of taking a stand. For example, in the situation above, if you asked your Amiable, "Can you think of any problems that might occur if you *don't* fire this person?" he or she might say, "Well, I think morale might erode—and you know, it might have a negative impact on my credibility as a manager. And other people are having to fill in for this person, so it's hard keeping our productivity up." If you then ask, "What good things might happen if you let this person go?" he or she might respond, "It would free up quite a bit of my time, actually—I spend so much time making up for his shortcomings and explaining him to other people. And I know that some people in the department would feel I'd done the right thing. And you know, ultimately, it would probably even be better for him—I know he's just waiting for the other shoe to drop, and it would be better for him to be in a job where he could excel." Having been helped to think through the situation like this, that is, to turn their awareness in a new direction, most Amiables will have an easier time making a difficult decision.

Building on this, when setting performance goals for Amiables, it's especially important to hold them accountable for making timely decisions. If you don't give them a clear deadline, not only for results but for the decisions intrinsic to those results, they may avoid making difficult but necessary decisions. Talking through all the possible consequences of those decisions and providing the assurance of your support for their decisions and actions will make this process significantly easier for them.

Analyticals

Any Analytical employees in your group are most likely to be the people you rely on for precision, accuracy, and a balanced presentation of the facts. I've noticed that many teams use their resident Analyticals as a kind of safety net—to keep them from running off half-cocked, or leaving things undone, or not considering important elements of a situation. Most Analyticals devote a lot of focus and skill to **getting it correct.** If you provide them enough information and time to do what you've asked, they will not only deliver excellent work, but with all the backup and contingency plans you could ever want! And if you, as their manager, also offer feedback—either about their performance or their results—in a calm and balanced way, they will generally be quite satisfied and productive working with and for you.

The flip side of this strength—as we've already seen with the other styles' strengths—is problematic. When taken to an extreme, the Analyticals' focus on detail and precision, on facts and backup, can turn into an unwillingness to decide quickly when necessary, or to consider intangibles, or to see how others might look at a set of facts and come to a different conclusion. They can then be seen as negative, inflexible, and/or risk-averse. You can help your Analytical employees avoid these problems by teaching them to share their thinking.

Here's how this works: many Analyticals don't share their thinking because they don't see why it's necessary. They tend to believe that everything can be decided factually, and that if two people look at the same set of data, they will come to the same conclusion. "Selling an idea" is a foreign concept to many Analyticals. You need to help your Analytical employee understand that letting people know how they came to a conclusion, or why they are taking a certain course of action, or how a project is progressing, will make it much more likely that others will understand and support their efforts. When Analyticals start to see this positive impact of sharing their thinking, they are much more likely to want to continue doing it.

Teaching your Analytical employees to make decisions more quickly when necessary will be very helpful to their careers. Interestingly, I've found that getting them to share their thinking about where they are in a decision-making process often helps them to decide. For example, when asked where she is in creating next year's plans, an Analytical marketing person might say, "I haven't decided the best way to approach the marketing plan for next year" (or worse yet, not say anything to anybody until the decision is made!). Instead, encourage your Analytical to share where she is in the decision-making process and what she will need to move forward. If she then said, for instance, "We're waiting to find out whether we're going to have the same budgets we had last year, and I don't yet know how the salespeople are going to use the fourth-quarter tools we gave them," you or others might be able to provide information or alternatives to help her move forward, or you might be able to encourage the Analytical to think about how she could make some assumptions that would allow planning before all the data is in.

A very powerful skill for Analyticals—perhaps as powerful as listening is for Drivers—is to learn to lead with the positive. Because their focus is on balance and precision, if they hear someone talking about the potential benefits of an approach, they will feel honor-bound to redress the imbalance by talking about constraints and possible downsides. This can make others think that the Analytical is negative or risk-averse. Teach your Analytical employees to respond to new ideas or information by using the Likes, Concerns, Suggestions approach I explained above. It's a great way to share their thinking while still building positive relationships, and letting people see that they are hopeful and results-oriented. (And it will really appeal to their Expressive colleagues!)

In setting performance goals for your Analytical employees, be especially careful to agree on reasonable timetables for results. If you don't specify a deadline, many Analyticals will assume that they can take as long as it takes to get it right. On the other hand, if you specify a deadline that the Analytical believes is unrealistically tight, he or she may not say so (not sharing their thinking). So it's important to set time frames and deadlines that seem appropriate and realistic to both of you.

About Versatility

It's important to note that, the more versatile someone is, the easier it will be for him or her to accept the idea of doing things differently—highly versatile people are those who have already discovered how shifting their behaviors can create better relationships, and help them overcome their own shortcomings. So, while it may be more difficult to use the growth strategies outlined above with employees whose versatility is low, it will be especially useful to them: helping them learn to "stretch" in these ways will significantly increase their versatility.

TRY IT OUT

OK, now let's put this into practice. You've already taken a pass at profiling your employees (above, on p. 112). Select the person you would most like to work on managing more effectively.

Below, write his or her name and Social Style:

_____

Now, referring to the chart on page 116 and the more in-depth paragraphs about this person's style that follow the chart, decide and write down for yourself the following:

- One or two specific ways you can give this person more of how they like to be managed:

_____

_____

_____

_____

- One or two specific actions you can take to provide for them what they need but may not like, in order to help them develop in their style-based area of growth:

_____

_____

_____

_____

Putting It All Together

I'd suggest that you try this out over the next few weeks with this first employee, and see how it works and what you may have to do differently. Then, based on what you've learned (about yourself and your employee) you can use this same simple, practical approach to take advantage of what you've learned in this chapter to manage each of your employees more effectively.

Here's a way to create a simple structure for yourself to help assure that you continue to explore and refine your use of Social Style as a tool. First make a copy of the Social Style "map" you created on page 114 that includes you, your boss, and your employees. Create a folder for your current files (or whatever system you use to keep track of ongoing stuff) called "Social Style" and slip in the map. Now, use this folder to keep track of efforts you make (like the process you've just gone through, above) to manage and develop people in ways that acknowledge and build upon their Social Style. Any time you have an insight about someone's Social Style, or want to think through a conversation about how to take advantage of a person's style-based strengths or help them overcome their style-based weaknesses, put it in the folder. After a few months, you may find you no longer need a separate folder, and that you will automatically factor in an employee's style when interacting with and coaching him or her.

Before We Continue

I have to admit I feel a little uncomfortable leaving this topic here. I could definitely write an entire book about the Social Style model and how to make use of it, and not think I was devoting too much time to the topic. I've found this model to be a tremendously useful tool for insight and behavior change in my own life, and I believe my own relationships with colleagues and clients, as well as with friends and family, have benefited from my understanding of this approach. Given that, I feel I've shortchanged you—as though I've given you a first-aid kit versus a medical degree! Fortunately, even a first-aid kit can be extremely useful, and I feel confident that you'll make good use of this. If you'd like to find out more about Social Style, I encourage you to explore some of the books available on this topic, including *People Styles at Work,* by Bob and Dorothy Bolton.

Oh, by the way, Ms. X was profiled as a D2 Analytical, and Mr. Z was profiled as a B4 Expressive. How did you read their styles?

One more thing . . . as you get into the habit of looking for the Social Style clues to your employees' management needs and wants, it's likely that you'll start to notice there are some things that all employees need, whatever their style, background, or experience. The next chapter focuses on those "maintenance" skills—the often underappreciated but essential skills that apply to every flower in the garden.

BIG IDEAS

Once a gardener has planned and planted a garden, he or she needs to stay attentive to it, in order to make sure each plant gets what it needs to continue to thrive. A manager, once he or she has established a strong team, also needs to stay usefully attentive to everyone on that team, in order to assure each person's growth and productivity. Staying usefully attentive means:

Directing your attention toward those things that will yield the best information about how to support your employees' growth

The Social Style Model provides an approach to what to look for, and how to use what you see, so that you can manage each employee in the way that will be both most enjoyable and most helpful to him or her.

Drivers: are task- and goal-focused, compelled toward *getting it done.* They want clarity and autonomy from their managers, and they need to learn to *look for others' perspectives.*

Expressives: are relationship- and forward-movement-focused, and passionate about *getting it further.* They want interaction and freedom from their managers, and they need to learn to *do reality checks.*

Amiables: are relationship- and team-focused, and they're most satisfied by *getting to it together.* They want support and structure from their managers, and they need to learn to *take a stand.*

Analyticals: are task- and information-focused, and they feel most strongly about *getting it correct.* They want emotional balance and reasonable time frames from their managers, and they need to learn to *share their thinking.*

CHAPTER 7

Staking and Weeding

I sit back on my heels and wipe a not-too-clean gardening glove across my sweating (and now dirt-smeared) forehead. "Wow, it's looking great," I note, surveying my friend's garden in all its full-blown late-summer splendor.

My gardening friend, equally grubby and pleased, nods. "This dead-heading stuff is easier than I thought it would be," she says. "And I'm really glad we staked the bee balm."

Now, for those of you who haven't done much gardening, rest assured my friend and I aren't doing anything violent. "Deadheading" means clipping the spent flowers from a plant to neaten it up and encourage it to bloom more, and "staking" just means providing some kind of support for a plant to lean against so it doesn't fall over. These two tasks, along with a few other things, like watering, weeding, and mulching, fall into the category of "ongoing garden maintenance." If you recall, at the beginning of the last chapter, I taught my friend how to be sensitive to the unique needs of her different kinds of plants. This visit, we decided to focus on teaching her to do a few very common and relatively straightforward things that all gardens need in order to stay healthy and productive over time. They are the gardening equivalent of taking vitamins or wearing your seatbelt.

These standard tasks for maintaining a garden aren't difficult or complicated, but they're not very thrilling. And you have to do them regularly and well, or all the hard work you've put into planning, planting, establishing a helpful mind-set, and understanding the needs of your individual plants can end up in the compost heap with the skeletal remains of your garden.

I'm sure you feel a metaphor coming on, and I won't disappoint you. As a manager, there are employee maintenance tasks that will keep your team flourishing. They aren't complicated or strenuous, but they're not always much fun. It's worth your while to learn to do them well, and to motivate yourself to do them regularly—because not doing them can yield very unhappy results.

Listening as Mulch

One of these tasks—you'll be happy to learn, since you already know how to do it—is listening. Listening is like mulching (stay with me here). In the first chapter, when we talked about the foundational importance of listening, we compared it to the need for preparing and enriching your soil before you plant, to create an environment in which any plant can flourish. In the garden, mulching (which means putting a yearly layer of organic substance, like shredded bark or leaves, over the bare ground between the plants) not only keeps the weeds down, holds in moisture, and protects the plant roots from extremes in temperature—it eventually dissolves and releases more nutrients into the soil. Simple mulch, as you can see, does a pretty dramatic job of maintaining a supportive soil environment for your garden.

In the same way, continuing to listen to your employees regularly not only assures an ongoing environment of respect and mutual support, but also helps to protect your employees (and you) from the extremes of corporate life. For example, when things get crazy—insane deadlines, unrealistic budgets, difficult customers—listening can help ensure that people have a chance to air legitimate concerns, and that everyone is working together efficiently to find solutions to those concerns.

TRY IT OUT

Here's a quick activity to help you think creatively about how to use "listening as mulch." Jot down ten situations where you want to use listening regularly to keep your team motivated, avoid miscommunication, and protect against mistakes and conflict (examples: staff meetings, responding to customer complaints):

_____   _____
_____   _____
_____   _____
_____   _____
_____   _____

Agreements: A Stake in the Ground

When my friend said, "I'm glad we staked the bee balm," she was talking about how much better and healthier tall, flexible plants look when they have something holding them up. By the end of a growing season, many plants, especially those with relatively long stems and heavy flowers, flop over and look pretty bad. They sprawl all over their neighbors and are likely to be less healthy and productive because they're not getting the light and air they need.

Making clear performance agreements is the management equivalent of staking. Without a clear and agreed-upon understanding about what an employee is supposed to be doing, it's all too likely he or she will have problems either "sprawling all over his or her colleagues" by working on things that are others' responsibility; or putting energy into less important tasks; or not accomplishing necessary results.

So, what constitutes an appropriately defined agreement about performance? It not only needs to be clear, it has to be headed in the right direction. In order to be effective on an organizational as well as an individual level, the agreements you make with your employees need to line up with three things:

- your company's vision and strategic goals
- your department's part in reaching the vision and goals
- your employee's understanding and ability

For example, let's say you're head of the design group for a jewelry manufacturing company, and your organization's vision includes rapid growth in fashion (read: costume) jewelry for young, hip women. When you're making performance agreements with your designers, you'll need to keep all that in mind. So, for instance, if you have one designer who is particularly good at coming up with wild, fun ideas that often have a lot of consumer appeal, you might clearly define that person's responsibilities to include submitting a certain number of design ideas every month, or leading design brainstorms for the group.

Once you're sure you're making the right agreements, you need to assure you're making them in a way that will work. There's a very straightforward three-step process you can use to help assure you're making a clear, mutual agreement that will work well.

MAKING CLEAR AGREEMENTS
Clarify
Commit
Support

Clarify

In the first step, you work with the employee to create a clear and compelling mental picture of what needs to be done, describing the goal or responsibility in specific, measurable terms and providing as much detail as is appropriate. (This will be different for different employees; we'll talk more about this in a minute.) You make sure the employee knows why this area of performance is important to the company, to him or her, and to you. You listen to discover the employee's understanding and ideas, and to get clearer on his or her ability in this area. Finally, you make sure the agreement is doable: that the employee has the necessary skills, knowledge, and resources (or can get them), and that any other obstacles to fulfilling the agreement can be overcome.

Commit

In the second step, you make sure that you and the employee understand each other, are agreeing to the same thing, and will have some way of checking to see whether the agreement is working. You do this by summarizing what each of you has agreed to do (what the employee has agreed to accomplish, and what support you have agreed to provide), then setting benchmarks (to check how the agreed-upon work is proceeding) and any necessary deadlines.

Support

No matter how clearly and well you and your employee move through the first two steps, without the third step it's unlikely the goal will be accomplished or at least unlikely that it will be accomplished well. This step is what happens after the agreement-making conversation. First, you and the employee both honor whatever commitments you've made. You provide feedback about how the employee is doing relative to the agreed-upon goal or responsibility. Most important, you create and maintain in yourself the mind-set of a coach (remember chapter 5?)— believing in your employee's ability to fulfill the agreements you've made together, and wanting to help him or her succeed.

Using this model will result in clear, mutually agreed-upon goals and responsibilities. Your employees will have the "stake in the ground" they need to support them to be committed and productive.

Step 1: Clarify

Let's look at the Clarify step in more detail. Here are the key elements:

- Create a clear mental picture
- Establish context and rationale
- Listen to your employee's perspective
- Check for obstacles

Clear mental picture
Ask yourself, "What specific information does this person need from me in order to succeed in this area?" With a new or inexperienced employee, you'll need to communicate a greater level of detail, and to focus more on how something is to be accomplished. With a more experienced or higher-level employee, you'll allow more room for creativity and initiative by focusing on what needs to be done (outcomes, deadlines, etc.), giving them more freedom to decide the "how."

Context and rationale
In addition to creating a clear mental picture for the employee, you'll offer your understanding of why this area is important. First, before the conversation, take time to clarify in your own mind why this area is important to you, and to your employee's current and future success within the context of your company's vision and goals. Then, during the conversation, you'll be able to share your perspective simply and directly.

Listen
Listening lets you gather the employee's insights—about what you've said, the history of this issue or area, ideas about how best to fulfill the agreement. Listening also helps establish the employee's competence in this area. You can start listening with an invitation to talk (e.g, "So, based on what I've shared so far—what are your thoughts?").

Check for obstacles

Make sure the employee has (or can acquire) the resources, skills, and/or knowledge needed to fulfill the commitment. Look for any obstacles and how to overcome them.

I'm going to give you a chance to try this out, but first let me offer a "demonstration": here's how this conversation might sound between the design manager and the jewelry designer we discussed earlier.

Andy, the director of design for Lobo Jewelry, hears a tap on his open door and looks up. Josie, one of his best designers, is standing in the doorway with an expectant look on her face, and Andy realizes it must be 4 P.M.—just when he asked her to come and meet with him. "Hey, Josie, thanks for stopping by. Come on in."

He gets up from his desk, and, walking over to his little seating area, gestures her to a chair. As soon as both are comfortably settled in, and after a bit of small talk, Andy says, "I wanted to talk to you about shifting your focus in a way that will take advantage of your skill at initial ideation. You interested in hearing about it?"

Josie nods. "Sure."

"OK. Well, here's the top line. You know that this year we're really wanting to create a big buzz in the industry. They're giving us more design money than ever before, and we want to come to the major shows with some exciting new stuff. Now, you also know, since we've worked together for a while now, that I love getting ideas from all the designers. And I've noticed, particularly over the past year, that you're really great at coming up with original ideas, and that you've got a great hit ratio . . . a lot of your design ideas have become popular pieces for us. You also don't seem to mind having the other designers take your initial ideas and work them to come up with something that's cost-effective to produce. Are you with me so far?"

Josie nods again. "In fact, I like having the other designers—especially Jim and Tanya—make my ideas workable. They're much better at that part of it than I am."

"Good, that's great," Andy adds. "So here's what I'm thinking. I'd like to have you spend more of your time focusing on that pure ideation part of the job. For example, I'd say you probably bring me two ideas a week that we feel are solid possibilities. I'd like you to double that. It would really support the direction the company is going this year, and it can only help your professional profile to have design credit for so many of our new pieces. We can talk about what else would have to shift for you to have the time to do that, but what are your initial thoughts about this direction?"

Josie, who's a little shy and laid back ordinarily, is clearly excited. She's sitting up straight in her chair, and her face is lit up. "I'd really like that," she says. "It's the part of the job that's most interesting to me, and that I feel I'm best at."

"OK, great. I'm also open to any other ideas you might have about how to get more great design possibilities in the pipeline. Have you thought about anything like that?"

Josie smiles. "Well, there is something I've been doing with Ed. You know, he and I are good friends, and sometimes he'll bring me an idea he's working on that just isn't jelling for him. And then I can suggest something—often it's just something subtle, like a change in texture or material, or rethinking the weight of a line—and it seems to help him get 'unstuck,' if you know what I mean."

"I do, and I love that idea. How about if we look at it this way: the agreement we're making here is that your key responsibility shifts to getting as many initial design ideas to me—from you or others—as possible. And the part of your job that's been focused on taking ideas from concept to production-ready, we can distribute among the other designers. That would free up about ten hours a week for this 'generating great design' responsibility, right?"

Josie looks thoughtful and nods slowly. "I think so. Yeah, I think that's probably about right."

Andy rubs his hands together. "I like how this conversation is going. Do you have any concerns about this, or are there any other resources you think you might need to make this work?"

Josie thinks for a minute. "Well, the only thing I guess I'm concerned about is, I want to make sure it's OK with everybody else. I don't want them to feel like I'm taking anything away . . . I want them to understand this makes me available to help them with their designs, as well—you know? And maybe they don't like the production-ready part of things so much, either. That could be a problem."

"Hmm, good point. How about if I sound out everybody on this individually, and see what they think. I suspect, as you say, that Tanya and Jim will be cool with it, and Ed, too—as long as they know that taking on the production specs for your designs means they get you helping them with their designs! The other two designers are more junior, as you know, and are mostly assisting and making models, so I don't think it will affect them so much. But I appreciate your concern for the team, and I'll check it out with everyone. Anything else?"

"Well, I hesitate to mention it, because I think this is a great opportunity, but I'm kind of concerned about promising you a set number of design ideas—you know, the creative flow isn't exactly predictable."

Andy nods. "Oh, I get that. Look, I trust your work ethic. Let's just keep it that your responsibility is to ensure that as many great ideas as possible land on my desk. No set 'quota.'"

Josie nods, looking pleased . . .

Now remember, this is just the Clarify step (I'll talk you through the "Commit" step next.) This part of the conversation would only take about ten or fifteen minutes (including time for chitchat!), and Andy has a pretty sound initial agreement that Josie is clear about, and feels ownership of—she helped create it, and her concerns were addressed.

One thing I want to point out is that Andy's explanation mixed together "context and rationale" with "clear mental picture." That is, he didn't just do "clear mental picture," followed by "context and rationale." He led with a kind of "clear mental picture" headline: "I wanted to talk to you about shifting your focus in a way that will take advantage of your skill at initial ideation." He then offered some great context about company direction, and then went back into the "clear mental picture" part, giving her a clearer sense of what he was asking of her. And he finished up with more context—how doing this would help the company and her professional profile. I wrote it this way on purpose, because that's how it tends to happen in real life. When you're preparing for the conversation, I've found it's helpful to think through the two parts—context and rationale and clear mental picture—separately, and then when you're having the conversation, the order you say them in doesn't matter so much as making sure you cover your main points.

TRY IT OUT

OK, now it's your turn. Think of an employee with whom you'd like to make a new performance agreement. You might want to choose a situation like the one above, where you're asking someone to focus more on a particular responsibility or take on a new project. Another possibility might be making sure a new employee has initial clarity about a key job responsibility.

· **Clear Mental Picture:** in the space provided below, write the particulars of a performance agreement you'd like to make with one of your employees. Create a clear mental picture of what you're asking the employee to do. Focus on the specific information this employee needs in order to succeed in this area:

_____

_____

_____

_____

_____

· After you've created, in the space above, a clear mental picture that you believe offers all the information the employee needs, check it again to make sure it's specific, understandable, and doable.

· **Context and Rationale:** Think about and note why this performance area is important to the employee, to you, and to your company. Remember to link your comments to your company's vision and/or strategic goals:

_____

_____

_____

_____

_____

· **Listening to Your Employee:** Now, think about and write down a few questions you could ask to elicit any important information your employee might have about the agreement you're requesting:

_____

_____

_____

_____

_____

· **Possible Obstacles/Solutions:** Finally, think about obstacles: a lack of skills, knowledge, or resources; time constraints; other people's conflicting agendas or resistance to new ideas. Jot down both any possible obstacles and ways you and/or your employee might overcome them.

When you've finished the written practice above, I suggest you imagine yourself talking through the main points with your employee, just to see how it feels and sounds. Will it be clear to the employee what you're asking him or her to do? Will he or she understand why it's important? Will the employee feel that you genuinely want to hear and address his or her ideas and concerns? If not, think about how you can revise your message to achieve these goals.

(By the way, if you're an action-oriented type, and want to race right out and try this with the employee in question, I suggest you wait until we've worked through the Commit step—that comes next—then you can have the complete conversation.)

Step 2: Commit

When both you and your employee are satisfied with the clarity of the agreement you've made, it's time to find out whether you're agreeing to the same thing! The second step of making agreements involves checking your understanding and setting time frames—to make sure that both you and your employee really agree on what's going to happen and when. The key elements to committing are:

- Ask the employee to summarize:
    - What s/he has agreed to do
    - What you have agreed to do
- Set benchmarks and time lines

Summarize

I suggest that you ask your employee to summarize his or her understanding of the agreement reached during the Clarify step. It may feel a bit awkward to ask for the summary, but the problem is, if *you* summarize, you still only know what you think the agreement is—you don't really know what the employee understands. Hearing the employee's version of the agreement will help you see immediately if there are any misunderstandings or gaps, so that you can keep working toward the same understanding.

Set benchmarks and time lines

Agree on a benchmark date or dates for touching base about how it's going. Next, set clear deadlines for meeting the goal.

It's important to note here the difference between agreement and expectation. An expectation is one-sided: for instance, the vice president of sales who leaves a meeting expecting that his team will "upgrade the sales force" to his satisfaction—without having asked for or received their commitment. An agreement is two-sided: both parties understand and agree to something specific. When goals and responsibilities are based on agreements, they are much more likely to be fulfilled to the satisfaction of everyone involved.

Let's go back to Josie and Andy, and see how Andy completes the Commit step. We'll pick up the conversation just where we left off:

Josie nods, looking pleased.

Andy says, "OK, let's make sure we're on the same page here. How about if you just summarize what we've agreed to, so we know we're thinking the same thing?"

"Oh, OK." Josie looks a little surprised, but not bothered by the request. She thinks for a minute. "Well, I guess the main thing I understood is that we're saying I'm going to be shifting my focus away from getting my designs production-ready and toward generating new, good ideas. And helping other people with their ideas, if they'd like my help. And that you're not holding me accountable to a set number of design ideas—you just want more. More good ones, that is. I guess you'll let me know whether we're giving you the kind and quantity of ideas you're expecting as we get into it." She pauses, frowning. "You know, maybe we *should* have some kind of goal in terms of quantity. This feels a little too loose to me."

Andy's smiling. "Well, first of all, you and I think we're agreeing to exactly the same thing, so that's a good beginning. And as to quantity, I think you're right. So, how about this. We've been averaging about four or five 'pursuable' ideas from the group every week. How about if we shoot for seven a week as our new average?"

"That seems really doable," Josie replies. "And I wonder if we should share this new approach at the next team meeting, once you've had a chance to talk with Jim, Tanya, and Ed individually?"

"I think that's a great idea," Andy agrees. "I'll make it a point to go over this with them before the meeting, and then I'll 'unveil' your new focus and the team's new 'idea goal' at next week's staff meeting. How's that?"

Josie's blushing, but she's smiling, too. "That's good."

"And then let's give it few weeks to get rolling," Andy adds. "Do you think it's reasonable to expect our idea output to be up to seven a week by the end of next month? That's just about five weeks from now."

"Yes, that's really reasonable." Josie sounds confident. "Maybe we could incorporate that into our weekly one-on-one. You telling me what the week's 'pursuable idea' total is, I mean. And that way, if it's not on target, I could ask your advice about how to increase it."

"Josie, this sounds great. And I love how you're making it your own. I have a lot of confidence this will work out and be a good thing for you and the team. So, if Jim, Tanya, or Ed have any concerns, I'll let you know—otherwise, we'll share our plan at next Tuesday's staff meeting."

They both get up, and as Josie gathers up her things, she looks up at her boss. "Andy, I really appreciate this. I feel like you've really found a way to support me, the team, and the company all at the same time. Thanks."

Andy grins and waves a hand, mock-dismissively. "All in a day's work," he jokes. "And you're welcome."

I want to point out one interesting thing about this conversation before we go on. Josie's understanding of the agreement was right in line with Andy's. But did you notice that as she was talking through the plan, she improved it? She realized that having no specific goal felt too loose to her. This is a common side benefit of having the employee summarize the agreement; they'll often make suggestions for slight revisions—both improving it further and continuing to take more ownership in the process.

You'll also notice that they spent the rest of the conversation "time lining" the agreement very naturally; they agreed on when the next steps would happen, on a date for the new agreement to take effect, and on an ongoing way to check in with each other about it. [Invisible bonus points for assessing Josie's and Andy's Social Style. Answers are at the end of this "try it out" . . .]

TRY IT OUT

Now you'll have the chance to finish thinking through the Agreement conversation you began earlier in the chapter. You may want to read over what you wrote and then complete the Commit step, below.

Think about and note how you'll ask your employee for his or her understanding of the agreement made in the Clarify step:

_____

_____

_____

Write down any key benchmarks or deadlines you want to establish relative to this agreement.

_____

_____

_____

Congratulations! You've now got the "bones" of a good, clear agreement. So, go for it—have this conversation with your employee. Afterward, you can use the self-assessment tool below to reflect on how it went. Good luck!

Agreement Self-Assessment Tool

Clarify

How did you create a clear mental picture?

_____

_____

_____

What did you do to establish context and rationale?

_____

_____

_____

What did you do to listen to your employee?

_____

_____

_____

What did you do to check for obstacles?

_____

_____

_____

Commit

How did you invite the employee to summarize the agreements?

_____

_____

_____

How did you set benchmarks and time lines?

_____

_____

_____

What was the outcome of the conversation?

_____

_____

_____

How did the employee respond, overall?

_____

_____

_____

What did you like about what you did?

_____

_____

_____

What do you intend to do differently, next time?

_____

_____

_____

[Social Style: Josie's an Amiable and Andy's an Expressive—how'd you do?]

Step 3: Support

If the Agreement conversation you just had with your employee went well, I imagine it was satisfying to you. There's a feeling of connection and completion: your employee is clear and motivated, and both of you are confident that the goals will be met—achieving excellent results and helping the employee develop at the same time.

Unfortunately, all this clarity and good intention can be lost unless both of you follow through after the initial conversation. The employee is clear about what he or she needs to do, and the majority of the responsibility generally falls on him or her. However, you as the manager have responsibilities as well. You need to do some things to support the agreement. This third step of the agreement process, Support, is where the goal is reached or lost. The key steps in supporting the new agreement are:

· Honor your commitments
· Offer feedback
· Maintain the mind-set of a coach

In other words: do what you said you were going to do, let the employee know what you see happening relative to the agreement, and believe in his or her ability to succeed.

Simple doesn't necessarily mean easy, though—time constraints, workload, mental habits, organizational crises, and a host of other factors can conspire to make supporting the process seem difficult, if not impossible.

To help you recognize and break through some of these obstacles, let's do a quick brainstorm focusing on how to support agreements in your real day-to-day world.

In the left column of the table below, list some of the things that might get in the way of you supporting agreements you make with your employees. I've written in a few to get you started.

Possible Obstacles	How to Overcome Them
Priorities change.	Let my employee know. Talk through how it changes the agreement.
I don't have time to do the things I said I'd do.	Apologize and rework the agreement. Don't commit to do things I don't have time for.

Now, in the right column of the table above, jot down a few ideas for things you can do to overcome your own obstacles to support the agreements you make. Again, I've written in some possibilities for the first two to give you some ideas.

Corrective Feedback

So, you've mulched, you've staked. The garden's looking pretty good. Now, there's one kind of maintenance task we've yet to talk about, one about which most gardeners feel somewhat skittish. It's the group of tasks that involve cutting: pruning, deadheading, dividing. There's just something a little scary about taking an implement with a sharp edge and using it on a live plant. I remember the first time I went out into the garden, encouraged by my trusty gardening book, and lopped the dead flower heads off a group of daisies. I really thought I was hurting them, on some deep primal level. They did look a lot better afterward, but still . . .

Then, almost magically, within a couple of weeks those daisies were happily abloom again, outshining their neighbors whose heads I hadn't removed. I've since moved on to dividing (cutting apart a plant that's grown too big for its space, and replanting the pieces in new places) and pruning. Although pruning still creeps me out a little.

Anyway, the management equivalent of "pruning" tasks, I've decided, is giving corrective feedback. Managers resist doing it—it seems hard, unkind, like it can't possibly make the situation better—and yet it's essential to an employee's growth.

Giving positive feedback is much easier for many managers; it's mostly just a matter of remembering how important it is to most people, and being specific enough that employees know what it is you're pleased about (e.g., "Thanks for staying late to finish this, Jack. And it's really excellent too; very well-thought-through and persuasive," versus, "Thanks Jack—great job."). We'll talk about positive feedback a bit at the end of the chapter—but for most of us, giving corrective feedback is the challenge.

A good gardener knows when and how to prune or deadhead; that's the art of it—cutting in a way that helps the plant, rather than hurts it. My husband, in a burst of gardening enthusiasm, once pruned a rose-bush back so far that it languished in a state of shock for most of the season before beginning to put out a few tentative leaves.

In the same way, the art of giving corrective feedback lies in giving it in a way that supports the employee's development, rather than impeding it. I'm going to offer you an approach to giving feedback that helps create the highest likelihood that the employee can hear, understand, and act on the feedback you give.

Over the years, I've noticed people tend to approach giving corrective feedback in a handful of ways, most of which don't work very well. It seems that they do one of five things. They either provide:

· No feedback
· Delayed feedback
· General feedback
· Feedback given with no urgency, or
· Specific, timely feedback that includes the impact.

The first four possibilities above have something in common, though they may seem very different: They don't give people the information they need in order to improve. That's pretty obvious with the first one, **no feedback.**

Delayed feedback may provide information, but it's too little, too late. One really common example of this approach to feedback is the performance review where an employee finds out he or she has been doing something incorrectly or not up-to-standard for months, but the manager was "waiting for the performance review." What is that about? Cowardice on the manager's part, I'd say. Even if the feedback is accurate, the person will likely be so angry and resentful that you didn't say something earlier, thereby giving no chance to correct the behavior before the review, that he or she won't be able to hear the truth in it.

General feedback is not much better—if someone says to you "You really messed that up," you don't get much insight about how to improve. This approach to feedback is especially popular, unfortunately, when managers are trying to give feedback about interpersonal or attitudinal issues. Thousands upon thousands of employees have heard, "You're not a team player," or, "I don't feel like you're really committed"—and are left not only no clearer about what they're doing or not doing that isn't working, but feeling defensive and misunderstood in the bargain. (We'll talk in depth about how not to do this in a few minutes.)

Feedback given with no urgency doesn't let people know the importance attached to their actions. All too often, managers try to soften the impact of corrective feedback by making it seem as though "It's not a big deal." But if it's not a big deal, why should the person change? They've probably got a lot on their plate, and something you communicate as a nice-to-do is likely to fall off the edge.

Finally we come to the approach that does work. **Feedback that's specific, timely** (given as soon as possible), **and includes the impact**—that kind of feedback is not only easiest to hear and understand, it provides the information people need if they are to improve their performance.

"Timely" is pretty self-explanatory, but what do we mean by "specific" and "includes the impact"?

Includes the Impact

Managers often say, "I gave the feedback, but nothing changed." The employee may not have acted on the feedback simply because the manager didn't make clear its importance; he or she may have "softened" the feedback by talking about the behavior as though it doesn't matter that much, or by saying "do this" without including any rationale. Talking about the impact means letting the employee know two things:

· why this feedback is important and
· how important it is.

First, explain why changing this behavior is important to the business, to the department, to their teammates, or to their own current or future success. Then, let them know how important it is (e.g., is it key to their success, a possible derailment factor, or simply something they should be more aware of?). Including the impact in this way helps assure the employee's motivation to change; it helps employees connect their individual performance to the bigger picture and understand both its impact on their own success and their part in the success of the whole.

Be Specific

The third element of effective feedback, being specific, is probably the most often overlooked. Specific feedback has two important characteristics:

- it focuses on particular examples or instances (e.g., "Yesterday I noticed that you . . ." rather than, "You always . . .").
- it describes behaviors—not attitudes or characteristics ("You didn't complete the report," rather than, "You're not on board").

This specificity is critical because feedback is actionable only when it's behavioral. I'll say it again, because it's really important: someone can only act on feedback when it focuses on behaviors. For instance, if you say to an employee, "Jennifer, I don't feel you're really pulling together with the team—you've got to give it 100 percent," what does she know about what you want done differently? Nothing, basically. Even if she goes out and does her best to "pull together with the team" and "give 100 percent," you'll be getting *her* interpretation of that, and it may or may not be what you want her to do. If, however, you were to say, "Jennifer, I noticed that you've come late to the last two team meetings, and that you haven't completed your agreed-upon part of the team's work over the past two weeks . . ." she would have a clear basis for changing her behavior and results.

Camera Check

There's a method for making your feedback behavioral that's simple and nearly foolproof: we call it "camera check." Here's how it works: When you want to give feedback to someone, imagine you have a video camera recording the behavior that needs changing. Then play the "tape" in your head and notice what you see and hear the person doing. Then give your feedback based on what's "on the tape."

For instance, a video camera wouldn't show someone being "aloof and uninvolved" at a meeting, but it *would* record the person not making eye contact, doing paperwork when others are talking, or not responding to invitations to contribute.

Again, this translation into "camera check" behaviors makes the feedback actionable. If you told someone he or she was "aloof," they'd have no basis for understanding or acting on the feedback. If you told the person the things you observed—that they didn't make eye contact, did paperwork while others were talking, and didn't respond to invitations to join in, they'd know exactly what you want changed.

Another almost equally powerful benefit of using camera check is that it automatically removes most of the interpretation and judgment from the feedback, making it far less likely that the person will get defensive. Here's what I mean: when you tell someone they're "aloof," you're making a pretty big—and fairly negative—assumption about their state of mind. You're implying that they don't care about other people, or that they believe they're superior to others. It feels as though you're telling the person he or she has a character flaw. You're almost guaranteed to get a defensive response—most people will feel such a strong urge to convince you that they're not "aloof" that they will be unable to hear anything else you've said, and the conversation will run right off the rails.

When you tell that same person, however, that you've noticed they tend not to look at others during meetings, and to complete unrelated paperwork, and not to speak up even when invited—it still may not feel great, but it's a heck of a lot easier to hear than the alternative. With camera check, you're telling them what you see them doing—you're not trying to tell them what they think or feel. Defensiveness goes down dramatically.

Here's an initial practice to help you learn to do the "camera check." The list below consists of some common words and phrases managers use when trying to give corrective feedback. (You may have used or heard them yourself.) Your goal is to imagine a video of someone behaving in these ways, and based on what you see on the video, create camera check phrases to give the feedback in a way that's behavioral, specific, and hearable:

· Once you've envisioned the "video" for a statement, and converted it into a few camera check phrases, check to make sure you're not just substituting another, slightly less interpretive word or phrase. For instance, if after "nonleader" you wrote "too laid-back"—that's still fairly interpretive, and not very specific. You can ask yourself, "What would laid-back look like?" and you might come up with, "Doesn't respond quickly when there are tight deadlines," or, "Seldom offers a definitive point of view about what course of action to take." Those are actual behaviors, images you would see and hear on a videotape.

· Practice with as many of the feedback words below as you want.

· I've done the first one for you, just to get you going. (Please feel free to add other things your own "videotape" might show for this first word.)

Common Feedback	Camera Check Feedback
Arrogant	Doesn't speak to colleagues in the halls. Rolls eyes, shakes head while others speak. Interrupts to disagree with others' ideas.
Nonleader	
Micromanager	
Not a Team Player	
Bad Attitude	
Rigid	
Uncommitted	

· When you've finished translating these nonbehavioral words into camera check feedback statements, take a few minutes to think about employees of yours who may benefit from any of this feedback. Write the employee's name or initials next to the camera check statements that apply. You can come back to this later as a resource when you're preparing to give feedback in this way.

When to Give Corrective Feedback

Before we put the camera check skill within the context of an overall approach to giving feedback, I want to help you close one more escape
hatch for yourself. Even when you know how to give corrective feedback in a clear, behavioral, respectful way, it's still easy to avoid doing it.
It's just no fun to tell somebody that they need to do something
differently—especially if it's really complex or problematic. So, just to
make it a little harder for you to convince yourself that "you don't really
need to have that conversation," here are three signs that you need to
give corrective feedback:

· What you say about the other person turns negative
· Your self-talk about the other person turns negative
· Your relationship with the other person turns negative

In other words, if you find you're bad-mouthing someone—
downplaying his or her strengths and focusing on weaknesses, or making uncomplimentary jokes or remarks—that's a sign you need to give
some feedback. Or if you're running over and over in your head what he
or she has done or not done; having extended mental monologues with
yourself about the person and what he or she should or shouldn't be
doing—that's another good indication. Finally, if you find that you're
distancing yourself from the person—making less eye contact, avoiding
him or her, being less supportive—it's probably also time for some corrective feedback. If you don't pay attention to these signals, all these dy-
namics will probably continue on their downward spiral. The issues
won't magically get resolved without your saying anything (which most
of us seem to hope in situations like this), and a situation that could be
set back on the right track will probably continue to deteriorate.

How to Give Corrective Feedback

OK, now that I've given you a clear way to motivate yourself to do the right thing at the right time, let's go back to the "how." The approach below builds on what you've learned so far and adds some important new elements. Using this model for giving corrective feedback continues in the direction we've taken—reducing defensiveness and increasing the likelihood that the employee will be able to hear, understand, and act on your insights.

HOW TO GIVE CORRECTIVE FEEDBACK
Introduce the topic
Get the other person's point of view
Build on what you've heard, making your feedback
specific and timely and including the impact
Agree on next steps

Rather than explain these steps to you, let's try another approach. We'll go back to Andy and Josie, and I'll show you how these steps look in an actual conversation. Then we can deconstruct the conversation to look for the steps.

Before I take you back to observe Josie and Andy, I want to note two things. First, sadly, Andy's agreement with Josie about her new focus on design isn't going so well. They've checked in as they agreed, but the number of design ideas hasn't increased. He's noted that, and Josie recommitted to the original agreement, but it's been six weeks now, and it still hasn't changed. It's time for some corrective feedback.

I also want to note that this is the proper order of events: First, you make an agreement with someone. Then, you provide feedback—if he or she keeps the agreement you offer positive feedback; if he or she doesn't, you provide corrective feedback. It's not fair to hold someone accountable for something he or she hasn't agreed to do, so make sure the person has committed to do the behavior you're requesting before you give corrective feedback.

"Hey, Andy." Josie has arrived for her weekly one-on-one with Andy, and she's feeling anxious. She's pretty sure the number of new design ideas hasn't increased the way they agreed it would.

Andy looks up and smiles. "Hey, Josie, come on in." As soon as they're both seated, Andy gets right down to the issue at hand. "So, there's a lot going on right now, and there's lots we need to talk about, especially with the big show in Philly coming up at the end of the month. Today I want to talk with you about our 'new design' agreement, though. I have some concerns about whether it's working the way we hoped. What's your sense of how it's going?"

Josie's somewhat relieved to have the chance to talk first. She doesn't want Andy to think she's oblivious to what's going on, but she also wants him to know what she's up against. "Well, I don't think we've been able to increase the number of new design ideas. We might even have had less this week. I know I've only given you two that I think are any good, and one each that I've been trying to help Ed and Tanya with. And Jim's been so busy getting ready for the show . . ." She stops and bites her lip.

Andy just nods. "What else?" he asks. Reassured that he's really listening and interested, Josie continues. "I don't want to sound like a whiner, but this is harder than I thought. I feel like now I'm responsible for everybody's ideas, not just mine. I'm not sure what to do . . ."

Andy is listening carefully. "OK, so it sounds like your own output of ideas has gone down, rather than up, as we agreed it would. And that you're feeling more burdened rather than less. Right?"

Josie nods.

Andy nods, too. "OK, that's pretty much what I thought was going on. I've noticed a couple of things you're doing that I think might be getting in your way, and I want to share those with you."

Josie takes a deep breath, looking unhappy. "OK."

Andy leans forward. "Look, I have every confidence you can do this, Josie. So this is me helping you, right?" She smiles a little and nods. "OK, here's what I'm seeing," Andy says. "The first thing goes right along with what you said about feeling responsible for everybody's ideas. I've seen that when you're working on ideas with Ed and Tanya, you're using words that imply that completing the design is your responsibility. For instance, I overheard you talking to Ed yesterday about his pendant idea, and you finished the conversation by saying, 'Let me work on this, and I'll bring something back to you tomorrow.' And Ed just nodded and let you take it . . . by doing that you're communicating to him that it is your responsibility to finish the design."

Josie looks a little confused. "Well, I'm just trying to help . . ."

"I know you are—you're a very supportive person. Here's the distinction I'm trying to make. It's still his design, and his responsibility to move it forward. My understanding of your and my agreement is that you would offer options and ideas; not that you would take over the idea and work on it."

"Oh, I get it. You're right. I need to be more like, 'Why don't you try this or that,' and then let them work on it."

"Exactly!" Andy replies. "Just giving input."

Josie nods thoughtfully. "OK, that's helpful."

"All right, good. The other thing I've noticed is that you're still working on developing production specs for your designs."

Josie's clearly embarrassed. "I know, I know . . . but Jim's so busy, and I just don't feel comfortable giving Ed and Tanya more to do."

Andy shakes his head, smiling. "Look, all three of them agreed to this; I think they're really fine with it. This agreement is only going to work if you're willing to turn over your designs to them.

Otherwise, it will seem harder rather than easier, and you won't have time to focus more of your attention on designing."

Josie sighs. "You know, it's a lot tougher for me to give work to other people than I thought it would be. I'm not quite sure how to get good at this."

"All right—I think we're on to next steps. So, we've talked about changing two things here: not taking on too much responsibility for the other designers' ideas, and actually passing on your production work. How would you suggest we handle these things?"

"OK, well, the first one I'm pretty clear about. I just need to remember that my role is to give input, to offer ideas for improving or 'unsticking,' rather than taking on the responsibility to improve the design myself."

"Exactly; I completely agree. And, I'm happy to keep noticing and let you know when you do it well and when you're drifting."

"Good, that would be helpful." She makes a note for herself. "Now, the second thing—about how to feel comfortable asking Ed, Tanya, and Jim to do the production work on my designs . . . I'm not sure how to do that."

"I've got an idea." Andy looks at his watch. "Look, I've got to go to a meeting now, but I'd be happy to teach you an approach to delegating that I think would be reasonably comfortable for you. We can also talk about how to think about the whole situation differently, so that it's not so daunting."

Josie blows out a big breath. "That would be really good. When can we do that?"

Andy and Josie pull out their calendars to find a time . . .

I want to talk you through this, but first, I'd like to encourage you to reread it, looking for each step of the model: (1) introducing the topic,

(2) inviting the employee's point of view, (3) building on what you hear to give a specific, timely feedback message that includes the impact, and (4) agreeing on next steps. Andy did a great job here, so you can see the steps of the model pretty clearly!

This conversation may have seemed unrealistically friendly and easy— but, in my experience, it's a fairly accurate description of how a corrective feedback conversation goes when you use this model. Of course, if someone is very defensive or un-self-aware, it will be somewhat more difficult, but still productive.

Now, let's focus on the ways in which this approach is different from what most people do when giving feedback. The first thing that may have seemed odd to you was when Andy took the time to find out how Josie saw the situation before giving her his specific feedback. If you notice, he set it up simply, so she'd know what the conversation was about. "Today I want to talk with you about our new design agreement. I have some concerns about whether it's working the way we hoped." And then he invited her point of view in a single sentence: "What's your sense of how it's going?"

When you get the other person's point of view first, all kinds of good things happen. First, no matter what the content of their response, their defensiveness will go down because they'll feel heard and respected. Second, you'll find out a lot of valuable information. Are they aware there's a problem? Do they see their own contribution? Are there other, extenuating circumstances you might not be aware of?

Generally one of three things will happen as you're listening to the other person's perceptions. Worst case, they won't see the problem at all. Even in that situation, they'll feel heard (again, lowering their defensiveness) and you'll know that you have to start at square one in offering your feedback. "Building on what you hear" will mean summarizing their point of view and then respectfully disagreeing!

Second—and much more common—they may see a piece of the problem, like Josie did, but not see how they're causing it or how to behave differently. In this case, you can do exactly what Andy did: acknowledge and agree with what they do see, then build on their perceptions to offer them specific, behavioral, camera check feedback.

Finally—this is definitely best case, but it happens more often than you would expect, if you give people a chance to speak first—the person will say pretty much what you were going to say. Then you're in the wonderful, nonconfrontational position of going straight to coaching: acknowledging what they've said and focusing immediately on "what to do about it."

The next important thing I'd like to mention about this approach is the incorporation of camera check—"here are the specific things I saw or heard, and here's the impact they had." For instance, at one point, Andy said, "I've seen that when you're working on ideas with Ed and Tanya, you're using words that imply that completing the design is your responsibility." Then he gave a specific example of this. This was a great example of how much easier feedback is to hear when it's behavioral and nonjudgmental. Andy's summary of "the impact" was also very clear: "Otherwise, it will seem harder rather than easier, and you won't have time to focus more of your attention on designing."

Finally, you notice that Andy didn't just stop with giving the feedback; he went on to invite Josie to cocreate next steps—to find a solution together. This is how the behavior will get changed, and it makes practical what he said at the beginning of the conversation, "I have every confidence that you can do this, Josie."

TRY IT OUT

Now you'll have a chance to experiment with giving corrective feedback, based on a real situation you want to address with an employee or colleague. I hope you'll actually be giving this feedback to this person; this is your chance to prepare, so that using this new model goes as smoothly as possible.

· Think of an employee of yours to whom you need to give some corrective feedback. Summarize the problem below:

_____

_____

_____

- Write a sentence or two you might use to **introduce the topic** in a simple and nonthreatening way (e.g., "I've noticed you've had some problems in the area of_____; I'd like to talk about it.").

_____

_____

_____

- Decide on a brief, nonthreatening question to **invite the other person's point of view** (e.g., "From your point of view, what's going well, and what could you be doing differently?").

_____

_____

_____

- Now, write what you believe this person's response might be when you ask for his/her point of view on this topic. (Watch out for limiting assumptions: base what you write on any data you have about the person, his or her awareness of the problem, and how he/she tends to respond to feedback.)

_____

_____

_____

- Based on the situation and the other person's probable response, write your feedback message to this person. Work to **make your feedback message specific, timely, and to include the impact.** (Using the camera check method, note a recent example of the behavior and focus on the possible impact of changing or not changing the behavior.) Be sure to think of ways to incorporate the other person's probable point of view:

_____

_____

_____

· Finally, note below **next steps** you'd like to agree on with this
person to address the feedback.

I suggest that you have this conversation at your earliest con-
venience (remember the "when to give feedback" signals?). Once
you've had the conversation, reflect on how the model worked for
you, and what you'd like to do differently next time to make it
even more effective.

Positive Feedback

If corrective feedback is the managerial equivalent of pruning—helping
employees "cut away" parts of their behavior that don't serve their
growth, or the health and productivity of the organization—positive
feedback is like encouraging your plants to continue growing strong and
lush by making sure they can get enough sun in the direction they're
growing.

OK, I don't want to stretch the metaphor to the breaking point . . . I
still have five chapters more to wring from it. Suffice it to say that positive feedback is a simple, powerful way to let people know that they're
headed in the right direction and that you're noticing and appreciating
it. If given well and appropriately, positive feedback is extremely motivating. It also helps corrective feedback feel fair: if you regularly acknowledge your employees' contributions, they're more likely to feel
you have a right to let them know when their behavior needs to be
changed.

Unfortunately, as for corrective feedback, not all positive feedback is
effective. The same five feedback possibilities also exist for giving positive feedback (no feedback, delayed feedback, general feedback, feed-
back without urgency, and specific timely feedback that includes the
impact). And again, only one of them works: specific, timely feedback

that includes the impact. In positive feedback, the impact is the benefit or positive effect the other person's behavior has on you, on their success, or the company's success.

The "how-to" of giving positive feedback is easier than for corrective feedback. The first two elements (i.e., introducing the topic and getting the other person's point of view) aren't necessary, because very few people resist hearing good things about themselves. They may discount your praise out of embarrassment or learned modesty, but that's OK—you can be fairly sure they heard it and appreciated it. The third step—making sure the feedback is specific, timely, and includes the impact—is the only thing you need to focus on.

Being specific is particularly important. It seems the most popular approach to giving positive feedback (if it's given at all) is the great-job-keep-it-up approach. Employees don't believe this kind of "one size fits all" praise; it tends to sound glib and insincere—as though the giver could say the same thing to anyone. Giving people genuine, specific, positive feedback lets them know that you're really aware of their situation—and it tells them exactly what you'd like them to keep doing right.

Timeliness can make your positive feedback more effective, too. If you wait for months before commenting on something, people are apt to think you've got ulterior motives or to wonder why you didn't say anything at the time. ("Where was this when I needed it?") Timely feedback is "catching people doing something right," and it is both surprising and motivating.

Including the impact helps people see how their behavior is helpful to you, the company, or their own success, and it lets them know that you see it, too.

One other difference between corrective and positive feedback: whereas corrective feedback always needs to be given in private, positive feedback is fine to offer publicly. You might want to send around a congratulatory e-mail when a person or a team finishes a difficult project or gets excellent results, or to credit someone for work well-done in a meeting.

Below, I've given you an opportunity to balance the scales by thinking of some positive feedback you can offer to the same person to whom you've given corrective feedback above.

· Think about the same employee you used as the basis for your corrective feedback practice. What specific positive feedback could you give about his/her current performance? Using the space below, write one piece of positive feedback—specific, timely, and including a clear positive impact—for that person:

_____

_____

_____

I suggest you also share this feedback message with the person when you have a chance. One caveat—don't share both the corrective and positive feedback at the same time, or they will tend to cancel each other out. The seriousness of the corrective feedback may get lost, or the positive feelings of the positive feedback might be negated—or both!

It's Not as Hard as You Think

My gardening friend definitely looked daunted and somewhat overwhelmed the day I started explaining garden maintenance to her—staking, deadheading, pruning, and weeding sounded complicated and time-consuming. She has been much relieved to discover that, once learned, these maintenance procedures take only a few hours every week, and that she actually feels a sense of pride and accomplishment whenever she does them and sees how much they benefit her garden. I suspect that, with a little practice, you'll feel much the same about making clear agreements and giving feedback.

BIG IDEAS

Gardens need regular maintenance in order to stay healthy and productive. Managers also need to do regular "maintenance" tasks in order to ensure their employees and their teams continue to grow and thrive. In this chapter, we focused on two key, high-leverage forms of employee and team maintenance: making clear agreements and giving feedback.

Making Agreements

Clarify: offer the information needed to complete the agreement well, while engaging the employee's commitment.

Commit: make sure that you and the employee are agreeing to the same thing.

Support: honor your commitments, offer feedback, and maintain the mind-set of a coach.

How to Give Corrective Feedback

Introduce the topic: let the employee know what you'd like to talk about.

Invite the employee's point of view: to lower defensiveness and gather new information.

Build on what you hear, making your feedback specific (camera check!), timely, and include the impact: this will ensure the employee can accept and act on the feedback.

Agree on next steps: what, specifically, the employee will do to change the behavior.

Finally, remember to give positive feedback as well—it's like making sure plants get enough sun, and is as necessary to your employees' productivity and satisfaction.

CHAPTER 8

Letting It Spread

"I'm over here," my friend calls out, waving to me from her backyard. I've just dropped by for a visit and was heading for the kitchen
door—but she's out in the garden, as is more and more common
for her these days, and clearly wants to show me something. She starts
talking before I'm halfway there. "Look, look. This is so cool. Remember how you told me that some plants would reseed themselves if I gave
them the chance? Look what happened!" She points to the edge of the
garden, where a whole colony of Johnny-Jump-Ups—a sweet-looking
little violet relative—are peeking shyly out from between low-growing
sedums and silvery mugwort. Last year we'd planted a few Johnny-
Jump-Ups and I told her they might spread if she let them go to seed.

"It's kind of magical," she adds, nearly embarrassed by her own enthusiasm. "And look at how much the dianthus has spread since last
summer!" I just smile and nod, sharing in her pleasure at the exuberance
of her well-grown garden.

Watching a garden take hold and start to spread on its own is a real
pleasure for gardeners. Most plants have an amazing drive to expand
and propagate. If a gardener has done most of the things we've talked

about so far, the energy of nature will start to take over. At that point, success is more a matter of channeling the growth than trying to make something happen. For example, some plants get a little carried away and try to shoulder out their neighbors, spreading with such abandon that they use up all the available light and water, so that the other plants wither and die out. Other plants are shyer and need some help to get going—you may have to clear a space for their seeds to fall or gather some seeds and give them an early spring head start indoors.

A manager who has built a good strong team using his or her own common sense and dedication, along with the approaches and tools we've discussed throughout the book, will notice employees wanting to expand and thrive in much the same way. They may begin to naturally take on more ownership for their projects, to ask about the possibility of promotion, or to look into development programs available through Training or HR. Most people, like most plants, seem to have a built-in urge to stretch out, to explore new areas. Delegation is the skill of channeling that urge to growth so that it benefits the employee, the organization, and you.

I think if you asked most managers, they'd say it's important to delegate—but then I think most managers would also admit, somewhat sheepishly, that they're maybe not so good at it . . . that it seems to work only sporadically, or that it too often seems to be more trouble than it's worth, or that their people just don't seem as capable as they thought, or . . . well, you get the idea. When managers are asked why they don't delegate more of their responsibilities to those who report to them, the most common answer is some version of, "It's easier to do it myself."

Hmm. When a garden fails to spread well, it's generally because the gardener is either being too intrusive or rigid; trying to make the plants do exactly what he or she wants, without regard to their nature or stage of growth—or is just letting it all hang out; leaving the plants completely to their own devices. The first approach tends to yield gardens that are sterile and somewhat fragile, needing lots of attention and never really taking off. The second approach most often results in a survival-of-the-fittest garden; wild, untamed, and not necessarily what you had in mind.

Managers who haven't had much success in delegating tend to make these same mistakes. They may be too intrusive or rigid in their delegation, leading to demoralized employees who feel afraid of stepping "outside the lines"; or they may confuse delegation with abandonment, leaving employees to figure things out for themselves and, all too often, fall prey to their own inexperience or misunderstanding.

The end result of managers failing to delegate well is sadly predictable: an overloaded manager who becomes a bottleneck for his or her department's work, frustrated employees who feel they're not getting the chance to grow, poor morale, and declining results.

As you might have assumed by now, I'm about to offer you a way to approach delegation that steers between these dangerous shores, and takes best advantage of your employees' urge to grow and develop.

Delegation Defined

So, what is delegation? Let's start by talking about what it's not:

Delegation is not abdication.
Delegation is not micromanagement.
Delegation is not assigning tasks.
Delegation is not "making somebody else do it."

Delegation means transferring to an employee the responsibility for an area of work. This transfer of responsibility may be quick or gradual, depending on the employee's experience and learning style, and the area of work may be large or small, depending upon the needs of the organization and the employee's capability. It may also be a either a permanent transfer, as in the case of a promotion or taking on a new job responsibility, or a temporary transfer—for instance, completing a project or working on a time-limited cross-functional team.

It's your responsibility to make the hand-off well and skillfully, and it's the employee's responsibility to be there to receive it.

I'm sure you felt it coming, so here it is: a model for delegation that's simple and practical.

DELEGATION MODEL
Prepare
Discuss/Agree
Support

Prepare

This first step takes place before you meet with the employee. You'll take some time to define both the area of work you want to delegate and the levels of autonomy appropriate for this employee in doing this work. Looking at the area of work gives you a chance to think through the "size and shape" of this responsibility, so that you can communicate it to the employee in a clear and meaningful way. Defining levels of autonomy (which I'll explain in some detail as we go through this chapter) allows you to think in depth about where you feel most and least comfortable giving this employee autonomy, and how you want to work with him or her to make sure that (1) the levels of autonomy you agree on initially are appropriate and (2) you know how you'll work together to increase the levels of autonomy over time.

Discuss and Agree

In this next step, you'll first share with your employee the "area of work" (your definition of the work being delegated), and make sure there's mutual understanding and agreement. Then you share your "levels of autonomy" preparation in order to define the transfer of responsibility from you to him or her. This is the most critical part of the conversation; it allows you and the employee to discuss and agree on how the "hand-off" will take place over time. Finally, you'll ask the employee to put it all together by creating a document that briefly summarizes what you've agreed upon in this step.

Support

No matter how clearly you and your employee move through the first two steps, without the third step it's unlikely that the transfer of responsibility will work well. In this step, you and the employee both honor the commitments you've made in the delegation conversation, above. You also provide the employee with timely, balanced, behavioral feedback about how he or she is doing relative to the agreed-upon responsibility. Most important, you work to increase your levels of confidence in the employee, and therefore his or her autonomy—so that ultimately this person is fully responsible for this area, with minimal involvement from you. (As you can see, this is very similar to the "support" step in the Agreements model from the last chapter; both are about making sure that the intent—and therefore the goal—of the initial conversation you've had doesn't evaporate over time.)

Effective delegation is the single most powerful way for you to build trust in your employees' abilities. It allows them to demonstrate increasing levels of competence; you respond by offering them increasing levels of autonomy. They become more independent and capable and you'll be freed to take on new, higher-level responsibilities as well. Everyone wins!

The "Prepare" Step

Let's look at the two parts of the Prepare step in a little more detail.

Define the Area of Responsibility:

First ask yourself, "What is the scope of the area I want to delegate?" What you're trying to do here is to define the area as a whole, so that the employee gets a sense of the big picture. Often managers make the mistake of inundating the employee with step-by-step specifics when first trying to explain a new responsibility. Remember, you're not trying to teach the person how to do the responsibility in this delegation conversation, you're introducing them to it. In order to avoid going into too much detail, some of the things you'll want to talk about during this first conversation are:

- an overall definition of the responsibility;
- key people involved (and with whom your employee will need to interact);
- recent history of the project or responsibility (e.g., how it's being done now and by whom);
- important benchmarks, cycles, or other time frames;
- skills needed (you can let the employee know you'll be available to coach as necessary);
- results or standards expected, etc.

When thinking through the Prepare step, I suggest you write down these important aspects of the "area of responsibility" to use as a memory aid when sharing this information with your employee.

Define Levels of Autonomy

Once you've thought through what this area of responsibility entails, you'll draw a continuum like the one below:

Levels of my confidence / employee's autonomy

LOW_____ HIGH

Now you'll place each part of the project or responsibility along the continuum in the appropriate spot, based on your level of confidence in this person's ability in that area.

Here's an example. Let's say you're an account manager, and you're delegating a client account to an employee. You know this employee has had experience in dealing with high-level people, and you've seen her in action and been very impressed with her handling of these kinds of relationships. You'd put "client relations" at the far right of the continuum—meaning you have lots of confidence in her ability to handle this aspect of the account (I've done this in the example below).

On the other hand, you know that this person isn't so good with detailed follow-through. You'd put "detail orientation" at the far left of the continuum, as I've done below. (Note: a low level of confidence may arise either out of negative information—you know this person isn't strong in this area—or a lack of information—you haven't seen this person perform in this area, and don't know what he or she is capable of doing.)

Once you've arranged the various elements along the continuum, you then think about and write down how you want to interact with your employee in each element. Where you have high confidence, you'll offer more autonomy—minimal interaction or oversight. In the example below, I've written "monthly updates" and "trouble-shooting as requested" as possible interactions. Only checking in once a month implies that you feel a good deal of confidence that things aren't going to get too far off track here. And leaving it up to the employee to ask for help when needed implies that you have faith that he or she is both self-aware and skillful in this area.

In the elements where you lack confidence in your employee's abilities, for whatever reason, you will offer less autonomy—more frequent interaction, a voice in decision-making, opportunities for coaching, etc. "Review and provide feedback on client communications before they go out" is a great safety net when you're not confident about someone's detail orientation, as is "Go over 'to-dos' from client calls to agree on next steps."

The other important aspect of these proposed interactions is that they are great starting points for development. Your goal, in the elements where you believe the person is less capable, is to provide the support and oversight the person needs in order to improve—to, in effect, "move to the right." You want, over time, to be able to fully delegate; your goal is to end up with a high level of confidence and autonomy in every aspect of this responsibility.

Levels of my confidence / employee's autonomy

LOW_____ HIGH

Detail-orientation	Client Relations
· review and provide feedback on client communications before they go out	· monthly updates
· go over "to-dos" from client calls to agree on next steps	· trouble-shooting as requested

Before we go on, I'd like you to think for a minute about why the interactions listed above are appropriate for very different levels of capability. For example, imagine what would happen if you reversed them. What if you checked in only monthly and expected someone to know when to ask for help in an area where he or she isn't very capable or experienced? I'd say you'd be practically begging for trouble.

Or, imagine the reverse: someone who is experienced and skilled being asked to hand in every communication for review and feedback, or go over to-dos from each client call to agree on next steps. How would it feel to that person? Pretty demoralizing, right? An almost textbook case of micromanaging.

By proposing interactions that offer an appropriate level of autonomy in each key element of the work you're delegating, you can avoid the primary pitfall of delegation. And that is (drumroll, please) the one-size-fits-all approach. Most managers pick one level—high confidence/ autonomy, low confidence/autonomy, or somewhere in between—and use it in delegating every element of every responsibility for every employee. We've all seen or heard of examples: the manager who hands new employees a huge stack of files, says (in effect), "Good luck—I have great faith in you—let me know if you need anything," or the manager who checks every word of every report, no matter how capable or experienced the employee.

Using this approach allows you to delegate in a way that works for every employee, no matter his or her current level of experience or skill, and that supports moving toward full delegation of responsibility over time, in a practical way, as your confidence (and theirs) grows.

And full delegation is the name of the game: it helps create capable and motivated employees, and frees you up to do the more strategic work that will allow your whole department or company to succeed.

TRY IT OUT

Define the area of responsibility

In the space provided below, define a project or area of responsibility you'd like to delegate to one of your employees. What big-picture information does this employee need in order to understand what's being asked and to succeed in taking on this responsibility? Remember to focus more on defining the overall area of responsibility than on detailed "how-to"s:

_____

_____

_____

_____

_____

After you've created your overview of the area you want to delegate, check it again to make sure it offers a reasonably complete picture.

Define levels of autonomy

· First, arrange the key elements of the project or responsibility along the continuum below, according to the level of confidence you feel in this person's ability to complete this aspect of the work being delegated.

- For each element you've put on the continuum, define the initial level of interaction and oversight you'd like to have with your employee. Focus on offering the appropriate level of autonomy for each element, given your current level of confidence.

Levels of my confidence / employee's autonomy

LOW_____HIGH

_____

_____

_____

_____

_____

When you've finished, I suggest you review what you've written, to make sure that the interactions you've proposed toward the left side of the continuum will provide the initial support the person needs in order to develop his or her capabilities in these areas.

The "Discuss/Agree" Step

When you're satisfied with your definitions of the area of responsibility and the levels of autonomy, it's time for the second step of the Delegation Model: the conversation with your employee.

Your goal is to leave this discussion with the employee feeling clear about what's being requested and how the two of you will work together, competent to take on this responsibility, and supported to succeed. This second step, "Discuss/Agree," involves the following:

- Offer Context
- Discuss the Area of Responsibility
- Discuss the Levels of Autonomy
- Put It All Together

Offer Context

Too often, managers delegate on the fly: "Say, Janet, why don't you take care of this from now on!" I recommend you start the delegation conversation by letting your employee know that you have something important (and positive) to discuss, and by making sure he or she has the time and energy to focus on the conversation. Then give a few sentences of what-and-why overview: what the topic is and why you want to delegate this responsibility—how it will be good for the employee, for you, and for the organization.

Discuss the Area of Responsibility

Your goal here is to make the discussion truly two-way, so that you know the employee understands what you're asking and that you've come to a real agreement. Doing the following will help you get there:

Share your definition: Start by sharing with your employee the overall definition of the project or area of responsibility that you created in the "prepare" step. Use your notes to help you paint a reasonably complete picture, without going into too much detail.

Invite employee's response: This is your chance to make sure the conversation is two-way. Invite your employee's thoughts and feelings by asking real curiosity-based questions, like, "So, what's your initial reaction to what I've just said?" or, "What do you think about taking on this responsibility?" (Unless you want your employee to feel coerced, avoid asking questions with a "right" answer, like, "Don't you think this will be great?")

Reach agreement: Once you have the employee involved, work to clarify any areas of misunderstanding or hesitation (for example, your employee may ask about how this new responsibility will fit into his or her existing job responsibilities), and reach agreement on the basic premise—that is, that the employee is ready and willing to take on this responsibility.

Discuss Levels of Confidence/Autonomy

At this point, the conversation gets into uncharted territory for most people. Talking about the area of responsibility may not have felt dramatically different (though I suspect your employee will be pleased about the clear, thoughtful, collaborative way you approached it!). However, you most likely haven't used "levels of autonomy" in delegating—and it'll be new to your employee, as well. Because it's new and different for both of you, this individualized approach needs to be done carefully in order to yield the results you want. These steps will help you move through it well:

Share your "continuum": First, let your employee know the principle behind this part of the discussion: that you want an initial level of involvement in this project or responsibility that will be most helpful to your employee, and that will allow you to build confidence in his or her abilities (and therefore delegate responsibility more fully) as quickly as possible. Once this is clear, walk through your continuum with the employee. We suggest you start at the "high" or right side of the continuum, to let your employee know where you have confidence in his or her abilities, and to reinforce your message about wanting to have everything end up "to the right."

Invite employee's response: Again, use your listening skills to invite the employee into the conversation; be especially sensitive to areas where the employee may have a different sense of his or her own competence (either higher or lower) than you. If the employee believes he or she is more capable in some element, you may want to say something like, "I invite you to demonstrate that to me. I'd love to be able to move our interactions in this area to a higher level of autonomy for you."

Reach agreement: Discuss and reach agreement about how you'll initially work together in each aspect of this area. Make sure that the employee is both supported and allowed to stretch.

Put It All Together

Finally, you'll ask the employee to summarize in writing all that you've discussed and agreed to above. This will serve three purposes: it helps the employee to take ownership for the process, it allows you to see whether or not you have the same understanding, and it gives you both a "stake in the ground" to refer to as you work toward more and more complete delegation of this area.

An Example: Jorge and SENSIA

I'd like to go back to our friend Jorge Lopez, from earlier chapters. You'll be happy to know he found an excellent director of HR for SENSIA's Central Region, Gloria Evans. Gloria's been with the company now for four months, and she's helped to hire most of the first wave of new employees for the manufacturing facility. She's hired her staff as well. Jorge is thrilled with the progress she's made, and he's decided it's time to turn over to her a responsibility he's always felt should be hers—but that he's kept on his plate simply because her time was almost completely devoted to staffing.

As you may recall, Jorge is a big fan of *Growing Great Employees,* and so he decides to try using the Delegation model outlined in the book. He starts by preparing for the conversation. Here are the notes he made on the practice pages earlier in the chapter.

Define the area of responsibility
In the space provided below, define a project or area of responsibility you'd like to delegate to one of your employees. What big picture information does this employee need in order to understand what's being asked and to succeed in taking on this responsibility? Remember to focus more on defining the overall area of responsibility than on detailed "how-to"s:

Gloria—Begin to take responsibility for the senior team meetings. Regular weekly meetings, and quarterly catch-up/strategy meetings. The main elements: (1) Facilitating to keep us on track and making clear agreements, (2) Point person for gathering agenda items pre mtgs and noting outcomes, and (3) W/ team, help make sure we're covering key strategic issues at quarterly mtgs. I'm main point of contact (as her boss and team leader), also want her to stay in touch with the other senior team members for ideas and perspective. Mtgs to be productive, fun, good use of everybody's time. Everyone to feel heard—and to come to decision on important issues. She needs to push us to think deeply, to decide.

Define levels of autonomy
· First arrange the key elements of the project or responsibility along the continuum below, according to the level of confidence you feel in this person's ability to complete this aspect of the work being delegated.
· For each element you've put on the continuum, define the initial level of interaction and oversight you'd like to have with your employee. Focus on offering the appropriate level of autonomy for each element, given your current level of confidence.

Levels of my confidence / employee's autonomy

LOW_____ HIGH

Keeping on Track

· Share techniques for keeping
  group moving
· Set up "silent signal" system
  for use during meetings
· Provide feedback after every
  meeting

Coming to Decisions

· Provide coaching on group
  decision-making
· Discuss decisions needed
  before each meeting
· "Safety net" her if she doesn't
  push us to a decision
· Provide feedback after each meeting

Strategic Thinking

· Share strategic thinking article with her
· Brainstorm issues before each meeting;
  discuss importance
· Include more strategic planning in our
  weekly one-on-ones

**Collaboration/
Group Involvement**

· Let her know if any issues
  arise
· She can come to me for
  feedback or support if
  needed

Prep and Follow-up

· Check agenda before first
  few weekly meetings
· Go over agreements and
  next steps after first few
  meetings

He did a good job, don't you think? Thorough and yet simple. He feels reasonably well prepared for the conversation. Now before he sits down with Gloria, he thinks through the Discuss/Agree step, as well. Jorge jots down a few notes for himself about how he'd like to offer context for this delegation, and thinks of a few curiosity-based questions he can ask to invite her into the conversation—both after he shares the overview of the responsibility and after he shares his "continuum." He also writes the four steps of the conversation on a piece of paper, just so he doesn't forget anything critical. Here's how it goes:

Jorge glances at his watch and realizes it's just a couple of minutes until his weekly meeting with Gloria. He takes out his notes for the Delegation conversation, and reads through them one more time. It's pretty straightforward, he realizes—it's just that he wants to do it right. Gloria's been very successful so far, and he wants to keep it that way. This is a chance for her to be seen as even more integral to the senior team.

Gloria sticks her head in the door. "Hey, boss!" she says, smiling. "Ready for me?"

Jorge nods and motions for her to come in. She sits down on the other side of his desk and pulls out a pad of paper. "So," she says, "I've got a great idea about how we can train the new line folks more quickly by using the most experienced folks as buddies/coaches. Now that I'm not completely sucked into staffing, I actually have time to think about other stuff!"

Jorge smiles. Gloria's enthusiasm is one of the things he finds most engaging about her. "I'd really like to hear about that, Gloria. A faster training cycle is definitely a good thing." He pauses. "I do have something else I'd like to talk about first, though."

Gloria chuckles. "Of course. Don't let me take over the meeting." She looks mock-worried. "I haven't screwed up, have I?"

"Actually, it's something good. I think you'll be interested and pleased." Jorge looks down at his notes and sees "offer context." "I want to talk to you about taking on a new responsibility—now that you're not totally in staffing mode—something I've been handling until now. I think you'll be good at it, and it will give you a new role on the senior team."

Gloria leans forward, clearly interested. "I'm all ears," she says.

"OK," Jorge replies. He underlines "discuss the area of responsibility" on his notes. "I'd like you to take over for me as facilitator for the senior team. The main things that entails are running the weekly meetings and the quarterly meetings, and being responsible for getting the agendas together beforehand. As the facilitator, I think the most important responsibilities are getting everybody's ideas on the table, keeping us on track with the agenda, and making sure that we come to decisions rather than just talking about things. Oh, and with the quarterly meetings, working with me to make sure we're focusing on the most important strategic issues." He looks up from his notes. "The only other thing, by way of giving you an overview, is that I'll be the main person you'll interact with on the strategic front, but you'll be connecting with the whole team for agenda items, follow-up, etc. Pretty much how we've been doing it. I know this may not sound like that much, but I consider it an important responsibility. As fast as everything is moving around here, our communication as a team is key—and this role helps ensure that." He scans his notes again, and draws an arrow pointing to the first "inviting" question he's prepared. "So, what do you think? How does this sound to you?"

Gloria's grinning. "It sounds great. This is right up my alley. I love facilitating groups, and I'd love to have this chance to support the team. Also, you've done a really good job, and I think there are some things I could learn from you." She shakes her head. "Boy, that sounds like I'm sucking up. But I really mean it. You're great at getting people to commit to something before leaving a topic. I could definitely be better at that."

Jorge says, "OK, so no problems or concerns overall with doing this?"

"None," Gloria says immediately. "Some questions about the specifics, when you want me to start and so on, but I'm very excited."

He checks off "Reach Agreement," and draws a line under "Discuss Levels of Confidence/Autonomy." "Well, let's get into that. I've put some thought into what I think will initially be easiest and most challenging about this for you—some of what you said, about getting people to come to decisions, and other things. I want to start out by giving you lots of freedom in those areas where I know you're skilled, and provide more support in the places where you need it. If we start out working together like that, then over the next few months I think you'll build your skills and I'll be able to completely turn it over to you with a lot of confidence that you'll be really successful."

Gloria looks a little puzzled. It's clear this is a new approach to her. Jorge takes out his continuum and gives her a copy. "Here," he says. "I probably should have shown you this before I started explaining it . . . but this way of delegating is new to me, as well."

Gloria quickly scans the page. "Oh, I think I get it—the stuff on the right is the stuff I'm good at." She looks up and waggles her hand. "The stuff on the left; not so much." Jorge laughs. "You're quick," he says. "Another thing you're good at."

He points to the words *Collaboration/Group Involvement* at the top right-hand corner of her copy. "You're really great at this. I've seen it already with your own staff; even the idea you came in here with today, about using staff to train other staff. So I think I can give you pretty much complete autonomy with this. I'll let you know if any issues arise, and you can come to me if you need to. Does that seem OK?"

"Yup, great."

"All right, so then there's *Prep and Follow-Up.* I suspect you're quite good at this, just based on how you've dealt with all the prep and follow-up tasks having to do with interviewing and hiring. But since we haven't done this particular kind of prep and follow-up together before, let's just check in before and after the first few meetings to make sure it's going all right." Gloria's already nodding.

"OK, so *Strategic Thinking.*" He points to it on the page. "You and I have already spoken about this, and I know you want to keep growing in this area. I think that facilitating the quarterly meetings will be a good opportunity for that. And I'll support you in the ways I've written down here." Gloria takes a moment to read, and then says, almost under her breath, "Yeah, this is good."

She taps the paper. "On this third bullet—I really want to do that. I'd like your help in making sure I'm thinking as strategically as possible with my team, too, about which people issues are most critical and how to approach them."

Jorge nods. "So, you can make notes on your copy. In fact, at the end of this conversation, I'm going to ask you to write up a summary, so we'll know for sure we're in sync." Gloria pens in a few notes for herself.

"All right, so now we're onto the two places where I want to give you the most support to begin with. One is the area you mentioned, *Coming to Decisions,* and the other one is related— *Keeping on Track.* If you look at what I've written, you'll see that I'm proposing a combination of teaching you some skills, having a 'signaling' system we can use during the meetings, and checking in with feedback after each meeting. That may seem like a lot of overseeing on my part . . ."

"No, it's good," she interrupts. Gloria pauses and bites her lip. "But . . ."

Jorge looks up. "Yes?"

"As I get better at this, you'll kind of—well, this sounds bad, but—back off, right?"

Jorge smiles. "Exactly."

"OK, good. Then I'm good."

Jorge checks off the second "Reach Agreement" on his notes and underlines "Put It All Together." "OK, just to make sure we're on the same page, could you write this all up? You can use this continuum thing as a starting point; why don't you just summarize your understanding of how we'll work together on this for the next month or so. Then, after a month, we'll relook at it and see"—here he stops and smiles a little—"how I can 'back off.'"

Gloria laughs. "You've got a deal. I'll write something up this afternoon and e-mail it to you. Can we have our first pre-meeting tomorrow morning before the senior staff meeting?"

"You bet. How about at 9:30—that gives us half an hour. More than we'll need ordinarily, I think, but you might have some first-time questions. And we have to get our signaling system together."

"Sounds good," Gloria says. She looks at her watch. "Say, we've still got time to talk about my peer training idea. . . ."

Good work, Jorge! I suspect that this transfer of responsibility is going to go really well. Now just in case you're thinking this is a lot of time and energy to put into getting Gloria to facilitate some meetings, let me play devil's advocate. First, this conversation would have taken about twenty minutes—plus ten or fifteen minutes for Jorge's prep time. Second, let's imagine for a moment how it *could* have gone, and what the result might have been. I just can't resist:

Jorge glances at his watch and realizes it's just a couple of minutes until his weekly meeting with Gloria. He remembers that he wants to talk with her about taking over the facilitator role with the senior team, among other things.

Gloria sticks her head in the door. "Hey, boss!" she says, smiling. "Ready for me?"

Jorge nods and motions for her to come in. She sits down on the other side of his desk and pulls out a pad of paper. "So," she says, "I've got a great idea about how we can train the new line folks more quickly by using the most experienced folks as buddies/coaches. Now that I'm not completely sucked into staffing, I actually have time to think about other stuff!"

Jorge smiles. Gloria's enthusiasm is one of the things he finds most engaging about her. "I'd really like to hear about that, Gloria. A faster training cycle is definitely a good thing." He pauses. "I do have something else I'd like to talk about first, though."

Gloria chuckles. "Of course. Don't let me take over the meeting." She looks mock-worried. "I haven't screwed up, have I?"

"Actually, it's something good. I think you'll be interested and pleased. I'd like you to start facilitating the senior team meetings—both the weekly ones and the quarterly ones. I think you'll do an excellent job. I have a lot of faith in you after the way you've approached our staffing challenges over the last four months."

"OK, great! When do you want me to start?"

Jorge considers. "Well, I guess tomorrow's meeting. Just use the systems we've been using. For gathering agenda items and following up. And you and I can talk about the strategic issues before the quarterly meetings."

Gloria nods. "OK—anything else you want me to know or watch out for?"

"You're the HR person," Jorge responds. "You're probably better at this stuff than I am. You'll be fine . . ."

CUT TO THE 4TH FLOOR CONFERENCE ROOM, FORTY MINUTES INTO NEXT DAY'S HOUR-LONG SENIOR STAFF MEETING:

Jorge looks around with a sinking feeling. Everybody's having a lot of fun except him. This is probably the most lively senior staff meeting they've ever had; Gloria started with a brainstorming exercise to "get everybody involved" that had nothing to do with the agenda. In fact, they've only discussed one of the four agenda topics, and they're nowhere near reaching closure on that one. Everybody seems really engaged, but they haven't accomplished anything. This is why, he thinks to himself, he doesn't delegate more. Sometimes it seems like the only way to get something done right is to do it yourself . . .

Jorge may have saved thirty or forty minutes by not going through the delegation process . . . but now he's paying full price for them. And then some.

Poor guy. No wonder people think delegation doesn't work.

(By the way, Gloria is an Expressive and Jorge's a Driver. Did you get that?)

The Last Step: Support

Let's assume our friend Jorge took the road less traveled, and this delegation is going swimmingly, and he is not kicking himself under the table. Now, he just needs to make sure he supports his very skillful delegation conversation in a way that will help make sure he continues to reap the benefits of having done it well.

When a delegation discussion goes well, it feels great to all concerned. The employee is clear and motivated, and both manager and employee are confident that goals and responsibilities will be met—achieving excellent results and helping the employee to grow.

Unfortunately, all this clarity and good intention can be lost unless both employee and manager follow through after the initial conversation. The third step of the delegation process, Support, is where the goal is reached or lost.

Supporting delegation is like supporting an agreement of any kind, and requires three very similar things:

· Honor your commitments
· Offer feedback
· "Move it to the right"

The first two are fairly straightforward: do what you said you were going to do in terms of interaction and support, and let the employee know how he or she is doing.

The third part is more complex and even more essential. Remember that, in delegating, your ultimate goal is to have the employee be fully responsible for this project or area of work, with only minimal involvement needed on your part. In order to realize that goal, you and the employee will both have to work to move those elements that start out on the left end of the continuum to the right. You do this by regularly assessing the quality of the employee's work in the elements where you have less confidence, and responding to improvements by offering more independence and less supervision.

If your tendency as a manager is to overdelegate (I call it the I-have-complete-faith-in-you school of delegation), be careful not to move to the right too quickly. Wait to see consistent demonstrations of the skills in question before you give more autonomy. If, on the other hand, your tendency is to underdelegate—if you admit to yourself that you are sometimes guilty of some version of micromanaging—make a concerted effort to give the person more autonomy once you see them getting the desired results. And remember, they don't need to do it exactly the way you would do it, they just need to do it in a way that achieves the agreed-upon results.

More Time for New Frontiers

The other day my friend told me she's thinking of starting a new garden at the front of her house, along the street. She's got all these extra plants, since lots of things are reseeding and spreading like mad—and now she's got some extra time, since the garden is flourishing largely on its own.

Delegating well not only helps your employees grow, flourish, and become ever more capable, it frees you up to do those things that will best support your success and the success of your department and the organization—from creating more streamlined processes, to hiring great people, to building stronger client relationships, or inventing new products. So, go on, plant a new garden . . .

BIG IDEAS

Smart gardeners work with the power of nature by supporting their plants' natural tendency to grow and spread. Smart managers work with the human impulse to grow and achieve by delegating well—providing the kind and amount of support their employees need in order to succeed in taking on new responsibilities.

Delegation Model

Prepare: carefully think through the "size and shape" of the responsibility, your employee's demonstrated capability in each aspect of it, and the level of oversight you want to provide initially in each aspect in order to best support his or her success.

Discuss/agree: have a thorough, two-way conversation with the employee, covering all that you've thought through above. End with a written summary to use as a starting point for the ongoing process of delegation.

Support: honor your commitments, offer feedback, and keep "moving it to the right."

Finally, remember that your goal in delegating is to hand off the responsibility as completely as possible—making for independent, capable employees and freeing you up to conquer new frontiers!

CHAPTER 9

Plants into Gardeners

O K, I'll admit it right away. This is the one chapter where my gardening metaphor breaks down, unless we venture into the realms of science fiction. Gardeners never have to deal with the possibility that their plants might someday become gardeners; managers deal with it all the time. In fact, if you're doing your job well, some of your employees will become managers; that's how companies grow and prosper. Even if they don't become managers, most of them—again, if you're doing your job well—will grow in a variety of ways; taking on bigger, more complex jobs, or developing new skills.

How do you help that transformation happen? Again, it's too bad we can't rely on a simple science fiction solution: zap your employees with electricity on a stormy night, and voilà—"Look, Igor, it's growing and developing!"

No, supporting employees' development requires focused effort over a period of time. The good news is that everything we've covered so far is a step along the path to supporting your employees' professional development. Let's assume that you've selected employees who are a good fit for the company and their jobs; that you've listened, made clear agreements, and provided feedback; and that you've begun to delegate thoughtfully. Let's say you're also working actively on maintaining the coach mind-set. Now you're ready for the next step: it's the step we call coaching.

What Is Coaching?

As we've already discussed, giving corrective feedback is telling someone what you see them doing and working with them to commit or recommit to a change in behavior. Delegation involves defining both a new area of responsibility for an employee, and the process whereby the transfer of responsibility will happen, and then working through those definitions in collaboration with your employee.

Coaching is both helping a person decide how to acquire new skills and knowledge, and—in most cases—being a part of that learning process. Coaching sometimes follows after feedback—you may discover that the person hasn't kept the agreement because he or she isn't capable of doing so. For example, remember our friends Josie and Andy? They made an agreement about her giving some of her work to her colleagues. When Andy gave her feedback about not having done this, they both realized that this was something she needed some support to learn to do. At the end of their feedback discussion, they agreed to get together later to decide how she could acquire this skill—which would be a perfect opportunity for a coaching conversation. (So perfect that we'll pick it up later in this chapter!)

Coaching also quite often arises out of delegation. When you're transferring a new responsibility to someone, they will usually need to gain new skills or knowledge in order to do it well, particularly in the areas where they start out "to the left." For instance, our delegation example in the last chapter involves some coaching; Jorge has noted on his continuum that he'll coach Gloria on group decision-making.

Finally, coaching can also arise independently of feedback or delegation conversations; you realize that an employee is ready to learn new skills in order to do his or her current job better, or to prepare for a promotion. Or an employee may come to you with a request for growth.

Whatever the impetus, coaching is your opportunity to help your employees develop new skills and knowledge. As a manager, you're in a unique position to provide your people with coaching. Your experience and knowledge, your perspective on their strengths and weaknesses, your insights into their interactions—all these give you the information you need to help them grow. You can probably have a greater positive impact on an employee's professional development than anyone else in that person's life. I'd go so far as to say coaching is a noble endeavor; true coaches help people become what they are capable of becoming. The benefit to the organization is clear: coaching creates more capable, highly skilled, independent, and committed employees. The benefit to the employee is equally obvious. But the personal benefit for you, the coach, is also powerful: you get the spiritual, mental, and emotional satisfaction that comes from helping someone grow.

Coaching Toolkit

Coaching requires three things; a coach's "toolkit," if you will. They are:

The Mind-set of a Coach
Appropriate Developmental Options
Coaching Skills

The Mind-set of a Coach

Good news: you've already learned the first one, the mind-set of a coach, in chapter 5. Just to refresh your memory, the mind-set of a coach is "believing in people's potential and wanting to help them succeed." (At this point, you might want to go back and read or reread the first couple of pages in chapter 5.)

Appropriate Developmental Options

Having a variety of developmental options to choose among is an important part of being a good coach. (Too many managers, if they think of this at all, simply default to a few favorites: a training, a book, a lecture.) Once you have such a list, making sure that you choose the options most appropriate to a given employee's skill/experience level is critical.

Coaching Skills

Once you're armed with a supportive mind-set and a varied and level-appropriate list of developmental options, you need to know how to coach. I'll share (surprise, surprise) a simple model for helping your employees acquire new skills and knowledge.

What's Appropriate?

OK, let's assume you've worked on achieving the coach mind-set. Now we'll look at the second tool in the toolkit: appropriate developmental options. I want to target the word *appropriate*. Below you'll see a continuum showing employee skill or experience from low to high (this continuum should look familiar to you if you've read the previous chapter). Underneath the continuum I've noted the three major errors that arise from choosing options targeted to the wrong level of skill and experience. I give more detail below about these errors and the problems associated with them.

SKILL/EXPERIENCE

NOVICE_____ EXPERIENCED

(LOW)   (HIGH)

Error 1—treating LOW as if HIGH
Error 2—treating HIGH as if LOW
Error 3—leaving HIGH alone

Error 1: Treating LOW as if HIGH: This means coaching new or inexperienced people as though they are experienced. This error is epidemic in fast-paced, high-pressure companies. The rationale behind it is often, "We hire good people; they should be able to figure things out for themselves." New, inexperienced employees are coached (if they are coached at all) using options that would be useful only to a much more experienced person. For example, new employees might be briefly introduced to a system or approach and then left to figure it out for themselves—to sink or swim. Many sink; the company loses their potential and spends unnecessary time and money to hire and train their replacements. Those who "swim" have probably spent more time and energy getting up to speed than necessary. In the process, they may have also learned unintended negative lessons: that it's every man for himself, for instance, or that managers aren't there to support success, but only to judge failures.

Error 2: Treating HIGH as if LOW: This error happens most often when managers are "stuck" on a certain approach to coaching, and coach all employees as though they are novices. This can work wonderfully for the novices, but it's a real problem when dealing with an experienced and skilled employee. A manager "treating high as low" will use coaching options that are very directive or involve a lot of oversight, so that they end up always checking the employee's work, or teaching step-by-step, elementary approaches. A highly skilled or experienced employee who is treated in this way will almost invariably become demoralized. He or she may become resistant and push back, or do only the minimum expected, or begin to second-guess his or her own decisions or actions. Eventually this employee may leave the company. In any case, the organization loses.

Error 3: Leaving HIGH Alone: This error tends to happen when a company is growing quickly, or when a manager has a number of difficult or new employees. Very experienced or skillful employees are then likely to be thought of as low-maintenance, and are more or less left to their own devices; in other words, they may get no coaching at all. This approach may seem tempting, but remember—there's no way of knowing how much better, faster, more creative, or more motivated such a person could be with a little well-placed coaching—or how much others in the organization could benefit by learning from his or her excellence and expertise. Not only that, top employees are often the most motivated to grow—and if they don't get any coaching in their current job, they may start looking for a job where they will.

Right Option + Right Experience Level = Growth

In order to avoid all these coaching errors, we'll generate a good solid list of coaching options from which you can choose. As I said earlier, most managers have a couple of "pet" options they come to rely on. For example, one manager I know has a three-ring notebook of all the procedures in her department; she hands this to each new employee and encourages them to come to her with questions. That's her coaching option. Usually these default options are either things that have worked for the manager or are simply the path of least resistance. (In the example I just gave, it was both.) Unfortunately, this one-size-fits-all approach doesn't take into account how different people learn, or what's appropriate to various levels of experience.

Before we go any further, a quick definition: I define a coaching option as any means by which a person might acquire new skills or knowledge. I suggest that, when considering possible coaching options, you think about all the ways you've learned throughout your life—from the most formal to the most informal. But don't stop there—also think about approaches to learning that you've heard about but haven't tried yourself. Starting from that point will really stretch your mind beyond the boundaries of the few coaching options that may be your "defaults," and get you started creating a much more varied and useful list.

Take five or ten minutes right now to think of at least twenty ways your employees might acquire new skills or knowledge. This is a brainstorm, so there are no bad ideas—feel free to get wacky. We'll sort them for feasibility later. (I've noted a couple of interesting possibilities to get you started.)

> Follow me around, taking notes; debrief every couple of hours.
> Set up a clearly defined simulation; go through it with them.
> Have them join an industry association.

All right, now review your brainstorm list above and:
1) circle those you think are feasible, given cultural, time, or budgetary constraints in your company,
2) for those that aren't feasible but that you really like, is there some other version of the idea that *would* be feasible? If so, alter the idea to its more feasible form and circle it.

Which Options for Which Level?

Once you've got a good starting list of coaching options, it's important to use them properly. In order to do that, you need to know what level of experience or skill your employee currently has in the area you're coaching. Sometimes you may already know, through observation or past work experience, but often you'll have to find this out from the employee. (We'll talk about how to do that when we go through the coaching model.)

Once you know the employee's skill or experience level in this particular area, how do you decide which coaching options are most appropriate? Knowing some key characteristics of learners at a low, medium, or high level of experience offers your best set of clues:

LOW (novices)—"Don't Know What They Don't Know"

In other words, people who are new to an area of skill or knowledge don't have enough experience even to know what they need to find out. They require fairly directive coaching options; ones that will lay out for them what's to be done, step-by-step, and why. Think about a skill you've learned as an adult: perhaps a new language, a sport, a dance step. You go into a beginner's class expecting that the teacher will tell you what you'll be learning and how to do it; otherwise, you wouldn't know where to begin.

MEDIUM (some skill and experience)—"Know What They Don't Know, But Don't Know What to Do About It"

People who have some experience or skill in an area will be more aware of their strengths and weaknesses, but probably won't know how best to address them. They will benefit from coaching options that give some choice about what to work on, but prescribe how to do so. For example, let's say you have an employee who is okay at managing his time, but wants to get much better. In coaching him, you might ask where he feels he gets off-track. He might say that he notices he tends to put too much time into low-priority tasks. You could then teach him some specifics for addressing that difficulty; perhaps a model for prioritizing, or helping him create a simple system for weighting his time use toward higher-priority tasks.

HIGH (skill/experience)—"Know What They Don't Know and Know What to Do About It"

People who are already skilled in a given area tend to be aware of how they need to improve and what that will require. With these people, coaching options that help them set realistic goals and provide the necessary resources are most helpful. Think of something that you're good at, but at which you want to be great. Let's say, for instance, that you're a talented amateur singer who has studied and sung quite a bit over the years. Your singing teacher might help you decide on a realistic "stretch" goal—to audition successfully for a semi-professional local chorus or dinner theater troupe—and then think through with you how to get the extra training or experience you'll need to achieve that goal.

TRY IT OUT

Now you'll decide how the options you circled from your brainstorm list, above, will work for different levels of skill/experience. Some will be fairly universally appropriate, while others will be far more useful with one level of skill/experience than another.

First, in the left-hand column below write the coaching options from your brainstorm you feel are most feasible for offering to your employees, given your company and your own skills and resources. Then, note the level or levels for which you believe the option would be best suited, using "L" for low, "M" for medium, and "H" for high.

Coaching Options	Skill/Experience Level(s)

We'll come back to these favorite options of yours later, when you decide how to coach an actual employee.

How to Coach

A quick review: we've talked about the mind-set of a coach, about the benefits and rewards of coaching, about being aware of coaching options, and knowing which option is appropriate for a given skill or experience level. Now I'll share a way to put it all together into successful coaching interactions with your employees.

COACHING MODEL
Explore
Commit
Develop

Explore

In the first step, you have a two-way conversation about the development opportunity you want to target and how to address it. You focus on the developmental area, listening to get a clear idea of your employee's experience in this area and to understand what's needed in order to improve. Then you work with the employee to explore coaching options to meet the needs, given his or her level of experience. You finally make sure there are no obstacles to implementing the option(s), or that they can be overcome.

Commit

In the second step you ensure that you and the employee understand each other, are agreeing to the same thing, and know how the developmental options will progress. First, you have the employee summarize what each of you has agreed to do to complete the options you've chosen; then, you set benchmarks and deadlines for the completion of the options. Finally, you have the employee write a summary of your joint commitments.

Develop

This step is where the rubber meets the road and you complete the coaching options. You and the employee will both fulfill the commitments you've made, and you'll offer feedback about how the employee is doing. Most important, you'll continue to nourish and maintain the mindset of a coach—believing in your employee's ability to improve or stretch in this area, and wanting to help him or her succeed.

The critical difference between this process and the somewhat similar process you learned in chapter 7 for making agreements lies in the third step. Supporting agreements is likely to be largely a matter of giving feedback, perhaps providing some resources, and keeping high positive expectations about your employee's ability to succeed. In coaching, the first two steps are simply the initial conversation to clarify how the coaching will happen. The third step, developing, is where the actual coaching and improvement will take place.

Step 1: Explore

The objective of this first step, for both you and the employee, is clarity: you need to become clear about where and to what extent the employee needs and wants to develop, how that might best be accomplished, and what might get in the way of its accomplishment. To successfully explore your coaching options you should:

- Define the developmental area
- Explore/define experience level
- Explore/define coaching options
- Check for obstacles

Define the developmental area: Before the meeting, clarify in your own mind the growth opportunity you see for this employee. Where can he or she develop? Why and how is it important to his or her overall success? Discuss your insights with the employee to help him or her understand your reasons for coaching. You'll also invite the employee's understanding of this area, and find out whether he or she wants to develop in this chosen area. Due to the two-way nature of coaching, this conversation may also be initiated by the employee—and often will be, if the employee is highly skilled and focused on self-improvement.

Explore/define experience level: This is where your listening skills will be put to use. You need to find out where the employee is starting from—his or her current level of skill or experience. You can use listening before the meeting, as well, to get others' perceptions of this employee's strengths and deficits in this area.

Explore/define coaching options: Once you and the employee are clear on the area targeted for coaching and the employee's current competency in the area, you can create solutions in the form of appropriate coaching options. By matching the growth area with options geared to his or her experience and learning style, you'll have the best chance for continued success and/or improvement.

Check for obstacles: Look for obstacles that might get in the way (they could be internal or external, involving you, the employee, or the organization itself) and how to overcome them.

I want to talk about one possibility that can arise here. In general, a coaching conversation is a very positive thing—you're working with the employee to figure out how he or she can be more successful and effective. However, when coaching arises out of a "failed" agreement—that is, where the employee has agreed to do something, and through subsequent feedback conversations you discover that he or she doesn't have the skill or knowledge to be able to do it—the person being coached can feel embarrassed, incompetent, or even angry (at himself or herself, probably, though it may seem that it's being directed at you). In those instances, it's especially important to maintain the mind-set of a coach and let the person know that you have every expectation he or she will be able to develop in the area you're discussing.

In fact, let's use Josie and Andy from chapter 7 to illustrate the coaching model, as they've found themselves in exactly this situation. Josie had agreed to give her design ideas to some of her colleagues to create production specifications . . . and she wasn't doing it. Andy gave her feedback and found out that she didn't really know how to do it, felt uncomfortable trying, and so was continuing to do that part of the job herself. A-ha! A skill to be developed. Let's go back to the tail end of their last conversation, and pick it up from there:

> Josie looks down at her notes. "Now, the second thing—about how to feel comfortable asking Ed, Tanya, and Jim to do the production work on my designs—I'm not sure how to do that."
>
> "I've got an idea." Andy looks at his watch. "Look, I've got to go to a meeting now, but I'd be happy to teach you an approach to delegating that I think would be reasonably comfortable for you. We can also talk about how to think about the whole situation differently, so that it's not so daunting."
>
> Josie blows out a big breath. "That would be really good. When can we do that?"
>
> Andy and Josie pull out their calendars to find a time to meet.
>
> Now imagine one of those cool old black-and-white movies where the hands of the clock spin around and around to signify the passage of time . . .
>
> Andy's waiting for Josie. It's a gorgeous day, so they've decided to meet in Union Square Park, just a few blocks from the Lobo New York offices, to have lunch and their coaching conversation. As he's been preparing for this, Andy has realized that the area Josie needs to develop in isn't really delegation; it's simpler than that—it's making agreements. Since attending a course last year called Encouraging Excellence, and since reading *Growing Great*

Employees, he feels pretty confident in his ability to teach Josie how to make clear agreements with her colleagues.

Josie wanders up to his bench, drink and sandwich in hand, clearly distracted by the signs of spring everywhere. She sits down, looking at the lilies of the valley in a planter next to them. "You know," she says, "we could make a very cool bracelet that looks like lilies of the valley. Really thin chain—small links, in a light green metal, and then a few little white-enameled 'bells,' like lily of the valley flowers. Or no, maybe not enameled, something lighter weight so they'd make a little jingly noise. Maybe hanging off in lined-up clusters, like they do . . ."

Andy's grinning. ". . . And then, we could ask Tanya or Ed to create the production specs for them!"

Josie looks momentarily startled—she really was off in design land, Andy thinks—and then she laughs nervously. "Right. The topic at hand." She unwraps her sandwich and takes a bite.

Andy sips his soda, then begins. "OK, so here's what I've been thinking. I've decided that you need to learn how to make agreements with Tanya, Ed, and Jim. At first I thought it was delegation, but it's simpler than that, I think. It's learning how to ask them to do a specific thing by a specific time, in a specific way." He stops and looks at her. "Does that capture it?"

Josie nods, chewing. As she finishes the bite, she adds, "Yeah, and not just them—I've been thinking about this, too, and I realized I'm just overall not so great at asking people to do things. My roommate, my sister, my friends—I could go on." She takes a swig of iced tea from her bottle, and shakes her head. "I don't know—sometimes I feel like I'm either a doormat or a control freak . . ."

"Neither, in my experience," Andy replies. "I think you just don't have a way to approach asking other people to do things that feels comfortable to you."

"Boy, if it was that simple, it would be great," Josie says.

"Well, then let's assume it is that simple, and go from there. OK?" She nods, and Andy continues. "All right, can we start from the point of agreeing that this is a new area for you; that you feel like a novice here?"

"Definitely."

"So I can think of a couple of ways for you to learn to do this. I could teach you, complete with role-plays—you know, I'm Jim or Tanya and you're you—or I could turn you on to this book I've been reading, which has a chapter with a simple approach for making agreements, or both. I could also hook you up with Debbie in production, who is really, really good at making agreements with people—I've noticed how clear she is about what she needs from us."

Josie drinks some more iced tea and sits looking out across the park for a few moments. "Actually, I like all three of those ideas. If I was going to do it in order, I guess I'd like first to read the book chapter, then have you teach me. Then maybe I could try it out for a while, and then talk to Debbie. I feel like if I talked to her now, I wouldn't even know what to ask her, or what to look for."

As he listens, Andy realizes she's right—the idea of talking to Debbie probably wasn't a great coaching option right at the beginning, for someone who's a novice like Josie—he's glad she caught that herself. "Josie," he says, "I think that sounds perfect—and you're right, let's save Debbie for later, when you can take better advantage of her as a resource." Josie's looking more confident, he notes, and less daunted by the whole topic.

"So, before we agree on the specifics of when and how we'll do this, let's make sure we're not overlooking anything. Can you think of anything else that might prevent you from learning to make agreements with your peers about doing your production specs?"

Josie thinks for a minute. "You're sure they're OK with this?" she asks finally.

"Absolutely."

"Well, then, other than me resisting the whole subject and just believing I should do everything myself," she says, smiling in a self-deprecating way, "which I know have to talk myself out of, by the way, I think we're good to go."

Andy replies, "You know, there's another chapter in that book about how to 'change your mind,' like, you know, your beliefs about things; maybe that might be good for you to read, too."

Josie laughs. "Wow, you're chockfull of helpful ideas today. Yeah, that does sound good . . . Let's do it . . ."

Before we go on to think about how you can use this approach with your own employees, I'd suggest that you quickly review Josie and Andy's conversation, looking for the four parts of the first step: How did they define the developmental area? Agree on her experience or skill level? Explore and agree on some coaching options? Check for obstacles?
Can you see it all? Great! Let's go on.

TRY IT OUT

Here's a chance to take a few minutes and think about how to help one of your employees grow, using this approach. I'll have you prepare for the Explore step below. (Then you'll learn and prepare for the Commit step—and after that, I'll encourage you to go and coach the person.)

· Think of an employee who wants or needs to develop in a certain area. Start with a relatively easy situation—a person who will be open to development, and an area where you feel reasonably expert. How would you define the developmental area?

_____

_____

_____

· How would you draw the employee out to get a sense of what he or she thinks the area is, and how he or she feels about growing in this area?

_____

_____

_____

· Write down a question or two you could ask to get a clearer sense of the employee's skill or experience level in this area:

_____

_____

_____

· What coaching options might you suggest (that you think are appropriate to the employee's experience level)?

_____

_____

_____

· How might you check for obstacles?

_____

_____

_____

Step 2: Commit

OK, hold those thoughts. Now for step 2. At the point in the coaching conversation when you and your employee both feel you know what's needed in order to develop in this area, it's time to make sure your understanding is in sync. As you know from previous chapters, that's what the Commit step involves:

- Ask the employee to summarize:
  What he/she will do
  What you will do
- Set benchmarks and time lines
- Have the employee write it down

Summarize: Ask your employee to summarize his or her understanding of the options you've agreed on. This is the time to make sure you're in sync and that you're clear on who's responsible for which actions. For example, if you've decided the employee needs training in a particular area, who's going to find out what's available? If you've agreed someone at the company is going to serve as a mentor, will you contact the person? Will the employee follow up?

As in the Commit Step of the Agreements conversation, I strongly encourage you to ask the employee to summarize. It's the best way to find out if you're thinking the same thing—and it also helps the employee take responsibility for the coaching; to feel that effort and success are in his or her hands.

Set benchmarks and time lines: Agree on a benchmark date or dates for completing each of the options you've chosen and a clear deadline for final completion. For example, if you've chosen the teaching option, you might set one date for getting together for an explanation and demonstration, and then another for discussing his or her experience putting the skill into practice and outlining any next steps. Whenever possible, the final deadline should include behavioral goals—that the person will be demonstrating changed behaviors rather than that they'll simply have completed the agreed-upon options.

Write it down: Since coaching often continues over a period of time or includes a number of steps, we suggest you have the employee write down all that you've agreed to above. This will help to remind you what you've committed to do, and will also give both of you a roadmap against which you can check progress over the weeks and months to come.

Let's listen in as Andy and Josie move through the Commit step and complete their coaching conversation. Remember, they've talked about Josie reading a couple of parts of *Growing Great Employees,* Andy role-playing the Agreements model with her, and finally—after she's had a chance to try out what she's learned—Josie using Debbie as a mentor/resource.

Josie laughs. "Wow, you're chockfull of helpful ideas today. Yeah, that does sound good. Let's do it . . ."

"OK," Andy says. He crumples up his sandwich wrapper and shoots it, one-handed, into the wire trashcan near their bench, then, turning to Josie with a smile, he says, "So, you're used to me asking this by now; why don't you summarize what we've agreed to, just to make sure we're on the same page?"

She laughs. "Nice shot. And yes, I figured you were going to ask me to summarize. So, you're going to lend me that book with agreements and belief stuff in it, and show me the relevant sections, and I'm going to read it. Then, we'll set up a time when I can talk over with you what I've read and we can do some role-playing. And then . . . then what?" She thinks for a moment as she gathers up her lunch leftovers and puts them in the trash. "Oh yeah. Then after I've tried doing this for a while, I'm going to ask Debbie for some pointers." She pauses. "Or do you need to ask her?"

"Nope, you can just ask her yourself. You guys know each other, right?" Josie nods. They've both gotten up and are walking back to the office together. "Good—well, then, you summarized it just as I would have; we're in agreement. Now, about timing. I can give you the book and show you the parts to read—of course, you're welcome to read as much as you want—as soon as we get back to the office. How about if we do our teaching/role-playing session next week at our one-on-one?"

Josie frowns and looks worried. "What?" Andy asks.

"Could we do it sooner than that? I've got two ideas sketched out and two more I'm thinking about—including this lily of the valley thing—and I'd really like to ask one of the other designers to do the specs on the two that are sketched."

"Great!" Andy says with genuine enthusiasm. "How about we meet day after tomorrow? I'm free after Eric's senior staff meeting— 2 P.M.?" Josie smiles and nods. "And now we have a real goal—for other designers to do the production specs on all four of these design ideas . . . the two you have, and the two you're working on. Right?" Josie nods again.

As they reach the front door of their building, Andy adds, "So, Josie, why don't you put this all in an e-mail and send it to me— that way we'll both remember what we've said, and have it to re-fer back to over the next couple of weeks."

"You got it, boss," she says as they step into the elevator. He no-tices she seems in a much better mood than when she first sat down in the park. "I'll just come with you to your office so you can give me that book . . ."

Seems like it's going to work out just fine. (We'll check in on them again later.) Now let's go back to your employee and think through the Commit step.

You might want to go a few pages back and reread your Explore step preparation; now you'll prepare for the Commit step with this same employee.

- How will you ask the employee to summarize what you've agreed to here: what he or she will do and what you will do?

_____

_____

_____

- How will you establish benchmarks and time lines—including final, behavioral goals?

_____

_____

_____

- Write down a few sentences of explanation to use when asking your employee to write up the coaching approach you've agreed on:

_____

_____

_____

If you, like Josie, want to get this moving right away, you can feel free to go and have your coaching conversation with this employee. Just be sure to mark your place in the book, so you can come right back to reading about the last step in the process.

Step 3: Develop

In the first two steps of the coaching process, you and your employee decide what the two of you want to work on and how you'll do it. Those are important steps in the right direction that often don't happen in business. The develop step, though, is where you actually complete the developmental options you've agreed on.

- · Complete the coaching options
- · Stay in touch
- · Maintain the mind-set of a coach

In other words: keep your coaching commitments, stay in contact with the employee to find out what's happening and let him/her know what you see, believe in the employee's potential, and be committed to helping him or her succeed.

Sounds pretty straightforward. Unfortunately, the same time constraints, workload, mental habits, and crises that can keep you from supporting agreements can be an even bigger problem here, because this step tends to require more effort on your part than supporting an agreement.

You may want to turn back to the Agreements section of chapter 7, and look at your brainstorm about the Support step; many of the same obstacles will come up in coaching, and you can probably overcome them in many of the same ways.

And just to help you out even more, here's some self-talk you can use to support your intention to coach: "By spending the time in this way, I'm working to create a loyal, motivated, competent, creative employee . . . what better resource could I have in my department and in the company?"

Teaching: An Important Coaching Option

Some coaching options will require minimal time on your part; recommending resources or helping the employee find appropriate training, for instance. Others will require more of your skill or time; for example, getting your employee onto a cross-functional team, or working together on a project.

However, the coaching option that will probably require the most effort and skill on your part is also the most common: sharing with your employees your own skills and knowledge. As a manager, you probably have expertise and experience that could benefit your employees. During coaching conversations, you'll often find that the best coaching option is for you to pass that expertise along to your employees by teaching them what you know.

Because this passing-on will require time and thought on your part, I assume you'll want to make sure that it "takes"—that the employee really learns what you're trying to teach. To help you teach your employees successfully, I'd like to offer you some ideas and guidelines for good teaching.

Fortunately, we can draw upon what we've talked about throughout the preceding chapters. (I believe in practicing what I preach, so I've made every effort to use the principles of good teaching in sharing these skills and ideas with you.) So, let's first go back to the LearningPath we discussed in chapter 4:

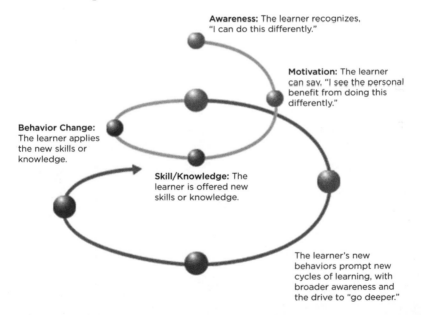

Awareness: The learner recognizes, "I can do this differently."

Motivation: The learner can say, "I see the personal benefit from doing this differently."

Behavior Change: The learner applies the new skills or knowledge.

Skill/Knowledge: The learner is offered new skills or knowledge.

The learner's new behaviors prompt new cycles of learning, with broader awareness and the drive to "go deeper."

The function of a good teacher is to help the student move along this LearningPath. So, rather than simply leaping into talking about the skill or knowledge (also known as the "so-do-this-and-this-got-it?-great" approach), an effective teacher will make sure that the student is aware that there's something to be learned, and feels that learning could benefit him or her. Then the teacher would offer the skill or knowledge. And finally, the teacher would make sure of the behavior change by giving the learner a chance to try the new skill or knowledge and reflect on how to make best use of it. Given that, here are the key elements of teaching:

· Involve
· Explain
· Practice
· Integrate

Involve

In this first step, you check initial levels of awareness and motivation, and then help to increase them, if necessary. The best way to do this is by asking curiosity-based questions. For example, if you were teaching delegation, you might ask, "How might it be helpful to you to learn to delegate more?" This one question would tell you a lot about the person's opening levels of awareness and motivation. For example, if he or she responds, "Ummm, well, I guess it would make me a better manager . . . ?" then you've got some work to do in increasing awareness and motivation.

You might do this by asking the learner to reflect on times when someone delegated to him or her well or badly, and how it impacted him or her, or by sharing some of your own experiences. Your goal here is to awaken employees to their own hunger to learn—at the end of this step you want them to feel, "I can learn to do this, and it would be helpful to me."

Explain

Next, you share with the employee what you understand or know. You can use a variety of approaches here, depending on what works best for you and the employee, and on the skill or knowledge being taught. Sometimes a simple definition or explanation will work; at other times you may need to offer a step-by-step "how-to." Demonstrating or modeling the skill is often valuable and sometimes essential. Especially in teaching complex or subtle skills (how to delegate, for instance), it's usually best to offer both verbal explanation and a hands-on demonstration. You can also use examples that hook the new skill to something with which the employee is already familiar. Whatever approaches you use, be sure to check with the employee during your explanation to find out whether he or she is with you—use your listening skills to check for reactions and understanding.

Practice

Someone may understand a skill or procedure conceptually, and yet not be able to do it. Offering practice opportunities gives the employee a chance to translate theoretical understanding into practical ability. Create a way for the employee to practice the new behaviors in fairly low-risk environments: you could set up a role-play between you and the employee, or you could let him or her try the behavior in a low-key situation with you there for backup. (Note: if you use this second choice, restrain yourself from jumping in and taking over at the first sign of trouble. Offer support only as absolutely essential. Your goal is, insofar as possible, to let the person learn from his or her own efforts.)

Integrate

This is where you help the employee reflect on what's happened and apply the learning to real life. You might have him or her self-critique the practice; you can offer your feedback and suggestions for improvement; you can lead a discussion about how to apply the new behavior day-to-day or in specific situations. You can also agree, at this point, on whether further teaching or feedback is needed.

I encourage you to remember, throughout each step of the teaching process, that the most important thing is not what you're sending, but what's being received. You may be very clear in what you're saying—but is the employee understanding and integrating it? That's the primary determinant of learning. That's why listening skills are so critical to teaching.

TRY IT OUT

To give you a chance to bat these ideas around in real life, I'm going to recommend you have a discussion about teaching with someone (or more than one person) who you feel is a good teacher. First, a little preparation:

· Think of something you'd like to and/or need to teach an employee. It should be something you know or know how to do well. Write the employee's name and the skill or knowledge you want to focus on:

_____

_____

· Refer to the section above for ideas about how to involve, explain, practice, and integrate. How might you use any of these in teaching your employee this skill? Write below your ideas about how to incorporate these ideas:

_____

_____

_____

_____

_____

· Think about what might be difficult for you in teaching your employee. Write down your concerns or questions to share with your teaching mentor(s).

_____

_____

_____

Once you've thought through the topics above, find one or more teaching mentors with whom you can share what you've written. Feel free to add their insights and suggestion to your notes above. After you've talked through your teaching "plan" with your mentor(s)—go do it!

Looking In on Josie and Andy

Before we leave this topic, let's check in once more on Andy and Josie. She's read the appropriate chapters in *Growing Great Employees;* she and Andy discussed what she'd read and then they role-played Agreement conversations with Ed and Jim (Josie felt Tanya would be easiest for her, and that practicing her conversations with Ed and Jim would be enough). We're eavesdropping on Andy and Josie's first one-on-one meeting after her initial try at having the real Agreements conversations with her colleagues—the two of them agreed they'd debrief her first effort at this meeting.

"OK, I'm on pins and needles," Andy says, practically pulling Josie into his office and closing the door. Josie smiles and shakes her head, rolling her eyes. "No, I'm serious," Andy adds, "I've been thinking about this all morning! How did it go?"

Josie shrugs, trying to look nonchalant. "It was OK."

"You're killin' me here. I want details!"

Josie laughs. "All right, all right. I'm pretty pleased, actually. Jim was OK, and my conversation with Ed went well—I'd say very well."

"Wow." Andy raises his eyebrows. "If you're saying it went very well, it must have been fantastic."

"Well, I wouldn't go that far . . . but it felt so—clear, I guess." She smiles. "I suppose that's why it's called the 'Clarify' step. And the thing I liked most was that it felt collaborative, that we were coming to it together."

"So you feel Ed knows what you're asking him and why, and agreed to do it." Josie nods. "And, you were less pleased about the conversation with Jim?"

Josie sighs. "It turned out OK, but I definitely made a few mistakes . . . fortunately, I didn't repeat them with Ed. I was trying to be way too careful with Jim not to have him feel like I was making him do something, and I ended up just being confusing."

"What did Jim do?"

"Luckily for me, he said something like—'Josie, just come out with it and stop beating around the bush. Are you trying to ask me to do the specs on this design?' So I got to start over. And then it was fine."

"Jim would definitely be the one to cut to the chase," Andy agrees, grinning. "So, it sounds like you didn't have that problem with Ed."

"No." She smiles again. "I learned from my mistakes. Just like with designs that don't work." Then Josie looks at him seriously. "You know, Andy, this is making me wonder—do you think I could ever be a manager . . . you know, manage designers?"

Andy leans back, a big grin on his face. "Well now, that's a whole 'nother conversation . . ."

Josie, as you can see, is moving merrily along the LearningPath; her behavior change has created a whole new level of awareness about what might be possible for her. A great example of how coaching can help plants become gardeners . . .

BIG IDEAS

In nature, even the best gardeners can't turn plants into new gardeners. However, in business, employees can grow into managers—or, if not managers, into doing bigger and more complex jobs. Coaching calls on all the skills you've learned so far; it's a powerful way to support the transformation of "plants into gardeners."

Coaching Toolkit

Mind-set of a Coach: believing in people's potential and wanting to help them succeed.

Appropriate Developmental Options: creating a list of ways to learn new skills or knowledge that work for a variety of experience and skill levels.

Coaching Skills: become familiar with the model below.

Coaching Model

Explore: discuss and define the area of development and the employee's experience level, select coaching options, and check for obstacles.

Commit: summarize the manager's and employee's role in the coaching, create benchmarks and time lines, and write it all down.

Develop: complete the coaching options, stay in touch, and maintain the mind-set of a coach!

When teaching, which is the most common coaching option, remember that learning happens within the learner—your job is to support the employee's journey along the Learning-Path.

CHAPTER 10

How Does Your Garden Grow?

By the third year, my friend has gotten quite comfortable with the dance of gardening—balancing her efforts with her plants' own efforts to grow and thrive. Since she started out by creating a supportive environment and choosing plants well-suited to her goals and situation, she's finding that her ongoing gardening tasks are, for the most part, a combination of removing obstacles (Japanese beetles, weeds), providing needed resources (stakes in the ground, enough room to grow), and getting out of the way.

There are only two places in her garden where this balanced approach isn't working—and it's driving her nuts.

"You know, I hate to say I told you so," I note, watching her carefully fertilize a woodland shrub she had fallen in love with at the garden center and decided she couldn't do without, "but—I told you so." Her shrub is beautiful but delicate, bearing tiny white flowers with a wonderful lemony fragrance. The tag told her it probably wouldn't survive through the winter in her area, and that it required quite a bit of shade and the kind of rich, deep soil that generally only exists on the forest floor. She's spent three years nursing it along, and it's alive—but just barely. Each year it looks a little more scraggly, and it's not much bigger than it was when she bought it. This year it's hardly bloomed at all.

"I know, I know," she grumbles, plopping into a chair beside me. "I've put more energy into that one stupid little bush than into the rest of the garden combined, and it's barely alive." She sighs and gestures toward the other side of the garden. "As opposed to those." She glares at a clump of bishop's goutweed that seems to take over more of the garden every year. "I feel like the other half of my energy goes into pulling out that stuff, so it doesn't kill off everything around it."

While most employees do just fine if put in the right job and managed well, some employees seem to require much more than their fair share of energy. This chapter is about finding the appropriate balance of effort and responsibility between you as a manager and your employees. In terms of your responsibilities as a manager of people, the things I've shared with you so far in this book are a good summary: to hire people who are a good fit for your vision, your organization, and the job itself; to listen to them, challenge your limiting assumptions about them, and deal with them as individuals; to create clear agreements with them, provide balanced behavioral feedback, and delegate appropriately and well; to coach them to develop in areas where they have potential and interest.

So then, what can you reasonably expect from your employees? What are the employee's responsibilities to you and to the organization?

I'm bringing this up, and devoting a chapter to the topic, because over the years I've seen too many good managers devoting way too much energy to those employees who don't hold up their end of the bargain. Employees who don't take responsibility for their own success and who over-rely on the manager to help and rescue them; or, conversely, employees who try to do too much—tasks for which they lack the requisite skills or experience, decisions they're not qualified to make, other people's jobs. Like my gardening friend, struggling with her woodland shrub and her bishop's goutweed, managers can end up feeling as though they're being held hostage to those few employees who are over- or under-responsible, giving way too much attention to them instead of to other employees or projects.

The Employee's Responsibility

Often managers struggle with this problem because they don't feel clear about what the employee ought to be doing. They end up second-guessing themselves . . . "Well, maybe I'm being too hard on him," or, "Have I really done everything I should/could for her?"

To help you avoid getting caught in this cycle, I'd like to offer you the "manager's bill of rights," those basic things that you have a right to expect from your employees. Responsible employees:

- Are responsive to feedback
- Keep their agreements
- Manage their own growth
- Are "Good Company Citizens"

There's a lot to think about in each of these; let's discuss them in depth.

Responsible Employees Are Responsive to Feedback

We can start by doing a camera check on the word *responsive*. What does "responsive" look like? Someone who's responsive to feedback would listen without interrupting, blaming, or accusing; ask questions for clarity; engage in discussions about next steps; and make efforts to change the behavior.

The person might feel defensive, but he or she would make an effort to manage the urge to respond to feedback with excuses or explanations. People who are responsive to feedback believe (and demonstrate this belief, in the ways I've described above) that they have things to learn, and that it's in their best interest to be open to feedback from their manager and others. They understand that by inviting and acting on feedback, they are clearly demonstrating their commitment, emotional maturity, and their ability to improve . . . all things a responsible employee wants his or her manager to see!

Now, even the best employees aren't always going to be perfect in this regard—they might be having a bad day, or you might not be doing such a great job of giving the feedback, or they may feel (and they may be right) that the feedback is unjustified or unfair. However, if you're making a consistent effort to provide balanced, behavioral feedback in a respectful way, and an employee is generally not responsive—is habitually defensive, or blames you or others for his/her own deficiencies, or resists discussing next steps, or changing the behavior—then I propose to you that person is not fulfilling his or her responsibility to you as an employee.

With employees like this, who consistently respond poorly to feedback, I suggest you begin by having an agreement conversation. Establish a clear, mutual agreement about responding to feedback (as well as the other core responsibilities we're discussing here). Then it will be completely clear to the person what you expect, and you will feel and be justified in holding him or her consistently accountable to being open and responsive to feedback.

Responsible Employees Keep Their Agreements

It may seem obvious that employees should be expected to keep agreements they've made, but I've had lots of conversations over the years with managers that go something like this:

> *Manager:* "I just can't get Ellen to answer the phone properly. Either she doesn't direct the caller to the right person, or she's too abrupt—and forget about taking messages; too often the number's wrong, or she doesn't communicate how important the message is. It's driving me crazy!"

> *Me:* "Have you talked to her about it?"

> *Manager:* "Are you kidding? Of course I have! We talked about it at her performance review, and I've had three conversations with her about it since then."

Me: "And has she agreed to change?"

Manager: "Every time!"

Reads like a bad joke, right? In fact, you may be cringing at this very moment, thinking about a similar conversation you've had about an employee of your own.

Let's be clear: if an employee makes an agreement that you know he or she is capable of keeping (that is, has the skills or knowledge needed to fulfill the agreement), and doesn't keep it, and then if you come back and have a corrective feedback conversation about the agreement a couple of times, and the employee recommits and still doesn't do what he or she has committed to do—that's not your problem. That person isn't fulfilling this part of his or her responsibility as an employee.

Some people learn, early on in life, that they can get away with problematic behavior indefinitely . . . as long as they continue to apologize and vow to change whenever someone calls them on it!

If someone doesn't keep important agreements, or only keeps them sporadically, it should be pretty clear to you that they're not the kind of person you want to have as an employee—again, it's not your responsibility to drag them along. However, if someone generally keeps their agreements, but is sketchy on just one or two, you have to decide for yourself how important that is to their overall effectiveness as an employee. For example, if someone is a fantastic salesperson and an excellent employee in most other regards, but is terrible at getting her receipts in on time, you may decide to work out something where the person's assistant takes over that responsibility. On the other hand, if a salesperson consistently doesn't meet his quota, or fails to learn to sell new products—well, those are clearly much more critical agreements; keeping agreements like that is every employee's responsibility.

Unfortunately the few employees who are consistently poor at keeping agreements often have the ability to convince you that it's somehow your fault they're not succeeding. Like the manager I noted above, it's all too easy to get sucked into an endless cycle of clarifying and reclarifying agreements. Just to help save your sanity, I've created a decision tree for using your management skills to address a performance deficit. Once you've worked through this decision tree with someone, and you've gotten all the way to the bottom, you can feel reasonably sure you've completed your responsibilities as that person's manager, that the employee hasn't completed his or responsibilities as an employee, that he or she isn't going to do so, and that it's now time to let him or her go.

Management Decision Tree

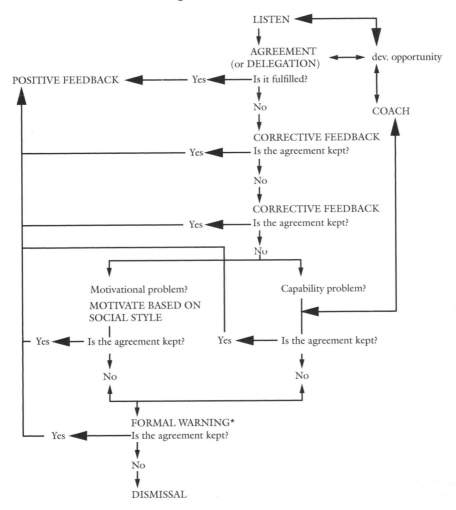

*Check with HR to find out your company's policy on this step. If you don't have an HR department, just be sure to document this conversation clearly.

Responsible Employees Manage Their Own Growth

What does it mean for employees to manage their own growth? Let me offer a couple of examples; first, of someone who is not managing her own growth, and then of someone who is.

Person #1

This person was hired with some of the skills needed to do her job; clear agreements were made about how and when she would acquire the rest. Though she didn't offer a lot of input to the discussion, she did state her intention to fulfill the agreement. Over the next six months, she learned some of the skills, but only with almost constant oversight from her manager. If he didn't encourage her to learn, then ask her when and how she planned on learning it, and finally follow up with her to remind her to carry out her plan—she wouldn't do it. Her manager also found himself having to review her work to make sure that she didn't repeat errors they had already discussed, or to make sure that she hadn't made other, similar errors.

She did some parts of her job reasonably well—things she seemed to like and feel most comfortable doing. However, she avoided doing those aspects of her job that required her to use new skills or unfamiliar approaches, or that she simply didn't like doing. When her manager gave her feedback about it, she would first become defensive, and then finally recommit to learning and doing the rest of her job. After almost a year of little or no improvement, he sat down with her and went over their original agreement point by point. He let her know she needed to decide whether she wanted to do her whole job, or find another job. After a difficult conversation, where she initially tried to convince him that she hadn't fully understood the initial agreement, and then that he hadn't given her the support she needed in order to succeed, they agreed she should leave the company.

Person #2

This person was also hired with only some of the skills needed to do his job. Again, clear mutual agreements were made about how he would acquire the remaining skills. However, this person was very much a participant in the discussion; he asked lots of questions about how and when things would happen, and who would be responsible for each step. He took the initiative in asking for a second meeting after a month to see how the agreement was going. During that meeting he noted some places where he had overcommitted and would need more time to fulfill the agreement, and other places where he was learning more quickly, and felt ready for more coaching and opportunities to try his skills.

Over the next six months, as he worked on completing his agreements, he also offered his help in other ways that both benefited the company and increased his skills. In addition, he actively invited feedback from his manager and others about how he was doing. The few times he made a mistake or didn't keep a minor agreement, he listened to the feedback and changed his behavior. Finally, he initiated conversations with his manager about potential career paths, sharing his aspirations and asking for her support in achieving them. At the end of his first year of employment, he had surpassed his manager's expectations and the original benchmarks in their agreement, and was well on his way to becoming a highly valued member of the firm.

These examples are based on real employees I've dealt with; I thought they would provide useful insights for you because the two employees' initial situations were so similar, and the outcomes were so different. So, the most interesting question for me was: what are the essential differences between these two people—the things that make the first person so frustrating and demoralizing as an employee, and the second so attractive and welcome?

Let's look first at the employee responsibilities we've already discussed—being responsive to feedback and keeping agreements. That's pretty clear: the first person wasn't responsive to feedback and didn't keep her agreements, while the second was and did. How about the third responsibility, managing one's own growth? Again, there's a critical difference between the two. I would point to their very different levels of personal responsibility. People talk about "responsibility" and "being responsible" a lot without defining what they mean. To avoid confusion, here's a definition that applies to this situation:

> *Responsible: (1) Liable to be held to account for discharging one's duty; (2) Able to make moral or rational decisions on one's own and therefore answerable for one's behavior; (3) Able to be trusted or depended upon; reliable.*

Personal responsibility, then, implies that the person holding you accountable and to whom you are answerable is you. Taking personal responsibility, in the area of managing your career, means recognizing that you are the primary person accountable for your own success, and holding yourself answerable for doing everything within your power to make that success a reality. It also means that, when things go wrong, you look first to understand and correct your own errors (rather than looking first to blame others or outside circumstances).

Person #1 refused to hold herself to account for "discharging her duty." She didn't do those things that would have made her successful, and she blamed her boss or things beyond her control for her unwillingness or inability to do them. Based on her behavior, her mind-set seemed to be that it was her boss's responsibility to drag her along every step of the way—and that if the dragging didn't work, it was his fault. In the description of her time at the company, we don't see any examples of her taking independent thought or action to advance her career or to grow professionally.

Person #2's behavior, on the other hand, clearly demonstrates his belief that he is primarily accountable for his own success. He does everything asked of him and more; he looks for ways to be more valuable to the company and to find out whether his efforts are bearing fruit. He shares his vision of his own future with his boss, and requests her help in achieving it.

Person #1 may be a particularly bad example, and person #2 may be a particularly good one, but they do illustrate the importance of "managing their own growth" as a basic employee responsibility. Employees who consistently behave as though it is your responsibility to "make them successful"; who blame you or others for their lack of success; who don't take the initiative to learn and grow—these employees are not fulfilling a key part of their role. It's easy to get pulled into their worldview; that is, that their role is to be a passive observer of your efforts to "grow" them, and that it's your fault if it doesn't work. Managers spend years dragging employees through their jobs in this way, often with the employee doing just enough not to get fired. Having employees who demonstrate themselves to be consistently unwilling to manage their own growth saps your time and emotional energy. Use your agreements skills and the management decision tree (as person #1's manager did) to give them reasonable opportunities to change.

Responsible Employees Are Good Company Citizens

We haven't talked yet about the employee who does too much (rather than too little) or who does the wrong things—the human equivalent of the bishop's goutweed my friend was struggling with at the beginning of the chapter. Most often, these employees seem *overfocused* on what they need and prefer, or what will help them to succeed—rather than what's best for others or for the team. If you remember the Social Style discussion in chapter 6, these employees are, as a group, low-versatile. They are more concerned with resolving their own tension and meeting their own needs than they are with making those around them more comfortable, or helping them to succeed.

I believe every employee has the responsibility to learn and practice a certain level of interpersonal versatility; to be a good "citizen" of the larger group. I'm not even saying that everyone has to be a skillful team member, because for some individual contributor jobs, that's not a requirement. So, what's the key difference between a good citizen of a group and a poor one? I find that the most useful place to draw the line is at the issue of others' rights. Employees who respect others' rights are aware of where they stop and the other person starts; they don't habitually do things that undermine, inconvenience, or intrude upon others.

For example:

- A salesperson who respected a fellow salesperson's rights wouldn't call on her clients without getting her permission—even if he thought he could close a deal that she couldn't.

- A boss who respected her assistant's rights wouldn't commit his time and effort on a project for another person without checking with him first—even if she thought it would get her brownie points with the person making the request.

- An employee wouldn't miss a deadline in order to change the format of an important report without checking with his boss—even if he thought the change was a needed improvement.

Let's be realistic, though. I'm sure each of us has at various points in our lives inadvertently stepped on someone else's toes—either literally or metaphorically. I'm talking here about a *pattern* of disregard for others' rights. I love scenarios (as you know by now); they provide such great examples. So, here's a conversation between a boss, Elaine, and a salesperson named Janet who is consistently overstepping her bounds with clients, and doesn't seem able or willing to watch out for the "boundaries."

Elaine sits in her office, staring out the window. She's the SVP of sales for Genex, a software development company, and she's about to have a conversation with Janet, one of her three East Coast account managers. She's not looking forward to it. This is the third time in as many months she's had to speak to Janet about what Elaine thinks of as her "overenthusiasm," and this time it has really created a problem.

Janet breezes into the office, sits down, and starts talking. "Elaine, I'm so glad we're meeting today! I've had the best meeting with

George, from Novis. They're interested in buying fifteen of the new X7 software packages, and he wants them by the end of the month! Isn't that great?"

Elaine thinks, "Here we go again." Taking a deep breath, she says, "Janet, I love that you're so focused on your clients." Janet beams and nods. "I do have one concern, though. I spoke to Al, the head developer for X7 this morning. My understanding is that they're still in beta testing and won't be ready to ship until October."

Janet looks a little taken aback, but then smiles and waves her hand dismissively. "I'll talk to him. It'll be OK. I'll get him to give me some advance copies."

Elaine shakes her head. "Janet, this is what I wanted to talk with you about. It's not OK, actually. It's not OK to promise software to a client before the ship date, and it's not OK to assume Al is going to be able to have copies that are bug-free before that date, and it's not OK to give a client software that hasn't been fully beta-tested. I don't want to dampen your enthusiasm—but you really need to learn to follow the rules on this one."

Janet frowns, looking a little rebellious. "So, you'd rather I lose a sale to an important client than inconvenience Al?"

Elaine feels herself starting to get irritated. "Janet, come on. Long-term, it's better for George to wait another month or two and get a fully tested, guaranteed product."

Janet either doesn't hear or ignores her boss. "I always thought this was a sales-driven company. This is a perfect opportunity— George has a big project coming up next month and the X7 is the ideal application. It's $200,000 worth of software!"

Now Elaine is definitely irritated. "Janet, I'm tired of your concern about your commissions getting in the way of our commitment to quality. You know we . . ."

"Hey, that's not fair! My concern is for the client's priorities . . ."

Let's tiptoe out of the room—it just heads downhill from here.

The problem with employees like Janet is they can always argue they're trying to do something positive. But I agree with Elaine (even though the *way* she said it was almost guaranteed to start an argument). Janet's clear concern is to get the sale: she's focused on what works for her. She can say that she's only concerned for the client, but it's not really true. She obviously hasn't thought about how the client will be inconvenienced by getting buggy software, or by getting the software later than she's promised. And she's not thinking about Al's needs and rights, those of his developers, and her own boss's commitment to fulfill the company's promises to the client (bug-free product, no vaporware).

So, how do you deal with an employee who doesn't respect others' rights? As usual, I believe the first step is making a clear agreement. But with these employees there's an added complication; it's often hard for them to see the problem, because they're so focused on their own needs. I'm sure Janet genuinely thinks she's acting for the best. (When I've coached executives who fall into the "don't respect others' rights" category, they often go on at great length about how they're the only ones who care about quality, are getting anything done, or respond to the client, etc., etc.) In order to overcome this myopia, when you make agreements with these folks about respecting others' rights, you have to first help them to think about what those rights might be.

With Janet, for instance, I'd suggest that Elaine ask her to think through: (1) what the client needs (beyond delivery by month's end); (2) what the development group needs; (3) what she (Elaine) needs; (4) what the company needs; and (5) what Janet needs. Then, she can make an agreement with Janet about balancing those (sometimes conflicting) needs. Here's how it might look and sound:

Elaine sits in her office, staring out the window. She's the SVP of sales for Genex, a software development company, and she's about to have a conversation with Janet, one of her three East Coast account managers. She's not looking forward to it. This is the third time in as many months she's had to speak to Janet about what

Elaine thinks of as her "overenthusiasm," and this time it has really created a problem.

Janet breezes into the office, sits down, and starts talking. "Elaine, I'm so glad we're meeting today! I've had the best meeting with George, from Novis. They're interested in buying fifteen of the new X7 software packages, and he wants them by the end of the month! Isn't that great?"

Elaine thinks, "Here we go again." Taking a deep breath, she says, "Janet, I love that you're so focused on your clients, and it's great that George is interested in the X7." Janet beams and nods.

"Let's step back from this for a minute, though," Elaine continues. "This is a somewhat complicated situation, and I want to look at the whole picture."

Janet looks a little taken aback, but nods and smiles tentatively.

"Let's look at everybody involved in this, and what they need to make it work. Now, what does George need in this situation?"

Janet looks puzzled. "Fifteen X7s by the end of the month."

"OK. What else?"

"Well . . . he needs it to do what it's supposed to do. He's got this big project."

"So he needs it bug-free, and he needs to get it when we promised it." Janet nods. "OK, what do Al and his group need in this situation?

Now Janet looks really puzzled. "Al? Oh, the development group. They need to get George the fifteen copies."

Elaine smiles a little. "Well, that's what you need them to do. What do they need?"

Janet shakes her head. "Gee, I don't really know. That's their thing."

"It affects you, and the client, so let's think about it. For one thing, they need the time to beta-test it, right? My understanding is their ship date is October 15."

"Well, yeah, but if a client is ready to buy . . ."

Elaine holds up her hand. "Bear with me for a moment. Right now we're just focusing on what Al and his folks need."

"OK, well—yeah. Time to follow their process and get it right, I guess."

"I agree. And how about me?" Elaine asks. "What do I need?"

Janet grins. "For me to meet my quota. Happy customers. That's what I need, too."

"Yup. You and I also need to fulfill our client promise: 'No bugs, no vaporware.'"

Janet nods, looking thoughtful. "Hmm, right."

Elaine leans back. "The company also needs for us to fulfill that promise, so that customers stay happy over the long term. And, Genex needs us to balance client needs with the realities of development and financial constraints, so that we can both serve our clients and stay profitable."

Janet looks serious. "I think maybe I kind of blew it, promising George the X7 by the end of the month."

Elaine nods, sighing. "Yes, I agree. We'll figure out how you can go back to George, and make this work for everybody. But first let's make an agreement about these kinds of situations. I'd like you, before you make a commitment to a client, to think about how that commitment affects the other people involved: the development group, me, the company, the client's long-term needs, and—if relevant—the other salespeople. And then, only make the commitment if it won't have a significant negative impact on anyone . . ."

Again, let's tiptoe out . . . I feel confident Elaine will make a good, clear two-way agreement.

Now, whether Janet will keep it is another story. Too often, in my experience, employees who don't fulfill this part of their responsibility are remarkably resistant to changing their mind-set. Fortunately, Elaine knows the management decision tree, and can give Janet every reasonable chance to learn to be a good company citizen.

The Bottom Line

This understanding of what you can reasonably expect from your employees is an important tool in your Growing Great Employees toolbox. I've found that this problem, of employees not fulfilling one or more aspects of their basic employee responsibilities, accounts for more manager stress and anxiety than anything else. I've seen hundreds of managers held hostage to employees who aren't responsive to feedback, or don't keep their agreements, manage their own growth, or behave as good company citizens. By "held hostage" I mean the situation continues, often for years, draining the manager's mental and emotional energy, wasting his or her time and effort—with the manager frustrated, not knowing how to address it, and having no clear strategy for requesting a change.

Having these responsibilities in your head, you can use your Agreements skills and the management decision tree to make it clear that you require a change in behavior, to support the person to change, to hold them accountable for changing—and finally, to have a clear and fair basis for letting them go if they're not able or willing to change.

My gardening friend finally dug up her woodland shrub and gave it to someone who had a moist, shady spot under some high-branched trees, where it's doing very well.

That leads us to the next chapter; dealing with those truly unfortunate situations where the employee is simply not willing or able to change in order to succeed in his or her current job. When you've made every reasonable effort, and have determined that the employee isn't going to change, how do you let him or her go in the same spirit of clarity and respect? Let's see. . .

BIG IDEAS

Most gardeners have a few plants that take an inordinate amount of their time and energy: those that have to be coaxed to grow and those that have to be prevented from overrunning the garden! Most managers have similarly high-maintenance employees—those who do too little or too much.

Just as you are responsible to your employees to provide the support and direction we've discussed throughout the book, so they have basic responsibilities to you and to the company. These responsibilities are what you can expect from every employee. Being aware of them can keep you from being "held hostage" to employees who don't hold up their end of the bargain.

Responsible Employees:

Are responsive to feedback: they listen, engage in dialogue about how to change, and make effort to do so.

Keep their agreements: they do what they've committed to do.

Manage their own growth: they recognize they are primarily responsible for their own success, and take independent action to learn and improve.

Are good company citizens: they consider others' needs and preferences, as well as their own, when speaking and acting.

CHAPTER 11

Some Plants Don't Make It

"You're looking very smug," I say to my friend one fine fall Saturday. "What's up?"

"Come out and look at the garden," she replies, smiling mysteriously. We wander out the back door, breathing in the cool, apple-scented air. Her garden really looks wonderful, the honey-colored autumn light lengthening across the plants. Everything's vibrant and healthy; asters and mums add their yellows and reds to the leaves just beginning to fall.

"Wow," I breathe. "It looks great. It's really come together. Next year it will be even more beautiful."

"Notice anything different from last time you were here?"

I look more closely. "Oh, my gosh! You got rid of that ratty little shrub—and the goutweed!" I turn to her, smiling. "Very brave. Such decisive action. I guess you finally got tired of having those two plants take up half your gardening time?"

"Exactly. What a relief. I took the goutweed out carefully, as it had twined itself into so many other plants. And then I put some of it out back by the woods; I figured it would look pretty at the edge of the forest, and it could spread without killing anything—I gave the shrub to a friend who's got a shady, protected spot where it ought to do fine." She looks at her garden thoughtfully. "It seems weird that just taking out those two plants would make such a difference to me, but it has. Don't get me wrong, it's still work—but now I don't get that 'zing' of frustration whenever I come out here." She laughs. "Am I nuts?"

"Not at all," I reply, " I know just what you mean," and proceed to tell her one of my own stories about finally calling it quits with a frustrating plant . . .

It's one thing to pull out a plant. It's something else entirely to fire somebody. Unless the person has done something horribly wrong, or is just a nasty human being, you're going to feel somewhere between badly and really badly about it. In fact, a friend and client of mine, a successful CEO and a great guy, once said to me, "The day it's easy for me to fire somebody is the day I should quit."

And yet, occasionally it's the right thing to do. Let's say you've made every reasonable effort—done all the things we've talked about here, including making clear agreements about employee responsibilities, and working all the way through the management decision tree. There you are at the bottom of the tree, where it reads:

FORMAL WARNING
↓
Is the agreement kept?
↓
No
↓
DISMISSAL

Big sigh. You know it's your only real alternative. At this point, keeping the person on is bad for the company, bad for the team, bad for you, and even—I would argue—ultimately bad for the person. So, how do you fire this person in a way that's clear and final, but also respectful and as painless as possible, while minimizing the negative effect on the team, the company, and the person you're firing? That's what my friend did with her goutweed and her shrub—and that's the focus of this chapter.

Get Very Clear

Knowing what you're going to say and do in this situation is essential. For both emotional and legal reasons, you *really* don't want to wing it here. Imagine a doctor going in to operate on someone. He or she will prepare carefully, perform the operation with the highest standards, and then make sure there's the proper follow-up to promote healing. Think of this as an operation to separate the person from your team: you want everybody to live! We'll look at each of these steps to letting someone go separately.

HOW TO LET SOMEONE GO
Prepare Carefully
Perform Impeccably
Follow Up Properly

Prepare Carefully

Are you sure? I suggest you begin by making sure that you are truly committed to this course of action. You may know rationally that this is the right thing to do, but unless you're sure, on a visceral gut level, that this is what you *must* do . . . you will make a mess of it. I know that sounds a little extreme, but I've seen it too many times. It's like that old saying, "You can't leap a canyon in two tries." You have to be 100 percent sure—head, heart, and guts—that this is what you must do. Which is not to say that you have to feel good about it; just that you have to feel it's necessary.

How do you feel? The next thing I suggest—and this may sound contradictory—is that you reflect on how you feel about the whole situation. As I said earlier, sadness, anxiety—even anger, guilt, or resentment—are completely normal and understandable in this situation, even when you know it's the right course of action. Acknowledging and accepting any negative feelings you may have will make it easier for you to stay on track, even if those feelings persist or get stronger during the process. Being in touch with how you're feeling will also make it harder for the person you're firing to manipulate those feelings (if that's the sort of person he or she is).

What will you say? Now you'll craft your message. It needs to be simple, clear, and definitive. You can include an acknowledgment that this is a difficult message, then make a clear statement of termination, followed by a single sentence of "why." (Clearly, this will almost never be the first time you're talking about this; you're summarizing primarily for legal purposes.) Then, tell the person exactly what he or she must do next. You don't want to leave him or her at loose ends here. Omit any language that's blameful or accusatory: you're not trying to make the person see the error of his/her ways, or feel bad—you're simply making it clear that they no longer have a job with the company, and telling them what will happen next. At the same time (and this is sometimes harder) you need to leave out any language that's positive or hopeful. Here's an example of a good termination message:

> "Joe, I imagine this is very difficult to hear, but I'm letting you go. As you know, you've been on formal warning for three months, and I haven't seen the improvement we agreed was necessary. We'll go to HR and you can complete the necessary paperwork, and then I'll come with you to gather up your things."

What might go badly? Having decided what to say, sort through some possible difficulties: ways in which the person might react badly to your message. How might you feel, and what will you do? For instance, what if he cries? What if she starts insulting you? What if he begs for another chance? Yikes. All distinct possibilities, and all very difficult—for you and for them. Feeling and thinking your way through these situations beforehand, and deciding how you would respond, will help you not to be caught off guard, so you can continue to be professional and appropriate no matter what. I'll also offer some specific advice about responding appropriately when we discuss "performing impeccably."

Below, I'll pull out the key elements of this termination message, and you can write one of your own. If there's someone you know you need to fire, try preparing the message with him or her in mind. It might help you move ahead. If not, prepare the message based on someone you should have fired—or should have fired differently, or would have fired if you'd been his or her boss (most of us have somebody like that in our past).

"Joe, I imagine this very difficult to hear . . ."
   An acknowledgment that this is a hard conversation (note: this must NOT be an apology):

_____

_____

". . . but I'm letting you go."
   A clear statement of termination:

_____

_____

"As you know, you've been on formal warning for three months, and I haven't seen the improvement we agreed was necessary."
   Why you're firing him/her:

_____

_____

"We'll go to HR and you can complete the necessary paperwork, and then I'll come with you to gather up your things."
   What you want him/her to do right now:

_____

_____

This may seem incredibly cut and dried, but it's essential to keep it this simple and neutral. We'll talk more about the message, and why it has to be this way, in the "perform impeccably" section that follows.

Is it legal? Your legal preparation is best done with someone from HR, if you have an HR department. You will generally have had some conversations with HR about this person, so it shouldn't be a surprise. Now that you've decided to let the person go, talk through the situation with your HR person. Tell him or her what you plan to say so he or she can make sure your message is legal and appropriate. If there are unusual circumstances (the person is in a protected class, for instance) your HR person will help assure you're doing everything you can to reduce your company's risk and exposure to legal action.

Perform Impeccably

When and where: When you're ready to have the conversation, pick the time and place very carefully. Most people choose to terminate people at the end of the day; the most common day is Thursday. The rationale behind these choices is that if you do it at the end of the day, the person is less likely to run into colleagues on the way out, and doing it on a Thursday (and asking that he or she not come to work on Friday) gives the person a long weekend to begin to go though his or her emotional reaction. Out of common courtesy, I suggest you not fire people within a couple of weeks of Christmas, Thanksgiving, or their birthday.

As far as place, choose a completely private space, with no chance that someone else will intrude on the conversation. Your office may be best, but a conference room with a locking door is OK. Again, out of common courtesy, don't have the conversation in the person's office. It will feel to most people much more invasive and personal—no matter how skillful you are—if it's on their own turf.

Please: never, never, never take someone out for a meal and then fire him or her. One of the worst corporate horror stories I've ever heard involved a network executive who took a vice president to dinner, wined and dined him, chatted amiably throughout the meal, called him a car—and then fired him while they were waiting for it to come. It reminds me of the stories of medieval kings inviting neighboring noblemen to a feast and then slaughtering them on the way out.

Also, always fire people in person. There is no legitimate excuse, in my mind, for firing someone by phone, fax, e-mail, or sky-writing. I know it's deeply uncomfortable, even painful, to have this conversation, but don't let yourself off the hook by not doing it face to face: making it harder on the person being fired in order to make it easier on yourself is, in my opinion, not acceptable.

Delivering the message: So, you're sitting in the room with the person. What now? The following approach will keep the conversation simple, focused, and brief:

· State your prepared message.

· If the person reacts calmly, thank them for their professionalism and continue on to the next steps you've outlined.

· If the person reacts emotionally, restate (very briefly) his or her feelings, without agreeing or disagreeing, and repeat your message. (For example, "You feel this is unfair, and that I haven't given you a chance to improve. Joe, I know this is difficult, but I'm letting you go. The three-month formal warning period is over, and I haven't seen the improvement we agreed was necessary.") Then continue on to the next steps.

· If the person becomes insulting or abusive, say, "I'm finished with this conversation now. I'm going to leave the room, and when you're ready, you can come out and we'll _____ [whatever you've outlined as the next step]." If you feel endangered in any way, call security. If you don't have a security person or staff, call the police. (Fortunately for all of us, this is almost never necessary. I know of only three situations in all our client companies over the past fifteen years that required this kind of intervention.)

· If the person asks you to reconsider, say, "I've made my decision on this, and it's not open for discussion. I know it's difficult. Now let's _____ [whatever you've outlined as the next step]."

· When you've completed the next steps, as quickly and efficiently as possible, wish him or her good-bye and good luck in the future (if you can do it genuinely).

Please, resist the temptation to soften the message by telling them ways in which they've been a good employee, or a nice person, or by offering any other positive feedback. It may seem cruel, but adding these things in can be risky legally, and it can also be confusing (If I'm a good employee, why are you firing me?). In addition, it sends the message that you're open to engaging in dialogue about this—and you're not. Unlike every other situation we've talked about in this book, this is the one place where it's completely appropriate—necessary, in fact—to have a quick, one-way conversation.

On the other hand, resist any temptation to punish or get back at the person verbally, even if this person has been a particularly difficult employee. Avoid elaborating on their bad behavior, talking about how hard they've made your life, contrasting them with other, better employees, etc. It may feel momentarily good to vent in this way, but again, it's risky legally—people have been sued for less—and it's cowardly; it's like hitting someone when they're down. Let them retain as much of their dignity as you possibly can.

Finally, this is not the time for corrective feedback. You're firing them at least partly because they didn't respond to feedback, right? Even if it's well-intentioned (for example, you want to leave them with some self-awareness that will help them in future endeavors) it's extremely unlikely that they'll even be able to hear it, and—again—it communicates "This is a dialogue," a message you don't want to send.

OK, you did it. Congratulations on being an honorable human being and doing a very difficult thing to the best of your ability.

Follow Up Properly

Taking care of the company: Over the next few weeks, make every effort to dot all the Is and cross all the Ts. Check to make sure the person has completed any and all legal and HR requirements. Make sure all of the employee's company-issued personal items have been returned. Document the firing in whatever way HR asks. Stay in touch with your boss about the whole situation, including any complications or planned follow-up.

Taking care of the person: Most important, resist the temptation to say negative things about the person to others in the company—especially your other employees. It's unprofessional and unnecessary—and it makes you look bad. It will also make your remaining employees feel even less trusting and more paranoid around you than they already do. Let's talk about that . . .

Taking care of your team: This is by far the most critical part of following up a termination. Even if the person you've fired was universally disliked, it's still going to be upsetting to people. Remember, this situation reminds your employees that you actually have the power to fire them—which is pretty scary, and probably not something they think about very often if you're managing them well. Most people are likely to feel vulnerable, and worried about their own success. Here are three things I recommend you do to help people through this time:

Announce the firing in as neutral, honest, and hopeful a way as possible. For instance: "Joe and I agreed it was time for him to leave the company. His last day was Thursday." (Or, even more neutrally, "Joe has left the company as of last Thursday.") "I very much hope he finds a job that suits him and where he can really succeed." If the person was highly placed, and you need to make a public announcement, your PR group will probably help you craft the message; "Left to pursue other options" or, "Submitted his resignation" are much-used phrases that save face for everyone involved.

Let the team know what's next. They will want to know how the person's job will get done, and—though they'll feel a little guilty to be thinking about this—some people will be wondering whether the person's leaving might benefit them. So, as quickly as possible, make a clear statement of next steps. This might be something like: "We're going to be posting his job, internally and externally, at the end of the week, and we'll discuss in our next team meeting how to cover his work during the interim," or, "Darlene will be taking over for him and we'll be looking internally to fill her job, so let me know if you're interested."

Renew their belief that you are reasonable and fair. Even though it's not appropriate to talk to your other employees about why the person got fired, you can still reassure them that it wasn't arbitrary. You can do that by being as consistent and balanced as possible over the next few months. Be careful, for instance, to offer appropriate support (listening, positive feedback, coaching, delegation) while consistently holding people accountable (agreements, corrective feedback, delegation). Be especially attentive to keeping any agreements you've made; and if something changes, explain what's happening and why. You want to demonstrate to people that there is no mystery about succeeding on your team: those who fulfill their responsibilities as employees—who respond to feedback, keep their agreements, manage their own growth, and are good company citizens—will continue to be valued members of the team.

Finally, let me offer some cautions about style-based mistakes to avoid in this situation:

If you are an Expressive, I'd suggest that you not take a "buddy-buddy' approach during this time. Don't, for example, have parties, or behave in a more friendly or personal way than usual toward your employees. This may feel right to you, as a way to soften the negative vibe, and make people feel better—but it's all too likely to ring false to people, and leave them with the uncomfortable feeling that they have to "play nice" with you, or act as though the firing hasn't affected them. Some Expressives might be OK with it, but your other employees generally won't. Instead, channel your impulse toward the positive into a "let's start fresh" approach: craft a meeting focused on how to work more effectively as a team, or how you can work together to reach a particularly challenging goal.

If you are an Amiable or an Analytical, you may be tempted to avoid announcing anything publicly and "just let people come to you on their own." You may feel this will keep people from being uncomfortable or from focusing on a negative situation. You're partially right—some people will be relieved not to have the topic brought up. Unfortunately, there are likely to be a number of negative outcomes as well. First, if there's no public acknowledgment and explanation, people will tend to speculate—rumor and gossip will abound, and much of it may be far more negative than the reality. Also, people may not come to you for insight because they'll assume that you don't want to talk about it (since you haven't). Those who do come to you may communicate what they hear with their own spin, adding to the swirl of competing gossip. Add in people's inevitable skittishness and paranoia in situations like this, and voilà! A mess.

For instance, let's say Joe was a salesperson, and all anybody knows—because you're not saying anything—is what they saw of him, which is that he was a big spender and a big talker; he seemed to be taking clients out for dinner in expensive restaurants, etc. With no real information from you, this can easily turn into something like the following: "Hey, did you hear that Joe got fired because he was falsifying his expense reports?" "Oh, no, I heard it was much worse than that; he actually told his employees to pad their reports—and now the company's going to institute a system to check every line item of our expenses to make sure it doesn't happen again." "Are you serious? Oh my God, one person messes up and they stop trusting all of us . . ." And so forth. Please, give people the facts, even if it feels awkward and embarrassing. You'll save yourself a lot of unhappiness and confusion down the line.

If you are a Driver, avoid making any comments that make it sound as though firing the person was no big deal. An executive I coached once told his team that he was "glad" he had fired someone; that "now they could move on and really get results." Until I pointed it out to him, he hadn't thought at all about the impact that his level of indifference to that person's fate might have on his other reports. Even if you're one of those rare people who literally doesn't mind firing someone, at least acknowledge to your team that you gave it a lot of thought, that you hope the person is successful going forward, and that you recognize this may be unsettling, or uncomfortable, or a shock to the rest of your employees. Remember, from their point of view, you have just had a huge negative impact on the life and livelihood of someone like them—their peer and colleague. As I said earlier, they are now uncomfortably aware that you could do the same to them. If they get the feeling that this is not hard for you, they are going to be much more paranoid and less trusting; they may feel that you don't value or respect your employees. And, to put it bluntly, productivity tracks morale: a team that doesn't feel trusting, respected, or valued is significantly less likely to perform well.

Now for the Good News

Once my friend had removed the plants that weren't working, and her garden consisted only of those plants that were doing their "job" (i.e., that were reasonably easy to grow and maintain, and didn't overwhelm the other plants), she felt much better. Once you've gotten through the uncomfortable and difficult business of firing someone, and once you've reassured your team that you're not Attila the Hun, you will probably also begin to feel the beneficial effects.

The team will probably coalesce in a new and more effective way. The time you were devoting to working around or thinking about or trying to motivate the person you've fired will be given back to you—you may feel less overwhelmed, and you'll have more time to spend with other employees who deserve and can benefit from your attention. You may find that you feel much happier without the emotional drain that's often the result of dealing with a problematic employee. Finally, you and your team will be able—especially after you replace the person you've let go with someone better suited to the job—to get the results you want and need to achieve.

In short, you'll see that your decision was the right one, and you may feel a renewed energy and pleasure in your work. You can go "back to the garden" with anticipation and hopefulness.

BIG IDEAS

No matter how skillful and attentive you may be as a gardener, some plants just don't make it. If you want to salvage a plant that isn't working in your garden, you have to remove it carefully and quickly put it in a place where it can thrive, being careful not to damage the plants around it.

It's true of employees as well: even the best managers sometimes have to fire people. The trick is, as with plants, to do it quickly and carefully, with minimal damage to those around them.

Letting Someone Go

Prepare Carefully: prepare yourself emotionally, mentally, and legally, to insure everything that can go right *will* go right.

Perform Impeccably: choose a time and place, and deliver your message in a way that creates the greatest chance that this ending will be as dignified and cause as little pain for your employee—and you—as possible.

Follow Up Properly: make sure to take care of the company, the person you've fired, and—most important—your team, in order to minimize the negative impact of the firing, and allow you all to move forward.

CHAPTER 12

The Master Gardener

As I walk into my friend's garden unannounced, I see a very odd thing. There, deadheading the coreopsis, is a lanky teenage boy of fourteen or fifteen. With his wispy blond hair and bright green T-shirt, he looks oddly like the plants he's tending. I remember my own chapter on plants becoming gardeners, and wonder, briefly . . .

"Hey," my friend says, coming up behind me. "Hey," I reply, startled out of my reverie. The boy looks up. "Oh," says my friend, "this is Owen. He lives next door—Angie's son? I hired him to help out. You know, I've been taking that master gardener class you recommended, and I wanted to have time to try some new stuff, and Owen said he liked gardening. And . . ." She hesitates. "And I thought I could teach him a few things." I suddenly realize she is shy at telling me, her teacher, that she feels capable to teach someone else.

"Passing it on is a great way to keep learning," I reply. "Nice to have a willing guinea pig." She smiles.

Owen holds out a thin, somewhat grass-streaked palm, and we shake. "I'm kind of interested in gardening," he says. "Last spring my dad and I started some vegetables in the backyard. That's good and all—but I wanted to get into flowers, too." He looks down, a little abashed. "It's pretty cool."

"Very cool," I answer. "Something you could really get good at."

"Yeah," he says, looking at me speculatively; perhaps I might not be entirely old and clueless. "Something I could get really good at."

It's a basic human need, I think, to get really good at something. Although you might not agree, looking at the state of the world today, I do believe we human beings have an urge toward mastery. It manifests in lots of different ways—that kid on the corner who looks like a loser to you, but who can name every single car that goes by, what's under the hood, how it's put together, and how it will perform in every possible circumstance. The shy clerk at the grocery store whose border collie is the state Frisbee-catching champion. The guy who just won the gold medal in fencing. The old lady who has raised eight well-adjusted foster kids on a fixed income. The senior vice president who is such a good operator and such a great leader of people that, when the CEO retires, the board of directors asks her to take over the company.

Mastery arises—to paraphrase Jim Collins in *Good to Great*—when people feel a passion for something, when they see they could get really good at it, and when they believe it will give them something that's important to them. (In Jim Collins's corporate version, this third element of greatness is "drives their economic engine." My experience of individual human beings is that, unlike companies, our engine is not necessarily economic; we can be equally motivated by love, comfort, fame, the feeling of helping people, or any number of other things.)

Individual mastery is not singular; one person can attempt to achieve mastery in a variety of areas. For instance, someone could be passionate about excelling at his job, his marriage, amateur basketball, and having an impact on national politics, all at the same time.

I'm writing this final chapter for those of you who want to achieve a level of mastery in managing and growing employees. Now, I don't believe it's necessary to feel that pull toward mastery in order to benefit from the last eleven chapters. I've written them, as I said at the beginning, to provide practical insights and skills that any manager can use to become a better manager, the kind of manager who provides value to his or her company by hiring the right people and supporting them to do the best work they can do. If you've gotten what you need from the book, and feel capable of taking the skills and ideas I've offered and applying them to your own situation, I thank you very much for the honor of being useful to you. I'll say good-bye here; I wish you well and I hope this book will continue to serve as a helpful resource.

Now, for those of you who are left: I'm going to assume you're interested in mastering this area of growing great employees. That is, you feel passionate about it; you feel you have the capability to become really good at it; you believe it will give you something or some things that are important to you—monetary or otherwise. We're going to talk about how to take what you've learned here and build on it as a stepping-stone to mastery.

First, How Does Mastery Happen?

I've thought about this quite a bit over the years. I've closely observed a number of people who seem to me to have achieved a level of mastery in some area, from the best CEOs I know, to any child who's learned to walk and talk, to employees who've confounded everyone's expectations by succeeding when everyone thought they would fail. I've reflected on my own learning process and that of other people who have done well in a variety of pursuits.

I've come to the conclusion that mastery can be gained by doing the following things (by the way, this is the last of these little models you'll be getting from me, so appreciate it while you can).

MOVING TOWARD MASTERY
Don't Stop Yourself
Honor How You Learn
Practice

Don't Stop Yourself

I can't tell you how many times I've watched people talk themselves out of pursuing their dreams—dreams that seemed perfectly achievable to me. Someone very dear to me is a talented artist. He began to pursue mastery, quickly producing some amazing works in a very unique and personal style. When he was working, it looked to me like a classic mastery situation: there was the passion, the talent, and the intense satisfaction. Then he stopped. When I asked him why, he had a flurry of reasons. "I lost my studio space, I felt like I was repeating myself, I wasn't that good, I just wasn't inspired anymore," etc.

Now, I don't know the underlying reasons for his abandoning this passion. But I suspect he got uncomfortable. And he wasn't willing to push past his discomfort because he didn't have faith there would be anything on the other side.

I believe the process of achieving mastery, no matter what the field, requires confronting and surpassing your self-imposed limitations over and over again. Remember when I talked about the mind of a gardener in chapter 5? I used the phrase, "Believing in your people's potential, and wanting to help them succeed" as the essence of the coach's mind-set. In order to achieve mastery, you have to hold that mind-set about yourself. If you don't believe in your own potential, you will abandon your pursuit when the going gets rough. Your self-talk at that point— and this may happen on such a subconscious level, or be so habitual for you, that you don't even notice it—might be something like: "This feels bad/awkward/embarrassing/frightening/silly. I'm probably not going to make it anyway, so why endure the pain?"

It seems to me there is always pain—or at least discomfort—involved in getting really good at something. Think about it. Think of something at which you've really worked to excel. If it's something physical—skiing or ballet or running—there is the physical pain of pushing your muscles to their limits, of forcing them to perform new tasks, the pain of bruises and strains that come from turning wrong, or stretching too far, or falling. If it's something more cerebral, there's the mental strain of struggling to understand new ideas, to remember and integrate new concepts, to put into practice new ways of behaving. And with any kind of new endeavor, there is the emotional discomfort of feeling inadequate, of doubting your own capacity, of feeling embarrassed when you make a mistake or do something badly.

If you reflect on your own experience, I believe you'll find that, in those areas where you've excelled, you've come to those points of discomfort again and again—and you've chosen to keep going.

To come back for a moment to our gardening metaphor, think of a seed. The seed contains the full potential for the plant. In order to achieve that potential, the soft, living shoot has to break through the protective shell and make its way to the light of day. Achieving mastery requires breaking through the shell of your own limitations—both actual and imagined—and struggling up to the freedom and enjoyment of real skill.

TRY IT OUT

Let's apply this idea of "not stopping yourself." First, I'll walk you through a self-reflection exercise to help prevent you from talking yourself out of achieving mastery in some area you're already exploring. Then we'll do the same exercise as applied to mastering the art of growing great employees. Pick an area where you've already experienced "stopping yourself" at least once when you felt uncomfortable.

What's the area you're trying to master?

_____

Describe the experience you've had of "stopping yourself":
· What, specifically, were you doing or learning at the time?

_____

_____

_____

· Describe your discomfort (e.g., "I felt . . .")

_____

_____

_____

· How did you "stop yourself"; that is, how did you talk to yourself and/or what did you do?

_____

_____

_____

_____

What negative beliefs do you think contributed to your negative self-talk or actions?

_____

_____

_____

_____

Pick the belief above that you feel is most likely leading you to "stop yourself." Now, referring back to the "changing your mind" model in chapter 5, let's shift that belief:

Question: How could you turn your belief into a question?

_____

_____

Gather new data: Note any information that might answer your question in ways that challenge your negative beliefs:

_____

_____

_____

Test/revise: With this new information in mind, how might your belief change; and what would your new, more supportive self-talk be in this area?

_____

_____

_____

I'd like to share with you an example of how this exercise worked for my artist-in-the-making friend (you can use this example to prompt you doing the activity above, or you can do the activity first, then read the example). My friend noticed that the point where he started to get uncomfortable was when he felt as though his ideas outstripped his technique—that is, that he didn't know how to create what he could imagine. At that point, he felt inadequate and clumsy. He realized he was "stopping himself" by listening to and acting on this self-talk: "I don't know why I'm even doing this; it's just a hobby and I've got lots of other things I should be doing."

After he thought about it a little more, he decided that the key negative beliefs fueling this self-talk were that he wasn't that talented or capable—so that, if he invested the time to learn more technique, he still wouldn't be able to create the kind of art he wanted to make. And that would be deeply disappointing.

He "gathered new information" by simply looking at the existing information more objectively. He realized he had gotten a lot of juice about his initial pieces from some friends who were very knowledgeable about art, and that seemed like a good indication he had some talent. He also acknowledged he had no basis for believing that he wouldn't be able to benefit from learning more technique—because he hadn't tried it yet. Finally, he decided that being disappointed would be better than never knowing how good he could have been.

Armed with this "new" information, he changed his belief and his self-talk to: "I won't know how much talent or capability I have until I make the effort to develop it. Moving in this direction is scary, but I want to find out what's possible for me."

TRY IT OUT

Now that you've tried this in another area of mastery, and reflected on an example from someone else, let's apply "not stopping yourself" to the area of growing great employees.

Describe an experience you've had of "stopping yourself" as a manager; when you've turned away from a management or leadership challenge:

· What, specifically, were you doing (or needing to do) at the time?

_____

_____

_____

· Describe your discomfort (e.g., "I felt . . .")

_____

_____

_____

· How did you "stop yourself"; that is, how did you talk to yourself and/or what did you do?

_____

_____

_____

_____

· What negative beliefs do you think contributed to your negative self-talk or actions?

_____

_____

_____

Pick the belief you've noted above that you feel is most likely to be leading you to "stop yourself." Now, referring back to the "changing your mind" model in chapter 5, let's shift that belief:

Question: How could you turn your belief into a question?

_____

_____

Gather new data: Note any information that might answer your question in ways that challenge your negative beliefs (including things you may have read or tried from this book):

_____

_____

_____

Test/revise: With this new information in mind, how might your belief change; and what would your new, more supportive self-talk be in this area?

_____

_____

_____

I suggest that you write this new belief down on a Post-it and put it where it will remind you of your intention: that you want to master the art of people development. As you surface any other negative, "stopping" beliefs, you can go through the same exercise to shift them to more realistic and supportive beliefs.

Finally, over the next week or so, note the effect on your behavior. Do these new beliefs help you keep going, instead of stopping you? That's what you're going for here.

Honor How You Learn

Most people know at least one smart person who did poorly in school. However, if that person finds a passion and a way to pursue it outside the classroom, he or she might end up being very successful in life. People as varied as Steve Jobs, Whoopi Goldberg, and Albert Einstein come to mind as examples.

I offer this as a way to illustrate the second part of mastery. People learn differently, and in order to achieve mastery, they need to find out how they learn best, and use that approach (or those approaches) to learning even if other people are telling them they're "not doing it right." If your way of learning is nontraditional—that is, if you don't respond well to the standard classroom teaching approaches—you may have been called unmotivated, lazy, or even dumb or "slow," and that has probably insinuated itself into your beliefs and your self-talk to some extent.

And even if you did well in school, it may be hard for you to honor your way of learning; your success with traditional teaching may make you resistant to exploring other ways of learning that might be even more valuable for you.

If you remember in chapter 4, we talked about the LearningPath; the process all learners need to go through in order to acquire new skills and knowledge in a way that allows them to change their behavior. (You might want to refer back to p. 68 to review that model). However, within the "New Skills and Knowledge" step of that model, people take in and process information in a variety of ways.

However, before we talk about these different ways of learning, let me offer a piece of advice that connects back to "not stopping yourself." Whatever your past experiences with learning, I believe there are learning approaches that will work for you, and that it's a matter of experimenting until you find them. Please don't let past failures (or successes) with learning lead you to stop yourself from doing this experimentation, or from believing in your ability to find your own best learning style.

All right then: let's talk about learning styles. Quite a bit of research has been done in this area over the past few decades; we're much clearer about how people learn than we were a generation ago. At the risk of oversimplifying, let me offer you the main ways people seem to learn: doing, hearing, seeing, reading/writing, and reflecting.

Before I explain these, let me note that, in my experience, most people seem to have one or two preferred styles, a few styles that definitely don't work for them, and one or two about which they feel fairly neutral—in other words, approaches that would work okay for them, but aren't optimal. As you read through these descriptions, I invite you (I've even provided a place for it) to note whether each approach appeals to you (+), doesn't appeal to you (-), or doesn't create a strong reaction either way (0).

☐ **Doing:** People who like to learn by doing are the ones who say "Let me do it." They'll nudge the teacher away from the computer or the paintbrush or the ski slope and start trying the skill themselves, asking the teacher to tell them what's wrong when they run up against a problem. Learn-by-doing folks need to have their bodies engaged in learning. If it's a physical skill, they want to try it—often even before hearing the explanation. If it's a mental skill, they still need to engage their bodies: by talking about it, for instance, or by using objects to represent the ideas they're discussing. Traditional classroom learning generally doesn't work very well for "doing" learners—sitting in one place all day taking in information is not effective for them, to say the least.

☐ **Hearing:** These people learn best by listening to new information. They're the kind of people who can learn a new language by listening to Berlitz tapes, or who like to play "how-to" CDs during their commute. They do well in lecture courses, because they can take in the speaker's information easily, without getting distracted, and it's meaningful for them. Questioning is generally an important skill for these learners, because they've found that it gets them what they want—more information to hear! Much to the amazement of the learn-by-doing people, these learn-by-hearing people can often perform a process or follow a set of directions after hearing about it once—whereas the learn-by-doing person would be lost without trying it out.

☐ **Seeing:** People with this learning style use their eyes in much the same way the previous style uses their ears. If someone starts to explain something to them, they'll often say "show me." If they're trying to select a book on home design, for instance, they'll first look to make sure there are plenty of pictures that show the ideas discussed. If a set of instructions isn't illustrated, they'll find it much more difficult to use. These people find it very helpful to have more abstract ideas represented visually, as well. For example, when learning about a process, seeing it in the form of a flow chart works better for these folks than seeing it in outline form.

☐ **Reading/writing:** These people are the note-takers of the world. They generally like to take in information first by reading (and are capable of sorting through lots of written information to hold on to what's valuable for them). Then, people who use this approach need to write down the key ideas in order to really learn them. For example, when "reading/writing" learners are preparing to do a presentation, they'll start by reading through the information to be covered, but then they'll want to write it out in their own words, in order to feel like they fully know it. Once they've written it down, they often reread and revise it, in order both to deepen their understanding and to make sure it fully represents that understanding.

☐ **Reflecting:** People with this learning style take in information from a variety of sources, but for them, the learning happens primarily when they filter that information through a process of mental review and visualization. That is, they learn best by thinking through how they would do something. For example, if a learn-by-reflecting person needed to use a new process at work, he or she might want to read, see, or hear about it in order to understand it initially, but the critical learning step would be for that person to imagine him- or herself using the process. They use the same process for abstract ideas: after taking in the information, they think through it in order to assure they understand, and to integrate that understanding with what they already know. These people need time alone to learn.

For example, let's imagine five managers are learning to run meetings. Shawna, George, Jamie, Dawn, and Amy meet with their boss, who asks them all what would be the best approach for learning this skill. All five are aware of their best learning style, and are able to ask for what they need. The first person, Shawna, is a learn-by-doing person. She'd like a few tips, but then wants to try running a meeting (a low-risk one, maybe with her peers who are also learning) with her boss watching her and offering feedback afterward; then she'll want to try it again. George, the second person, a hearing learner, would most like to have someone talk him through the process of running meetings, and have the opportunity to ask lots of questions, before actually doing it. The third person, Jamie, learns by seeing. He would most like to watch someone else conduct a meeting or two, and then try it himself. Dawn learns by reading/writing. She would like to read some information about how to conduct meetings, then write up her own notes about how to use what she's read before conducting a meeting herself. Finally, Amy learns by reflecting. After hearing or reading about how to run a meeting, she'd like some time alone to visualize herself doing it, then she'll be ready to try it in real life.

Now, you'll notice that all five learners need to try doing the skill at some point. The differences come in when they get to that point. For the learn-by-doing folks, it simply comes earlier—it's how they learn. For everyone else, it's how they test out what they've learned.

TRY IT OUT

Let's apply any insights you've had about your learning style to the area of growing great employees. The skills we've discussed in this book are listed below. Circle the two or three you think could most improve your ability to grow great employees:

Listening	Changing your beliefs
Self-talk	Social styles
Creating core competencies	Making agreements
Creating job descriptions	Giving feedback
Interviewing	Delegation
Interview assessment	Coaching
Employee orientation	Firing

· Which of the five learning styles described above work best for you?

· Given your preferred learning style(s), how might you use this book and any other available resources to improve in the skills you've selected above?

Skill 1:

How I'll learn it:

Skill 2:

How I'll learn it:

Skill 3:

How I'll learn it:

Practice

The last part of mastery is the simplest and perhaps the hardest to do. To really change your behavior, you need to do the new thing over and over until it's a habit. This is true no matter what the learning—whether you're learning to speak German, to grow beautiful flowers, or to make clear agreements with your employees.

The first two aspects of mastery support practice. If you're not stopping yourself, and you're honoring your own way(s) of learning, you'll be much more likely to keep working on a skill until you're good at it.

The most frustrating and demoralizing part of practicing is also, ultimately, the most productive and gratifying: working on the things you're worst at. You can get pretty good at something just by focusing on improving in those parts where you already feel pretty comfortable. But, in my experience, mastery comes only when you gain fluency in those parts where you feel least comfortable. I'll give you an example. A CEO I coached for years was very good at the "positive" parts of management and leadership. He was inspiring, he articulated his vision clearly, he was great at supporting people so that they felt competent and trusted. He worked on getting even better at these things, and people acknowledged him for these strengths . . . from his direct reports, to stories in the press, to his company's board members.

What he wasn't good at, and didn't like, were the more "negative" parts of management: he avoided like the plague giving people corrective feedback, or telling them they couldn't do things about which they felt passionate. Lacking these skills kept him from mastery. He was a good leader, rather than a great one.

During the course of our working together, he began to see the negative consequences of his unwillingness to practice in these areas. Senior people working for him were less effective than they could have been, because he wasn't telling them when they were doing something wrong. In situations where two executives felt passionate about two different courses of action, time and effort were wasted because both executives believed he was supporting their point of view. It came to a head when it took him months to fire someone who everyone else saw as being extremely ineffective, and people began to question his ability to make tough choices.

He began to practice, first by using the model in chapter 7 to give corrective feedback. It was difficult for him at first, but it got easier fairly quickly because his direct reports, for the most part, thanked him—they had felt as though they had been "flying blind" and appreciated getting a clearer sense of how they were doing. Then he began to practice telling executives "no." This was tougher, because nobody thanked him! However, he soon began to see the benefits—since he was more often acting as the tie-breaker on these difficult decisions, much less time was spent with the senior team treading water, wondering what was happening on important initiatives.

Now, a few years later, he's much, much better at these things than he used to be. He'll never be as good at them as he is at the aspects of management that come more naturally to him—but he's skillful enough that these things no longer hold him back. His practice in these areas has moved him toward mastery of people management, and both his organization and his direct reports have reaped the rewards.

TRY IT OUT

In the activity above, you decided how you would go about learning the two or three *Growing Great Employees* skills in which you most need to improve. Now we'll focus on how you're going to practice them.

First, create one or two pieces of supportive self-talk that will encourage you to keep practicing these two or three skills, even when it feels difficult, embarrassing, or futile. (Some examples of supportive self-talk: "This is tough for me because I haven't done it before; it will get easier the more I do it" and/or, "Being able to do this is essential if I want to be promoted.")

_____

_____

_____

Of these two or three skills, which one do you think you'll most resist practicing? In other words, which one is hardest for you?

_____

Select a few situations you know about right now where you need to use this skill:

_____

_____

_____

Which of these situations might provide a good practice opportunity (not too high-risk, yet would provide a good benefit if dealt with well)? Circle that situation.

Below, make a statement of intention to yourself about how you'll practice your "hard stuff" in this situation:

_____

_____

Before we move on, I'd like to offer you a few other pieces of parting advice to support you in practicing growing great employees so that you can achieve mastery:

· Be kind to yourself—sometimes you'll do well, and sometimes you won't. When you screw up, reflect on what happened and why, and use your self-talk to support continued effort and future improvements.

· Remind yourself why you're doing this—focus on whatever it is that makes you feel passionate about wanting to be a great manager.

· Look for useful, challenging ways to practice, versus thinking that you "have" to practice. It's a mind-set shift based in curiosity that will change the way you feel about the process of mastery.

The Rewards of Mastery

Remember Josie and Andy, from Lobo, the jewelry design company? We last looked in on them in chapter 9, where Andy had coached Josie about how to make agreements with her peers. Josie has just talked with her colleagues, Ed and Jim, about creating production specs for her jewelry designs. Here's the end of that conversation (oh, just as a reminder—Josie's an Amiable and Andy's an Expressive):

". . . So you feel Ed knows what you're asking him and why, and agreed to do it." Josie nods. "And, you were less pleased about the conversation with Jim?"

Josie sighs. "It turned out OK, but I definitely made a few mistakes . . . fortunately I didn't repeat them with Ed. I was trying to be way too careful with Jim not to have him feel like I was making him do something, and I ended up just being confusing."

"What did Jim do?"

"Luckily for me, he said something like—'Josie, just come out with it and stop beating around the bush. Are you trying to ask me to do the specs on this design?' So I got to start over. And then it was fine."

"Jim would definitely be the one to cut to the chase," Andy agrees, grinning. "So, it sounds like you didn't have that problem with Ed."

"No." She smiles again. "I learned from my mistakes. Just like with designs that don't work." Then Josie looks at him seriously. "You know, Andy, this is making me wonder—do you think I could ever be a manager . . . you know, manage designers?"

Andy leans back, a big grin on his face. "Well now, that's a whole 'nother conversation . . ."

So, as in old movies, the pages of the calendar fly off, and eighteen months have passed. Josie is now managing Ed, Jim, and a new designer, Li. Andy is really amazed and pleased with her progress—it turns out she has a real talent for managing, and a passion for doing it well. And Josie has discovered that managing provides something that's really important to her—the ability to build a creative team where everyone supports and appreciates each other's skills and talents. She is on the path to mastery. Let's eavesdrop on a conversation with Andy:

"Hey, thanks for coming in . . . I've got something exciting to share with you," Andy says as he gets up from his desk and ushers Josie into his office.

Josie smiles. "That sounds interesting," she says. "What's up?" We notice that she carries herself differently than last time we saw her: she's standing up straighter, and she looks at Andy directly. She's also dressing a little differently; still casual and New York, but with a subtle "grown-up-ness" that's new. She sits on the couch across from Andy.

"Well, this is completely hush-hush at this point, but I'm leaving Lobo. I've been asked to head up the design group at a much bigger company in San Francisco. I can't even say which company it is yet, because they really don't want it to leak. But I'm definitely going. This is a big opportunity for me!"

Josie is silent for a moment. "Andy, I'm thrilled for you," she says finally, "but I'm not so thrilled for us. It's hard for me to imagine anyone leading this group as well as you've done it."

Andy grins. "How about you?"

"What?"

"I said, how about you? I'm planning on recommending to Ada that you take over for me. Are you up for it?"

Josie looks astonished. "Are you serious?"

Andy laughs. "Of course I'm serious! You're already managing more than half the group, and you did a great job when I was on vacation last month."

Now she's starting to look excited. "Wow. This is amazing. I guess I hoped you would ultimately feel I was ready for this . . . but, wow."

"So, are you in?" Andy is leaning forward, waiting for her response.

Josie takes a deep breath. "Yes. I am," she says clearly. Then she nods. "This is really what I want. I want to get really good at this. . . ."

Josie is well on her way to mastery. Before I say goodbye, I want to offer you one last support in your own quest for mastery. I encourage you to take some time to review all that you've read here. You can do that by looking back at the chapter overviews in the introduction, or by quickly leafing through all the chapters. Think about why you want to be a truly excellent manager of people. What's important to you about growing great employees? Why is that meaningful for you?

Now, in the box below, write a note to yourself. It can be one word, or a few, or a sentence or two—its purpose is to remind you of your core motivation for being a great manager. I want you to provide yourself with something that will support you in your efforts, at those times when things get crazy and it's hard to focus on anything beyond the crisis of the moment.

So, what will help you remember why you want to master the art of growing great employees?

When I coach executives, we work together to agree on the words or phrases for a reminder card like this, focused on what they want to do differently, and why. After the session, my assistant at Proteus creates a laminated version and sends it to the executive, who keeps it close at hand—on her computer, in his wallet, or wherever it will be easy to see and remember.

Though I can't create a laminated version of your reminder note for you, I'd like to encourage you to create one for yourself and keep it where it will remind you of your intention. I also hope that this book serves as a reminder, a reference, and a support for you.

Thank you for the privilege of spending this time with you; I hope that you achieve mastery in all the things that are important to you, and that you leave the world a better place than you found it.

BIG IDEAS

There are master gardeners, master mathematicians, and master managers. Human beings have an innate drive toward mastery; most of us want to be really good at something or some things. What is mastery?

Mastery arises when you're passionate about something, you have the capacity to excel in that area, and excelling in that area will give you some reward that's deeply important to you.

Moving Toward Mastery

Don't Stop Yourself: mastery requires consciously moving through your limitations—those points of development where you feel stuck, discouraged, or inadequate. Those who achieve mastery avoid sabotaging their own success.

Honor Your Way of Learning: each of us has learning approaches that work and don't work for us. Find out what works for you, and rely on those approaches to take you to mastery.

Practice: the core of mastery is doing new behaviors again and again until they become habitual. Practicing—and especially, practicing those things that are hardest for you—will enable you to achieve your hopes of mastery.

Proteus International

If you've enjoyed this book and found it helpful, I'd like to invite you to explore the other work we do at Proteus International. Some of it is directly related to what you've read here; for example, we conduct open-enrollment workshops in New York City based on some of the *Growing Great Employees* skills, and we also offer those workshops within our client companies.

In addition, my colleagues and I coach executives one-on-one to support them in achieving mastery as managers and leaders, using many of the approaches I've shared with you here.

We work with our clients on an organization-wide level as well, to help them clarify the future they want to create for their companies, and then move toward that future.

If you'd like to find out more about the work we do, and how it might benefit you or your organization, please feel free to explore our Web site, at www.proteus-international.com, or to contact us at connect@proteus-international.com.

Thank you once again for your time, your attention, and your curiosity!

Index